THE
ALLIANCE

REID HOFFMAN

BEN CASNOCHA

CHRIS YEH

THE
ALLIANCE

MANAGING TALENT IN THE
NETWORKED AGE

Harvard Business Review Press

Boston, Massachusetts

Library of Congress Cataloging-in-Publication Data

Hoffman, Reid.
    The alliance: managing talent in the networked age / Reid Hoffman, Ben Casnocha, Chris Yeh.
        pages cm
    ISBN 978-1-62527-577-6 (hardback)
    1. Organizational change.   2. Employee motivation.   3. Leadership.
I. Casnocha, Ben.   II. Yeh, Chris.   III. Title.
    HD58.8.H6444 2014
    658.3—dc23

                                                                    2014005468

Contents

Contents

THE
ALLIANCE

1

Employment in the Networked Age

Rebuilding Trust and Loyalty through an Alliance

Imagine it's your first day of work at a new company. Your manager greets you with warm enthusiasm, welcomes you to "the family," and expresses her hope that you'll be with the company for many years to come. Then she hands you off to the HR department, who sits you down in a conference room and spends thirty minutes explaining that you're on a ninety-day probation period, and that even after that, you'll be an "at will" employee. "At any moment, you can be fired. For any reason, you can be fired. Even if your boss has no reason at all, you can be fired."

You just experienced the fundamental disconnect of modern employment: the employer-employee relationship is based on a dishonest conversation.

Today, few companies offer guaranteed employment with a straight face; such assurances are perceived by employees as naive, disingenuous, or both. Instead, employers talk about retention and tenure with fuzzy language: their goal is to retain "good" employees and the time frame is . . . indefinitely. This fuzziness actually destroys trust—the company is asking employees to commit to itself without committing to them in return.

Many of your employees have responded by hedging their bets, jumping ship whenever a new opportunity presents itself, regardless of how much they profess their loyalty during the recruiting process or annual reviews.

Both parties act in ways that blatantly contradict their official positions. And thanks to this reciprocal self-deception, neither side trusts each other. Not surprisingly, neither side profits as fully as it might from their relationship. Employers continually lose valuable people. Employees fail to fully invest in their current position because they're constantly scanning the marketplace for new opportunities.

Managers, meanwhile, are caught in the middle. They're wary about even acknowledging the problem, much less solving it. Instead of thinking about how to facilitate growth in their employees in forward-looking ways, they worry about keeping their teams intact long enough to complete key projects. No one wants to risk being jilted, so no one invests in the long-term relationship.

Employers, managers, and employees need a new relationship framework where they make promises to one another they can actually keep. That's what this book aims to provide. And we think it will help build successful companies and powerful careers.

The old model of employment was a good fit for an era of stability. In stable times, companies grew larger to leverage economies of scale and process improvement. These titans offered an implicit deal to their workers: *We provide lifelong employment in exchange for loyal service.* "Maximizing employee security is a prime company goal," Earl Willis, General Electric's manager of employee benefits, wrote in 1962.[1] In that era, careers were considered nearly as permanent as marriage. Employers and employees committed to each other, for better or worse, through bull and bear markets, until retirement did them part. For white-collar professionals, progressing in one's career was like riding an escalator, with predictable advancement for those who followed the rules. Because both sides expected the relationship to be permanent, both sides were willing to invest in it and each other.

Then the world changed, both philosophically and technologically. The rise of shareholder capitalism led companies and managers to focus on hitting short-term financial targets to boost stock prices. Long-term investment took a backseat to short-term cost-cutting measures like "rightsizing"—or as we used to call it, *firing people*. Around the same time, the development of the microchip ushered in the Information Age, sparking a communications revolution and the globalization of business. Companies like the Big Three American automakers found themselves competing with leaner, hungrier competitors.

As a result of these shifts, the stability of the 1950s and 1960s gave way to rapid, unpredictable change, and once-stalwart companies began to be toppled out of the S&P 500 at a faster and faster rate.[2] Adaptability and entrepreneurship became key to achieving and sustaining success in business, their importance growing as the spread of computers and software imposed Moore's Law on every corner of the economy. Today, anyone with an internet connection has the power to connect with billions of others around the world. Never before in human history have so many people been connected by so many networks.

The traditional model of lifetime employment, so well-suited to periods of relative stability, is too rigid for today's networked age. Few American companies can provide the traditional career ladder for their employees anymore; the model is in varying degrees of disarray globally.

In response to these competitive pressures, many— probably most—companies have tried to become more flexible by reducing the employer-employee relationship to what's explicitly spelled out in a legal and binding contract. This legalistic approach treats both employees and jobs as short-term commodities. Need to cut costs? Lay off employees. Need new competencies? Don't train your people—hire different ones. "Employees are our most valuable resource," companies insist. But when Wall Street wants spending cuts, their "most valuable resource" suddenly morphs into their most fungible resource.

In the 1980s, a Conference Board survey found that 56 percent of executives believed "employees who are loyal to the company and further its business goals deserve an assurance of continued employment." Just a decade later, that figure had plummeted to 6 percent.[3] Remember GE's focus on maximizing employee security? By the 1990s, GE CEO Jack Welch was quoted as saying, "Loyalty to a company? It's nonsense."[4]

In the at-will era, employees have been encouraged to think of themselves as "free agents," seeking out the best opportunities for growth and changing jobs whenever better offers beckoned. The Towers Watson 2012 Global Workforce Study found that even though about half of employees wanted to stay with their current employer, most of them felt that they would have to take a job at a different company in order to advance their careers.[5]

"It's just business" has become the ruling philosophy. Loyalty is scarce, long-term ties are scarcer, but there's plenty of disillusionment to go around.

And so managers and employees end up staring at each other after the "Welcome to the Company" happy hour, knowing that their relationship relies on mutual self-deception, but unable to do anything about it.

As much as companies might yearn for a stable environment and employees might yearn for lifetime employment, the world has irrevocably changed. But we also can't keep going the way we've been going. Trust in the business world (as measured by the proportion of employees who say they have a "high level of trust in management and the organization" they work for) is near an all-time low.[6] A business without loyalty is a business without long-term thinking. A business without long-term thinking is a business that's unable to invest in the future. And a business that isn't investing in tomorrow's opportunities and technologies—well, that's a company already in the process of dying.

The Alliance

If we can't go back to the age of lifetime employment, and the status quo is untenable, it's time to rebuild the employer-employee relationship. The business world needs a new employment framework that facilitates mutual trust, mutual investment, and mutual benefit. An ideal framework encourages employees to develop their personal networks and act entrepreneurially without becoming mercenary job-hoppers. It allows companies to be dynamic and demanding but discourages them from treating employees like disposable assets.

The Alliance lays out a path forward for companies and their employees. We can't restore the old model of lifetime employment, but we *can* build a new type of loyalty that both recognizes economic realities and allows companies and employees to commit to each other. Our goal is to provide a framework for moving from a transactional to a relational approach. Think of employment as an alliance: a mutually beneficial deal, with explicit terms, between independent players. This employment alliance provides the framework managers and employees need for the trust and investment to build powerful businesses and careers.

In an alliance, employer and employee develop a relationship based on how they can add value to each other. Employers need to tell their employees, "Help make our company more valuable, and we'll make *you* more valuable." As Russ Hagey, Bain & Company's chief talent officer, tells recruits and consultants, "We are going to make you more marketable [in the labor market in general]."

Employees need to tell their bosses, "Help me grow and flourish, and I'll help the company grow and flourish." Employees invest in the company's success; the company invests in the employees' market value. By building a mutually beneficial alliance rather than simply exchanging money for time, employer and employee can invest in the relationship and take the risks necessary to pursue bigger payoffs.

For example, many HR leaders and executives get frustrated when they spend a lot of money on training and development programs, only to see employees walk out the door months later. If you think of your employees as free agents, the natural response is to slash training budgets. Why train a competitor's new hire? In an alliance, the manager can speak openly and honestly about the investment the company is willing to make in the employee and what it expects in return. The employee can speak openly and honestly about the type of growth he seeks (skills, experiences, and the like) and what he will invest in the company in return by way of effort and commitment. Both sides set clear expectations.

When a company and its managers and employees adopt this kind of approach, all parties can focus on maximizing medium- and long-term benefits, creating a larger pie for all and more innovation, resilience, and adaptability for the company.

Moving from Family to Team

In a famous presentation on his company's culture, Reed Hastings, the CEO of Netflix, stated, "We're a team, not a family."[7] He went on to advise managers to ask themselves, "Which of my people, if they told me they were leaving for a similar job at a peer company, would I fight hard to keep at Netflix? The other people should get a generous severance now so we can open a slot to try to find a star for that role."

We believe that most CEOs have good intentions when they describe their company as being "like family." They're searching for a model that represents the kind of relationships they want to have with their employees—a lifetime relationship with a sense of belonging. But using the term *family* makes it easy for misunderstandings to arise.

In a real family, parents can't fire their children. Imagine disowning a child for poor performance. "We're sorry, Susie, but your mom and I have decided you're just not a good fit for us. Your table-setting skills aren't delivering the exceptional customer service experiences we're known for. We're going to have to let you go. But don't take it the wrong way; it's just family." Unthinkable, right? But that's essentially what happens when a CEO describes the company as a family, then institutes layoffs. Regardless of what the law says about at-will employment, those employees will feel hurt and betrayed—with real justification.

In contrast, a professional sports team has a specific mission (to win games and championships), and its members come together to accomplish that mission. The composition of the team changes over time, either because a team member chooses to go to another team, or because the team's management decides to cut or trade a team member. In this sense, a business is far more like a sports team than a family.

Yet while a professional sports team doesn't assume lifetime employment, the principles of trust, mutual investment, and mutual benefit still apply. Teams win when their individual members trust each other enough to prioritize team success over individual glory; paradoxically, winning as a team is the best way for the team members to achieve individual success. The members of a winning team are highly sought after by other teams, both for the skills they demonstrate and for their ability to help a new team develop a winning culture.

The idea of a sports team defines how we *work* together, and toward what purpose, but the idea of a family still has relevance because it defines how we *treat* each other—with compassion, appreciation, and respect. (One benefit of establishing a corporate alumni network, for example, is how it allows employers and employees to relate to each other as a family, even after they're no longer under the same roof; more on this in chapters 7 and 8.)

Getting Value from Entrepreneurial Talent

We three authors come from a business environment where the employment alliance has already taken root—the high-tech start-up community of Silicon Valley. It's the best place in the world for adaptation and innovation, as demonstrated by its economic growth over the past decade. If you want your organization to be able to survive and thrive in an environment where change is rapid and disruptive innovation rampant, you need to develop the adaptability that is the hallmark of this ecosystem.

Obviously, not every industry works like Silicon Valley, nor should many established companies attempt wholesale adoption of start-up strategies. The question is *which* lessons from Silicon Valley are generally applicable. Mainstream media's coverage of Silicon Valley tends to focus on flashy details. But attributing the valley's success to four-star meals in cafeterias, Foosball tables, or even stock options is like attributing a Ferrari's power to its bright red paint job.

The real secret of Silicon Valley is that it's really all about the people. Sure, there are plenty of stories in the press about the industry's young geniuses, but surprisingly few about its management practices. What the mainstream press misses is that Silicon Valley's success comes from the way its companies build alliances with their employees. Here, talent really is the most valuable resource, and employees are treated accordingly. The most successful Silicon Valley businesses succeed because they use the alliance to recruit, manage, and retain an incredibly talented team of entrepreneurial employees.

Entrepreneurial employees possess what eBay CEO John Donahoe calls the *founder mind-set*. As he put it to us, "People with the founder mind-set drive change, motivate people, and just get stuff done." Our previous book, *The Start-up of You*, showed individual professionals how to develop the founder mind-set for any type of career, including a career spent working at one or two companies. Indeed, having a founder mind-set doesn't necessarily mean you are going to start your own company. Many people with such instincts are quite happy to work at companies like eBay or LinkedIn— provided such companies maintain an employment alliance that encourages entrepreneurial behavior. Having employees focused on the start-up of their career is a good thing; after all, employees who don't feel a pressing need to invest aggressively in their own careers probably won't be capable of the quick, decisive actions that your company needs to adapt and grow.

The founder mind-set, and the alliance required to incorporate it into your company, weren't always quite so critical. In the old economy—the stable one—efficiency was the cardinal virtue. Employers placed employees on fixed tracks so that they could develop ever-higher degrees of specialization. But when markets change, specialization often shifts from asset to liability, as in the case of the proverbial buggy-whip manufacturer. In the new economy of fierce competition and rapid technological change, the markets are constantly shifting.

Today, *entrepreneurial thinking and doing are the most important capabilities companies need from their employees.* As the competitive pace increases, it becomes more and more critical. Consider the effect of just a few entrepreneurial employees at two giants of innovation, Pixar and Amazon.

John Lasseter at Pixar

John Lasseter is the type of entrepreneurial employee every innovative company wants. If you've seen movies like *Toy Story*, *Finding Nemo*, and *Monsters, Inc.*, you know his work intimately. His movies have grossed over $3.5 billion in the United States alone, and have averaged over $250 million at the box office, making Pixar the most successful movie studio of all time.[8] What most people don't know is the story of how Disney, his original employer, fired him.

Lasseter began his career at Disney as a young animation designer in the days when animation was created with pen and paper, then converted into film. One day, a colleague showed him a video from a local conference about the emerging technology of computer-generated animation. Lasseter was struck by a vision—Disney should create an entire film using computer-generated animation. He went to managers and pitched the idea. They listened carefully to his pitch, then sent him back to his desk. A few minutes later, he received a phone call from the head of Disney's animation department—informing him that he was being fired. The rationale for his dismissal: he was too distracted with his crazy ideas.

Like many with the founder mind-set, Lasseter refused to give up on his dream. He joined George

Lucas's Lucasfilm, where he pursued computer animation as a member of Ed Catmull's computer division. A few years later, Lucas sold the then-unprofitable division to Steve Jobs, who named the resulting company Pixar. And in 1995, Pixar partnered with Disney to release the world's first computer-animated feature film, *Toy Story*.

In 2006, eleven years after *Toy Story* was released and twenty-three years after Lasseter was fired, Disney realized it had made a mistake by rejecting computer animation and ended up bringing Lasseter back. But it would cost them—the Walt Disney Company spent over $7 billion to buy Pixar. And that's how Lasseter ended up back at Disney as its chief creative officer of Disney Animation Studios.[9]

Disney's management hired an entrepreneurial talent like Lasseter, but they treated him as a commodity rather than an ally, and in the process, they lost their chance to develop a multibillion-dollar business. Lasseter would have been happy to develop that business within Disney, but his managers wouldn't let him.

Benjamin Black and Amazon Web Services

Amazon didn't make the same mistake as Disney. Recently, it used the principles of the alliance to generate a new multibillion-dollar business. Amazon has become a leader in the field of cloud computing, thanks to Amazon Web Services (AWS), which allows companies to rent online storage and computing power, rather than buying and operating their own servers. Companies ranging from *Fortune* 500 giants to one-person start-ups run their businesses on AWS. What most people don't realize is that the idea for AWS didn't come from Amazon's famed entrepreneurial founder and CEO, Jeff Bezos, or even from a member of his executive team, but rather from an "ordinary" employee.

In 2003, website engineering manager Benjamin Black wrote a short paper describing a vision for Amazon's infrastructure and suggested selling virtual servers as a service.[10] He realized that the same operational expertise that made Amazon an efficient retailer could be repurposed to serve the general market for computing power. Black and his manager, Chris Pinkham, pitched Bezos on the concept, and after a few more iterations, Bezos put Pinkham in charge of a project to develop what would become AWS. When Amazon's board questioned whether the company should tackle something so unrelated to online retail, Bezos defended the idea and pushed it through. Launched in 2006, AWS contributed an estimated $3.8 billion to Amazon's revenues in 2013.[11]

Unlike John Lasseter's bosses at Disney, Bezos was open to the entrepreneurial contributions of Amazon's individual employees—even when those ideas were outside what Wall Street (and even his own board of directors) considered the company's core business. AWS represents precisely the kind of value creation any CEO or shareholder would want from their employees. Want your employees to come up with multibillion-dollar ideas while on the job? You have to attract professionals with the founder mind-set and then harness their entrepreneurial impulses for your company. As Intuit CEO Brad Smith told us, "A leader's job is not to put greatness into people, but rather to recognize that it already exists, and to create the environment where that greatness can emerge and grow."

Having the Courage to Lead Honest Conversations

We wrote this book to share our vision for how the employer-employee relationship should work. Our concept of the alliance represents a potentially controversial departure from the standard take on corporate management. You may not agree with everything we have to say. But if you consider it a priority to recruit, manage, and retain the talent that today's organizations need to adapt and thrive, this book will offer both a framework and practical advice, including a detailed template for a statement of alliance as an appendix. We'll tackle questions like:

- How do I build trust and loyalty with my employees if I can't guarantee lifetime employment?

- How does the alliance apply to different types and levels of employees?

- How do I build a relationship with my entrepreneurial employees when our ultimate goals and values might differ?

- What kind of networking and personal brand building should I allow my employees to do in the workplace?

- How can I run an effective corporate alumni network given limited time and resources?

Adopting the alliance is ideally a companywide endeavor led by the CEO. CEOs or senior executives will find commentary throughout on how a company should think about these ideas. Some advice, like establishing a corporate alumni network, is best carried out with the support of the CEO's office.

But we also recognize that the people who bear the primary responsibility for putting the alliance into practice are, in fact, managers. If you're a manager, you'll find tools that will help you implement the alliance so that you can start transforming your department or team.

For individual employees, this book can help them understand what they can commit to and expect from the alliance they negotiate with their managers. (For more direct advice on how to transform an individual career using entrepreneurial principles, see our earlier book, *The Start-up of You*.)

The Alliance isn't just an argument that we need a new way of doing business. It's a blueprint for how to actually do it. It's a way to invest in the long-term future without sacrificing adaptability. The alliance makes employees more valuable by making them more adaptive and skillful, gives managers the tools and guidance to work better with their direct reports, and teaches companies how to effectively leverage and retain entrepreneurial employees.

2

Tours of Duty

Organizing the Alliance

How did David Hahn go from a twenty-three-year-old with no business experience to one of the most sought-after executives in Silicon Valley? The answer is the unique way he structured his nine years of working at LinkedIn. Over four distinct "tours of duty," Hahn transformed the company and his career.

His first tour was as a junior business analyst; his last tour was running all of LinkedIn's monetization products as a vice president. Each time, with a different manager, he scoped out a mission objective that led to long-term benefit for both sides. For the company, it shipped dozens of key products under Hahn's stewardship. For the employee (Hahn), he acquired the managerial experience he needed to fulfill his longtime aspiration to become a successful company builder (we'll discuss Hahn's values and aspirations in greater length in chapter 3).

As a manager at LinkedIn, Hahn was also explicit about tours of duty with his team members, encouraging them to rotate to new tours of duty within LinkedIn so that they could gain operational experience across multiple areas. Hahn did this despite that the fact that many of his team members were perfectly happy within his group. He saw it as his duty to help them grow. This seeming contradiction—regularly changing roles in the context of a long-term relationship—is the essence of the tour of duty framework.

The phrase *tour of duty* comes from the military, where it refers to a single specific assignment or deployment. Soldiers will typically serve multiple tours of duty during their military careers, much as employees will take on a number of different projects or initiatives during the course of their work at a particular company and throughout their careers.

Clearly the parallel is only partial—it's difficult and arguably unwise to run a business like a military unit, especially in today's world. You probably don't have the authority and tools of a commanding officer. When an employee leaves your company, he might get a farewell party. When a soldier leaves his unit without permission, he goes AWOL and gets a court martial (and probably several years in a military prison). Nor will most companies offer the job security and social safety net of the US military. But the metaphor conveys the key concept that both military and business tours of duty have in common: focus on honorably accomplishing a specific, finite mission.

In the context of the alliance, the tour of duty represents an ethical commitment by employer and employee to a specific mission. We see this approach as a way to incorporate some of the advantages from both lifetime employment and free agency. Like lifetime employment, the tour of duty allows employers and employees to build trust and mutual investment; like free agency, it preserves the flexibility that both employers and employees need to adapt to a rapidly changing world.

This approach can relieve the pressure on you and your employees alike because it builds trust incrementally. Everyone commits in smaller steps and, as with any kind of meaningful relationship, the relationship deepens as each side proves themselves to each other.

The tour of duty is a way of choreographing the progressive commitments that form the alliance.

By recasting careers at your company as a series of successive tours of duty, you can better attract and retain entrepreneurial employees. When recruiting top talent, offering a clear tour of duty with specific benefits and success outcomes beats vague promises like "you'll get valuable experience." Defining an attractive tour of duty lets you point to concrete ways that it will enhance the employee's *personal* brand—while he's at the company and if and when he works elsewhere—by integrating a specific mission, picking up real skills, building new relationships, and so on.

When Reid first founded LinkedIn, for example, he offered an explicit deal to talented employees. If they signed up for a tour of duty of between two to four years and made an important contribution to some part of the business, Reid and the company would help advance their careers, preferably in the form of another tour of duty at LinkedIn. This approach worked: the company got an engaged employee who worked to achieve tangible results for LinkedIn and who could be an advocate and resource for the company if he chose to leave after one or more tours of duty. The employee transformed his career by enhancing his portfolio of skills and experiences.

A few of the managers we spoke with for this book worried that the tour of duty framework might give employees "permission" to leave. But permission is not yours to give or to withhold, and believing you have that power is simply a self-deception that leads to a dishonest relationship with your employees. Employees don't need your permission to switch companies, and if you try to assert that right, they'll simply make their move behind your back.

The finite term of the tour of duty provides crisper focus and a mutually agreeable time frame for discussing the future of the relationship. It gives a valued employee concrete and compelling reasons to "stick it out" and finish a tour. Most importantly, a realistic tour of duty lets both sides be honest, which is a necessity for trust.

We recognize the irony of looking to Silicon Valley for lessons on building long-term relationships. After all, Silicon Valley is where an engineer can update her LinkedIn profile in the morning and have five job offers by lunchtime. But this is precisely why you can learn from Silicon Valley. This is one of the fastest-moving, most competitive economies on the planet. It's immensely difficult to retain quality employees, so the companies and managers that convince their people to stay must be doing something extraordinary. The talent management techniques—such as tours of duty—that work in this brutal environment are battle-tested. If they work here, they can work anywhere.

Building Trust through Honest Conversations

Mike Gamson is one of LinkedIn's most senior executives. He's risen through the organization over nearly seven years to the role of senior vice president, Global Solutions, where he oversees all sales operations. In part, his ascent is explained by his ability to develop talent, which is LinkedIn's number one operating priority. The headline he wrote on his LinkedIn profile says it all: "Passionate about investing in people."

Gamson said he builds trust through honesty: "I know my employees are likely to leave the company at some point. Recognizing that fact doesn't temper my interest in investing in them. On the contrary, it fuels it. Assuring them that it's more than OK to talk together about their career, even if it doesn't include LinkedIn, helps establish an atmosphere of open honesty, and helps them understand that we are aligned in our interest in making them better."

Honesty is only the first step in Gamson's strategy: "I explain how my job is to create career-trajectory-changing opportunities for them, and their responsibility is to take advantage of exposure to the experiences here to grasp that opportunity and create long-term value for themselves. In some cases, the value will manifest most explicitly later in their career after they leave. During the years we share at LinkedIn, we both win when they grow fastest. This shared interest is at the heart of my management style and my personal promise to my employees."

Another LinkedIn executive, senior vice president of engineering Kevin Scott, models the importance of honesty even more explicitly. He asks every person he manages, "What job do you envision having after you leave LinkedIn?" He asks the same question of folks who are interviewing for jobs at LinkedIn ("What job do you want after you work at LinkedIn?") in order to make sure the company can offer a tour of duty that will advance their future career.

Both Gamson's and Scott's approaches illustrate the fundamental paradox of the tour of duty: acknowledging that the employee might leave is actually the best way to build trust, and thus develop the kind of relationship that convinces great people to stay.

Rich Lesser, the CEO of The Boston Consulting Group, calls this building an "opt-in" culture. "The reality of being an employer is not that you make people feel an *obligation* to stay," Lesser told us. "You hire the best people you can possibly find. Then it's up to you to create an environment where great people *decide* to stay and invest their time. Since we made this an emphasis, our employee satisfaction scores have been better than ever, and our retention of top talent is substantially higher than a decade ago."

Different Types of Tours

The specifics of a tour of duty vary greatly based on the person, company, functional area, industry, and job title. To help understand these distinctions, we've classified an employee's tour of duty into one of three general types.

Rotational

A Rotational tour isn't personalized to the employee and tends to be highly interchangeable—it's easy to swap an employee in to or out of a predefined role.

The first flavor of Rotational is a structured program of finite duration, usually aimed at entry-level employees. For example, investment banks and management consultancies have defined two- to four-year analyst programs. Everyone is on the same basic program, generally for a fixed period of time and for a single go-round. These programs are often explicit "on-ramps" to transition new employees from school to work, or from their previous employers to the new employer's unique work environment.

Many of the leading companies in Silicon Valley have also adopted the Rotational tour model to hire and train entry-level employees in "classes." For example, Google's People Operations (HR) department hires recent college graduates into a structured, twenty-seven-month Rotational tour that allows them to try out three different roles in three, nine-month rotations.[1] Facebook follows a similar model for new product managers, who go through three rotations in three different product groups in eighteen months.[2] LinkedIn even has a cross-functional training program called RotateIn.

The purpose of this type of Rotational tour is to allow both parties to assess the potential long-term fit between employer and employee. If there seems to be a fit, the next step is to define a more personalized follow-up tour to maximize that fit. If either side doesn't see a fit, the employee will probably leave the company, but without stigma or relationship damage.

The other type of Rotational tour applies to employees at all career stages. These tours are highly structured and largely programmatic, but focus on maximizing the *current* fit between an employee and his role, rather than grooming the employee for a different role. Most blue-collar jobs fit into this category. For example, working on a particular assembly line can be thought of as a Rotational tour. A UPS driver is on a Rotational tour as well—it's routinized and structured, and the role is such that talent can be swapped in and out relatively seamlessly.

Transformational

Unlike the Rotational tour, a Transformational tour is personalized. The focus is less on a fixed time period and more on the completion of a specific mission. It's negotiated one-on-one by you and your employee. Most managers already spend a lot of time "managing" their people, but lack a rigorous framework for honest conversation and for defining specific expectations. The tour of duty framework lets you make this process structured and explicit, rather than vague and implied.

The central promise of a Transformational tour is that the employee will have the opportunity to transform both his career and the company. His LinkedIn profile (or résumé) should look considerably more impressive afterward! As a Transformational tour of duty enters its final stage, you and your employee can start to negotiate a follow-up tour of duty to keep the employee at the company. Because a Transformational tour represents a more intense forward-looking commitment than a Rotational tour, the default expectation is that both parties want to invest in the long term, and that there will likely be a follow-up tour.

A general rule of thumb is that an *initial* transformational tour of a duty lasts two to five years. It's a time period that seems to be nearly universal for any organization or industry. In the software business, the two- to five-year term fits with a normal product development cycle, allowing an employee to see a major project through. One reflection of this cycle is that Silicon Valley stock option grants typically vest over four years. In the consumer packaged goods business, companies like Procter & Gamble (P&G) start their new brand managers on a two- to four-year tour.

Making a real commitment allows an employee to accomplish something substantive. As Intuit CEO Brad Smith said, "Year 1 [of the tour] lets you gain the important context for the role, year 2 is about putting your definitive mark on transformational change, and years 3 to 5 are about implementing and growing your successes—or pivoting when assumptions don't play out the way you expect." Google chairman Eric Schmidt told us he also likes to define tours in terms of five years—a couple of years to learn, a couple of years to do the job, and a year to arrange the transition. As you strengthen the alliance with an employee, follow-on Transformational tours can be even longer in scope than the standard two to five years.

Arranging a series of Transformational tours within a company is also a way to offer employees meaningful internal mobility. Joan Burns, the senior vice president and head of resourcing for North America at HSBC, uses this internal mobility to improve employee retention: "In financial services, people can feel stagnant. People think career development means moving up the ladder, but moving from side to side can be just as valuable. We want to help people develop different skill sets that can help them and us." Here in Silicon Valley, Cisco's Talent Connection program, which helps current employees find new opportunities *within* Cisco, increased employees' satisfaction with career development by almost 20 percent.[3]

Foundational

Jony Ive at Apple. Fred Smith at FedEx. Ginni Rometty at IBM. These are people whose lives are fundamentally intertwined with their companies. These are people on a Foundational tour of duty.

Exceptional alignment of employer and employee is the hallmark of a Foundational tour. (We'll discuss the concept of alignment in more detail in chapter 3.) If an employee sees working at the company as his last job, and the company wants the employee to stay until he retires, he is on a Foundational tour of duty. The company has become the foundation of the person's career and even *life*, and the employee has become one of the foundations of the company. The employee sees his life's work as the company's mission and vice versa. The Foundational tour recognizes and formalizes that reality.

Certain types of employees are likely to be on Foundational tours. By definition, company founders and CEOs are Foundational. For example, John Mackey started Whole Foods in 1980 and is still going strong nearly thirty-five years later. Mackey is a veritable toddler next to Warren Buffett, who has been running Berkshire Hathaway since 1965—nearly fifty years. At LinkedIn, even though Jeff Weiner has only been CEO for five years, he has become so Foundational to the company that Reid refers to Weiner as a cofounder, even though Weiner joined the company long after its founding.[4]

Ideally, most of the top executives of a company should be on Foundational tours. The average tenure of the executives who report to the CEO at exemplars of adaptability such as Apple, Amazon, and Google is over a decade. When teams work together over many years, they share a common background of experience, enabling more rapid communications and decision making.

However, Foundational tours shouldn't be restricted to senior management. People on Foundational tours, wherever they are on the org chart, provide a company with continuity and institutional memory. These stewards of the company way are the intellectual and emotional foundation of the organization. For example, they take greater pride and care when it comes to product quality because they develop a sense of (nonfinancial) ownership. As the expression goes, no one ever washes a rental car. A Foundational employee would never allow the company to cut corners to meet short-term financial goals.

Think of a Foundational tour as a form of marriage—a long-term relationship that both parties anticipate will be permanent, in which both parties assume a moral obligation to try hard to make it work before ending the relationship. Like a healthy marriage, a Foundational tour still requires regular, explicit conversations to make sure both parties remain content. People and companies can change, and it's not guaranteed that employee and company will always be perfectly aligned.

Because the Foundational tour of duty requires a deep degree of trust and alignment, it's exceedingly rare that an employee will enter a company on such a tour. Entry-level employees will probably start with either a Rotational or Transformational tour, while higher-level employees will begin with a Transformational one. Employees who transition from Transformational to Foundational develop a sense of psychological ownership of the long-term company mission.

Consider the example of Intuit's Brad Smith. Smith was brought into the company in 2003 on a

Transformational tour of duty. When Smith first joined as the general manager of the Intuit Developer Network, both he and the company wanted to assess their long-term fit. Neither side assumed that Smith would one day become the CEO of the company. But during the course of that Transformational tour, and the two tours that followed, Smith and Intuit kept strengthening their relationship to the point that in 2008, he agreed to embark on a Foundational tour—this time as president and CEO. Anyone can see that Smith is on a Foundational tour just from his LinkedIn profile URL: www.linkedin.com/in/bradsmithintuit.

Blending Tours of Duty

We summarize the tour of duty framework with table 2-1.

There isn't one type of tour that is superior to the others; most large companies use all three types, albeit with different groups of employees. For example, a company shouldn't place the majority of its employees on Foundational tours. That's essentially returning to the old model of lifetime employment. Many star

TABLE 2-1

The tour of duty framework

	Design	Deal	Duration	Transition
Rotational	Incoming employees are onboarded programmatically	Assessment of potential future fit at the company; predictable employment	For typical analyst programs, usually one to three years; for other rotational tours: ongoing	Employee may start another rotation or shift to a Transformational tour; little to no moral onus for leaving the company afterward
Transformational	Negotiated individually	Transformation of employee's career; transformation of company	Determined by the specific mission; usually two to five years	Prior to completing the mission, employee negotiates a new tour at existing company, or transitions out
Foundational	Negotiated individually	For company, a steward of core values; for employee, deep purpose and meaning from work	Ongoing	Both parties anticipate the relationship will be permanent and make their best efforts to stay together

employees actually refuse to accept Foundational tours precisely because of their high career aspirations. Ambitious companies often try to recruit ambitious stars who want to run the show someday. If these companies are good at recruiting, they simply don't have enough CEO or general manager openings to satisfy all their stars' ambitions—which means these employees will one day have to leave the company to realize their ultimate goal. Recall what happened when GE tapped Jeff Immelt to succeed Jack Welch; the other top candidates left GE almost immediately to assume the CEO role at other companies (Bob Nardelli at The Home Depot, Jim McNerney at 3M).

Think of the different tours of duty as the ingredients in a metal alloy. Different mixtures lead to different capabilities, which are suited to different uses. We don't use the same alloy for building a skyscraper that we do for the parts in a jet turbine or for a fine chef's knife.

Rotational tours provide *scalability* by helping companies hire large numbers of employees into stable, well-understood roles. The standardized nature of these tours makes them easier to implement and recruit for, especially at scale.

Transformational tours provide *adaptability* by helping companies bring in the specific skills and experiences required. Dynamic industries usually have greater competition, faster-paced technological change, and a more intense war for talent. The founder mind-set is critical to success in these industries, which means companies in those industries need a higher proportion of employees on Transformational tours.

Foundational tours provide *continuity* by helping companies retain employees who focus on the long term. Your senior management team should consist of Foundational employees.

The optimal blend of Rotational, Transformation, and Foundational tours depends on the specific market conditions of your company. Silicon Valley companies, including start-ups, rely primarily (roughly 80 percent) on Transformational tours, with a small number of Foundational and Rotational employees. This allows them to field a high-performance, highly adaptable workforce. In contrast, a manufacturing company with a stable market and a quasi-monopoly would probably rely far more on Rotational tours (for routine, lower-value work) and Foundational tours (for tapping legacy knowledge).

Broadly, the need for adaptability has shifted the optimal blend away from the Foundational and toward the Transformational, and this trend will likely continue. Silicon Valley is less an exception than an early adopter. We have been dealing with global competition and rapid technology change for decades, and in reaction, we gravitated toward the Transformational model. Since Transformational tours represent the greatest departure from most companies' management practices, this book focuses on defining and implementing this type of tour. Thus, whenever we refer to a *tour of duty* or *tour*, you can assume that we're referring to a Transformational tour.

A Broadly Applicable Framework

No company could be more the antithesis of a Silicon Valley start-up than fast food giant McDonald's. The company is big, it's old, and it makes most of its money by serving the same hamburgers, fries, and shakes it served over half a century ago.

Yet despite these differences, McDonald's actually illustrates the spirit behind tours of duty. Len Jillard, chief people officer for McDonald's Canada, said, "Whether you're with us for one year or if you're here for more, we will help you meet your future.

We will invest in you and your growth. You can take many of the competencies we will help you develop in whatever it is you choose to do—whether it's with McDonald's or whether it's outside of McDonald's."[5] Some people, like Jillard himself, stay at the company a very long time. Most leave the company after a tour or two—but they can draw useful lessons from their experience. Before he was a famous CEO, a young Jeff Bezos flipped burgers for McDonald's. Years later, he said that his manager at McDonald's was "excellent" and taught him the importance of responsibility![6]

An organization doesn't have to be a for-profit business to use tours of duty to build adaptive teams. Endeavor is a global nonprofit that serves entrepreneurs; this makes adaptability essential. According to cofounder Linda Rottenberg, this need for agility informed her adoption of the tour of duty model as a talent strategy. "Tours of duty are how I set up Endeavor's employee alliances from the get-go back in 1997," Rottenberg said. "I wanted to hire entrepreneurial rock stars that could compete anywhere and could match the talent of the Endeavor Entrepreneurs in our portfolio."

Endeavor explicitly hired people expecting them to serve multiple Rotational tours of duty, and to maintain a lifelong relationship with the organization. "Young folks recruited from the very best US colleges typically do two two-year Rotational tours of duty, one in search-and-selection and another in entrepreneur services," said Rottenberg. "Nearly all then go on to a top-five business school, join a top-tier tech company, or start a company of their own—having been bitten by the entrepreneurship bug. They all remain loyal Endeavor ambassadors as corporate alumni."

Tours of Duty for the Corporate Middle Class

Companies have long devoted resources to crafting personalized roles and career paths for their stars. Companies such as General Electric rotate promising young executives through a series of assignments to help them gain experience in different functions and markets.

Yet it is possible—indeed, necessary—to extend this personalized approach to all employees using the tour of duty framework. As the world has become less stable, you can't *just* rely on a few stars at the top to provide the necessary adaptability. Companies need entrepreneurial talent throughout the organization in order to respond to rapid changes. Obviously, you will spend less time reviewing the tour of duty principles with a summer intern than with a senior executive, but the same principles hold true for both. Every employee relationship should be bidirectional in nature; it should be clear how the employee benefits and how the employer benefits.

The employees who sit between entry-level and senior management make up the "corporate middle class." For these employees, a successful tour of duty cannot always be attached to a certain job title or compensation package. A competent professional in the corporate middle class might complete multiple tours of duty without a change in job title. At LinkedIn, for example, there are hundreds of excellent software engineers. The company values them immensely, even though promotion into the managerial ranks isn't likely for (or even viewed as desirable by) many of them. The start and end of a tour of duty for them is marked by changes and growth in their network, progress in their projects, and changes in their skills and opportunities. (We'll cover some of these smaller transformations later in the book in chapter 4.)

What's more, rather than the manager doing all the work of planning tours of duty, the corporate middle class needs to play an especially active role in the process. They should be looking for potential opportunities to make a positive difference for the company and identifying ways they can invest in themselves to advance their own career. This isn't an imposition on employees: in 2012, the Career Engagement Group conducted a survey in which 75 percent of employees say that they're willing to use their own time to further their careers and take on additional learning that would benefit them at work.[7]

Table 2-2 shows how tours of duty differ for stars and the corporate middle class.

TABLE 2-2

Stars versus middle class

	Stars	Middle class
Job title	Regular upgrades	Not necessarily any change
Who leads the process	Their managers	Managers, but with employees taking a more active, proactive role
Employee goal	Advancing the company and their career by achieving aggressive goals	Maintaining employability by helping the company adapt

Longer-Term Alliances

By providing a structure for an employee to take on a series of different, personally meaningful missions, tours of duty help an employee build a long-term career at a company. Yes, a tour of duty has an end point, but a successful end to a tour of duty can be beginning a new tour of duty at the same company. For example, software maker SAS Institute "believes that its employees will have three or four careers over their working lives. The company wants them to have all of their careers at SAS."[8]

Each completed tour of duty builds the bond of mutual trust, and knowing when a tour of duty is drawing to a close allows you to begin the process of working with the employee to define the next tour at the company—before that employee starts to look elsewhere. Even if the employee wants to explore options outside the company, in a trusting alliance, he'll grant you the "Right of First Conversation," which means he'll discuss his plans with you before he approaches other employers. We'll discuss this concept in greater depth later. These planned transitions from one tour to another are like the expansion joints we build into buildings and bridges—they allow the relationship to bend as needed, rather than rupturing under the strain of trying to maintain a fixed configuration. Deina King, a global strategic accounts manager (and a top overall salesperson) at LinkedIn, illustrates the retention power of the framework. She's been at LinkedIn for more than five years. She told us, "I probably won't keep doing my current job for another five years—the current of transformation is so strong at LinkedIn, I'm sure I'll be pulled into a new challenge. In the future, I would like to make a move. I'd love to be able to stay at the company, and I've told my managers that." Not only has the company been able to build a high degree of trust with King, who has given her manager *years* of advance notice, she explicitly wants to sign up for another tour of duty. This is not the attitude of a job-hopper; it's the attitude of a high performer who's committed to continual professional development and challenge.

The importance of continuity will depend on the dynamics of your company and its industry, of course. The Boeing Company, for example, employs thousands of engineers and estimates that it has to train an engineer for a decade before he'll reach full productivity. Conversely, a Boeing engineer who spends a decade learning how to build Dreamliner aircraft has invested in a set of skills that are highly valuable to Boeing, but not nearly so valuable to other employers. To unlock the value of that training and those skills, Boeing and its individual engineers have to commit to long-term, essentially Foundational tours of duty. The point of the tour of duty framework is to enable a high-trust, high-integrity conversation that allows both sides to make wise investments, whatever the length of the tour.

Walking the Walk: How LinkedIn Uses Tours of Duty

Perhaps the best way to illustrate the flexibility and range of the tour of duty is with more concrete examples. Here are two such stories from Reid's experiences at LinkedIn.

Eda Gultekin: Building a Long-Term Relationship

Eda Gultekin is the global head of solutions in the Talent Solutions group at LinkedIn. Straight out of college, Gultekin fulfilled her childhood dream of being an engineer by taking a job designing sprinkler motors. While she enjoyed her work, she discovered that she liked talking with people better than sitting in front of a computer all day. Like many young engineers who want to make a transition, she went back to school, earning her master's degree in engineering and management from Stanford University.

After Stanford, she embarked on a classic Rotational tour of duty as a consultant at Bain. Her two and a half years there were a great experience, but she still felt that something was missing. "I'm an execution freak," Gultekin told us. "I love operational things, and I wanted ownership of results." As a top performer at Bain, she qualified for an "externship" opportunity. She wanted to gain hands-on business experience so she reached out to a former Bain colleague, Dan Shapero, who had joined LinkedIn the prior year.

Together with Mike Gamson, then the vice president of Talent Solutions, Gultekin and Shapero defined a six-month tour of duty for her. LinkedIn was worried that it might have a churn problem with some of its customers; Gultekin's objective was to determine whether or not this was the case, and if it was, to propose a solution.

Once Gultekin dug into the issue, she decided that the scope of her project needed to be broadened, which she discussed with Gamson. The results of her analysis ultimately led to a new sales team structure designed to improve customer management.

During the course of Gultekin's initial tour of duty at LinkedIn, it became apparent to all that she and the organization were a good fit. "Let's figure out your role," Gamson said, and he, Shapero, and Gultekin worked together to define a new Transformational tour of duty. This time, her objective was to help the sales team figure out how to sell new products. This would allow her to fulfill one of her career goals—gaining management experience—while helping LinkedIn improve in a key growth area.

As with her previous tour of duty, Gultekin redefined her mission along the way. The timing wasn't right to execute her original objective, so instead she set out to build LinkedIn's recruitment media business (known as Talent Brand) within the Talent Solutions group from the ground up. Because it was a brand-new area, she didn't yet have the support of cross-functional teams. In a classic example of entrepreneurial hustle, Gultekin did whatever was necessary to achieve the mission. She built a business case for investment in the area and built a team of employees. She taught herself SQL and learned Salesforce.com so that she would have the hands-on skills necessary to enhance the online stages of the sales process.

The results speak for themselves. In 2009, that particular business line had a $1,200,000 annual run rate. By the time Gultekin's tour ended in 2013, the run rate had increased to $200 million in annual revenues. Talent Brand is now 20 percent of LinkedIn's overall Talent Solutions business and the global team of presales consultants, analysts, and account managers she started in 2010 now includes eighty-five people.

Gultekin's first two tours of duty built an incredibly strong alliance between her, her managers, and LinkedIn, which helped them deal with the unexpected. Due to complications with her pregnancy, Gultekin had to start her maternity leave several months earlier than expected. Despite the stressful circumstances, Gultekin felt confident she could return to LinkedIn because of the strength of the relationship she and the company had built. After the birth of her daughter,

Shapero even encouraged her to take extra time for her recovery, which meant that she was away from the office for a total of eleven months—the final trimester of pregnancy and eight months of maternity leave. Gultekin did her part as well; she touched base with her manager on a monthly business to stay on top of the business.

When the time came for her to return to the office, Gultekin found the process of defining a new tour of duty smooth and nearly seamless. About three months before the end of her maternity leave, Gultekin and Shapero worked out her next tour of duty. "When I talked with Dan," she said, "it felt like I had never been gone. I thought I had the same opportunities I would have had before my maternity leave." After a brief period with her old team to help her transition back to full-time work, she embarked on another Transformational tour of duty, this time in the sales organization.

As with her previous tours, the process of defining the tour was a collaboration between Gultekin and her manager. "Dan always asks, 'What do you want to do in five years?' and we work backwards from there," Gultekin told us. "I want to be a general manager, so we decided that I needed to add sales to my toolkit. I had never done sales in my life but he knew that my fresh perspective could be useful." Notice how the mission had to serve the needs of both the employee and the business; Gultekin and LinkedIn have a strong alliance because they have the mutual trust to commit to a mutual investment (shifting to sales) that will provide mutual benefit (a more well-rounded skill set for Gultekin, and a fresh perspective for LinkedIn).

As you can see from Gultekin's example, the different types of tour of duty can work together to weave a career, from the classic Rotational tour she did at Bain, to the short-term exploratory tour she and LinkedIn used to get to know each other, to the Transformational tours she negotiated with Dan Shapero and Mike Gamson. The tour of duty framework offers the flexibility to deal with changes (such as all the different times Gultekin began a tour, then worked to redefine it) and unexpected external events (such as the complications with her pregnancy). Through it all, tours of duty have helped Gultekin and her various managers build a stronger, long-term relationship. Employers that offer attractive tours of duty *can* retain top performers for the long term.

Matt Cohler: Maintaining the Alliance After the Job Ends

Even when LinkedIn can't retain a top performer, the company still tries to maintain a mutually beneficial alliance. Consider the example of Matt Cohler, who left LinkedIn nearly a decade ago.

In 2003, at the age of twenty-six, Cohler left the high pay and brand umbrella of McKinsey & Company to join LinkedIn, then a tiny start-up that was living in the shadow of Friendster. Reid, as CEO, was his new boss and did something none of Cohler's previous managers had done. Rather than simply hiring Cohler into a particular job or position, Reid worked with the young consultant to define an explicit tour of duty that would help both employer and employee.

Cohler's goal was to become a venture capitalist. But Reid argued that gaining operational experience at a successful start-up was a better path to being named a general partner at a venture capital firm than trying to join a firm straight out of McKinsey. Reid pitched Cohler on a unique tour of duty. Cohler would act as Reid's right-hand person. In this role, he would learn from the company's CEO and get extremely broad exposure to all the functional areas in the business.

In exchange, Cohler committed to doing whatever it took to build the business, regardless of whether those projects fell under any traditional job titles or career paths. By completing this mission, Cohler would add both the LinkedIn and Reid Hoffman brands to his personal portfolio. Thus, even though Cohler's ultimate goal of becoming a venture capitalist necessarily lay beyond LinkedIn's boundaries, he and Reid were able to align their short-term aspirations and interests.

After three years at LinkedIn, Cohler approached Reid to tell him that he was thinking about leaving LinkedIn to join an even younger social networking start-up that called itself "The Facebook." While Reid didn't want to lose Cohler, he advised Cohler to accept the Facebook offer, since it would help him move closer to his goal of becoming a venture capitalist by giving him greater diversity of start-up experience. Reid also gave Cohler his last assignment: to find his own replacement at LinkedIn.

After four years at Facebook, Cohler left for a new tour of duty—this time as a general partner at Benchmark, one of Silicon Valley's top venture firms. Even today, Reid has Cohler speak with high-value LinkedIn employees to explain the benefits of undertaking a tour of duty at the company. Reid and Matt Cohler still have a close relationship; for example, they sit together on the board of Edmodo, a start-up they invested in together in 2011. Matt Cohler's tour of duty at LinkedIn presents a textbook case of a mutually beneficial alliance that persists even after the official employment relationship has ended.

More Online: Learn how to structure tours of duty for different industries and functional areas, and join the conversation about the framework at www.theallianceframework.com/ToD.

3

Building Alignment in a Tour of Duty

Aligning Employee Goals and Values with the Company's

In the Industrial Age, the company subsumed an employee's individual identity. The company offered lifetime employment and defined benefit pensions. In exchange, the employee put his head down, worked hard, and subordinated any personal aspirations and values to those of the company. In his classic book *The Organization Man*, first published in 1956, journalist William Whyte described the fundamental principle of this age: "What's good for the group is good for the individual." Of course, Whyte was a critic of this approach, calling it "the soft-minded denial that there is a conflict between the individual and society."[1] Sure enough, this "organization man" era didn't last.

Today, a modern company cannot expect its corporate purpose to become the sole purpose of the employee. Unless an employee is on the (rare) Foundational tour of duty, he will want to explore and cultivate interests outside the company. The most entrepreneurial employees want to establish "personal brands" that stand apart from their employers'. It's a rational, necessary response to the end of lifetime employment.

A company's purpose still matters a great deal. But an employee can buy into an inspirational company vision without thinking, "I want to spend the rest of my life pursuing this future" or "These company values encompass all of *my* values in life." Even the most focused and successful business leaders have values and interests beyond their day job. Larry Ellison is passionate about winning the America's Cup, while Amazon's Jeff Bezos has funded projects like the 10,000 Year Clock and bought the *Washington Post*. The goal isn't perfect congruence on all dimensions, but rather a healthy alignment for a finite scope and time frame.

Alignment means that managers should explicitly seek and highlight the commonality between the company's purpose and values and the employee's career purpose and values. Some obvious commonality emerges naturally: both sides thrive on progress. Companies want to launch new products, grow their market share, and expand into new markets; employees want to take on new responsibilities, increase their capabilities, and yes, make more money. In other words, both company and employee want to be on a winning team. But zoom in a bit more, and differences appear. Perhaps the employee has a side interest in early childhood education, but his tour of duty doesn't involve that kind of work at all. He does however value autonomy and flexible work hours, which the company can accommodate. There just needs to be sufficient alignment to make the alliance durable.

By focusing on building alignment for the duration of a specific mission, a tour of duty reduces the issue of aligning values and aspirations to a manageable scope. As described in chapter 2, at LinkedIn Reid hired a young Matt Cohler, despite knowing that Cohler's goal of becoming a venture capitalist meant that he would inevitably leave. But by defining a tour of duty that served both parties, Reid was able to recruit a valuable employee who helped transform the company.

Your task is to build alignment with regard to the employee's specific mission objective, not his entire life. As we've said, your company is not a family—you don't have to unconditionally support your employees' values and aspirations, but you do have to respect them.

Alignment for the Different Types of Tours

The required level of alignment varies based on the type of tour. For Rotational tours, it's possible to have relatively modest overlap between the employee's and the company's interests (see figure 3-1). For

FIGURE 3-1

Rotational tour of duty

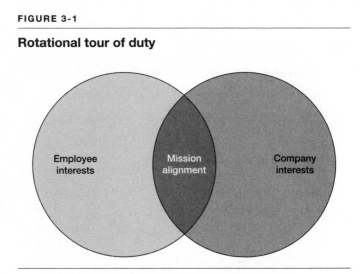

Employee interests

Mission alignment

Company interests

Transformational tours, there needs to be substantial overlap between both parties' values and interests (see figure 3-2). And for Foundational tours, the overlap is almost 100 percent (see figure 3-3).

Three Steps to Building Alignment

Achieving alignment is both an art and a science. Here are some principles of the craft a manager can follow.

1. ESTABLISH AND DISSEMINATE THE COMPANY'S CORE MISSION AND VALUES. Employees won't know where they stand with your company unless you can

FIGURE 3-2

Transformational tour of duty

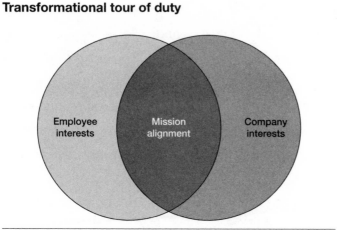

Employee interests | Mission alignment | Company interests

FIGURE 3-3

Foundational tour of duty

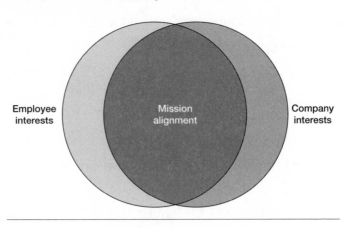

articulate what the company stands for. The core for any company is its mission. Unlike the tactical "Mission: Impossible" assignments we discussed when defining the tour of duty framework, company "mission statement" missions are guiding principles and goals. Great companies have specific missions that differ from those of their competitors.

Saying that your company builds great products and meets the needs of its customers is essentially meaningless because those aspirations could and should apply to any company. These are results, not purposes! Which specific needs? Which specific customers?

A good mission and values statement should be specific and rigorous enough so that some competent players will feel a strong alignment, while others will understand that the company just isn't a good fit. You may lose people who do not feel strong alignment with your company or group, but you *want* to lose those people—this allows you to build much stronger alignment with those who choose to join. Walmart's mission statement is clear: "Saving People Money So They Can Live Better." Exxon Mobil's, not so much: "We are committed to being the world's premier petroleum and petrochemical company. To that end, we must continuously achieve superior financial and operating results while adhering to the highest standards of business conduct. These unwavering expectations provide the foundation for our commitments to those with whom we interact."[2] Translation: win, but don't break the law. We were under the impression that that was true for any legitimate business!

For this discussion, it doesn't matter so much what your company's values are. It just matters that you have them, and that you and any other managers are able to articulate them. The goal is to enable employees to compare their personal values to those of the company or the work group. Even if you aren't part of the senior management team of the company, you can establish a set of aspirations and core values for your group or business unit.

2. LEARN EACH INDIVIDUAL EMPLOYEE'S CORE ASPIRATIONS AND VALUES. Asking about an employee's core aspirations and values may sound and feel awkward at first, but this activity isn't a matter of squishy good intentions. Talking about values is an important step toward building stronger trust and loyalty between employee, manager, and company. At eBay, John Donahoe has instituted systematic programs to learn about every employee: "We want to know their aspirations in life. We ask, 'Who do you look at and say, "I want to be her someday?"'"

Expect to encounter employees with varying levels of vagueness around their career aspirations and values. Some people (a minority) know exactly what they want in life. That's fine—the conversation with these folks is relatively easy.

Others have more abstract aspirations, usually centered on "making progress" in one of several different ways. That's fine too—as a manager, you want to help your employees discover what progress means to them for the specific tour of duty under discussion. Don't insist on perfect precision in their answers. For example, when Ben established an organization to support Reid's business, philanthropic, and civic interests and served as his chief of staff, Ben expressed broad aspirations, including honing his entrepreneurial skills to equip him to start more companies in the future; building relationships with intellectually stimulating people; and getting more exposure to international issues and opportunities. These goals were somewhat abstract, but they were clear enough for Reid and Ben to construct a mission that led to a fulfilling tour of duty.

Finally, some employees, especially entry-level ones, haven't reflected on their career aspirations at all. If the employee has a hard time articulating his values, here's a concrete exercise, via Anne Fulton from the Career Engagement Group, that you can use to jumpstart the conversation. First, ask the employee to jot down the names of three people he admires. Then, next to each name, the employee should list the three qualities he most admires about each person (nine qualities in total). Finally, he should rank these qualities in order of importance, 1 being the most important, 9 being the least important. He now has a list of personal values and can compare them with the company's values.[3] (To see how the three of us completed this values exercise, refer to appendix B.)

In general, you should expect that a company's mission and values will be clear and relatively unchanging, while an employee's career mission and values will be comparatively less well-defined.

3. WORK TOGETHER TO ALIGN EMPLOYEE, MANAGER, AND COMPANY. Once everyone's values and aspirations have been articulated, all parties should work together to strengthen the alignment between them. This is a collaborative rather than top-down effort. It's not just a job for you, but for the employee as well. The good news is, working together on this can actually help build the long-term relationship. John Donahoe emphasizes that after probing an employee's aspirations, "then we figure out how we link how you're spending your time at eBay to those aspirations."

For new employees, the process of alignment should begin during the hiring process itself. For example, Neil Blumenthal of eyewear retailer Warby Parker uses an unusual interview question to assess alignment: "One of our core values is to inject fun and quirkiness into everything we do. So we'll often ask, 'What was a recent costume you wore?' And the point isn't that if you haven't worn a costume in the last four weeks, you're not getting hired. It's more to judge the reaction to that question. Are you somebody who takes yourself very seriously? If so, that's a warning sign to us. We want people to take their work seriously but not themselves."[4]

Sometimes strengthening alignment will involve refinement or compromise. Remember, very few employees will have all of their core aspirations and values addressed by the company's purpose. For example, LinkedIn CEO Jeff Weiner is passionate about US education policy and serves on the DonorsChoose board, which plays a minimal role in LinkedIn's business. In Silicon Valley, many employees would like to be founders someday. Clearly, this means they will leave the company. But it's possible to align interests so that everyone wins over the course of a tour. For example, Reid tells LinkedIn employees who want to join a start-up that if they work at LinkedIn, they'll learn useful skills, and when they're ready to move on, and if they've helped the company, he'll help them get a job in the Greylock portfolio or elsewhere in Silicon Valley.

In all cases, you'll need to find the right lens for alignment; this might be a time frame, or it might be the scope or nature of the work (if the employee is looking to gain certain experiences). Remember, the employee and the company don't have to be aligned forever, just for the length of the tour of duty.

Ultimately, the alignment of interests, values, and aspirations increases the odds of a long-term, strong alliance between a company and its talent.

Walking the Walk: How LinkedIn Builds Alignment

Remember David Hahn and his four tours of duty at LinkedIn? LinkedIn retained Hahn for nearly a decade in a highly competitive talent ecosystem in part because his managers built strong mission alignment between him and the company during each tour of duty.

When he thought about how he wanted to build his career coming out of college, Hahn took inspiration from Theodore Roosevelt's famous dictum, "Far and away the best prize that life has to offer is the chance to work hard at work worth doing."[5]

To Hahn, that meant finding a way to have a positive impact on the world, and to do so at the largest scale possible. He started his career in Washington DC, thinking that he would achieve this aspiration through politics and policy, but realized the pace of change wasn't fast enough to satisfy him. He decided Silicon Valley's start-up ecosystem offered a better alternative. He set two initial aspirations: to learn from great leaders who had already built successful companies at scale, and to work for a company with a mission grander than just achieving its financial goals.

Hahn executed a plan that would let him make progress toward both of his goals. He used the very first version of LinkedIn (the product) to look up people who had recently moved from Washington DC to Silicon Valley and convinced one of them, former PayPal executive Keith Rabois, to hire him. Hahn joined Rabois at Epoch Innovations, a high-growth start-up that was trying to use technology to treat dyslexia—a seemingly perfect fit for his goals. In only a matter of weeks, however, he found out that the company was going under. Having already established a close relationship, Rabois and Hahn searched together for their next gig. During their search, Rabois introduced Hahn to Reid, his former colleague at

PayPal who had recently founded LinkedIn (the company). "It was clear from our first meeting that Reid would not only be an incredible person to learn from, but that he has a similar philosophy around impact," Hahn told us. Rabois and Hahn started at LinkedIn the following week.

Hahn was excited about LinkedIn's broader mission to deliver economic opportunity to the world's professionals. Hahn's manager, Rabois, also pointed out that their short-term professional values were aligned—by joining LinkedIn, Hahn would learn about company building from an executive team that had already succeeded at PayPal, and LinkedIn would get a smart generalist who could wear several hats. Four years later, when Jeff Weiner took over as LinkedIn's CEO, Hahn was able to learn from a seasoned executive about how to scale an organization from a midsize business to a global, publicly traded company.

Along the way, Hahn's managers at LinkedIn kept finding ways to define tours of duty that offered the promise of transformation for both his career and the company at large. For example, when Hahn was interested in building one of LinkedIn's early revenue streams from scratch, the company changed his tour of duty to go after that mission objective. Hahn applied the same principles to the people he managed. "At LinkedIn, the philosophy is to let our brightest go after areas that interest them, especially in areas where they will be a bit in over their head at first," Hahn said. "It's been a great strategy to keep our most talented folks motivated and learning as fast as possible."

HAVING THE CONVERSATION
Advice for Managers

The process of aligning values can be a long one, and requires establishing a deep level of trust during a series of consistent conversations. Each conversation should build on the foundation of the previous one.

DEFINE VALUES IN A GROUP. Almost every company has values that are written down. Most of them are composed of inoffensive platitudes such as "striving for excellence" that offend the intellect. If your company lacks meaningful official values, take the liberty of defining those values for your team. Of course, defining meaningful values works best when the *CEO* embraces the alliance and leads the effort.

The CEO and her executive team should create a rough draft of the company's values, present the draft to a broader audience of Foundational nonexecutive employees, and be open to feedback and refinement. Only when the Foundational core of the company agrees should the CEO expand the process to the entire company.

A CEO can't convene all one thousand employees in an auditorium and ask them to define the values from scratch, but she can't do the opposite either, by carving her preferred values in stone and then asking for "voluntary" buy-in.

If the company is larger than seventy-five people, break employees up into smaller cross-functional groups and have each one hold a separate meeting to discuss the draft values. The assumptions you uncover during these honest conversations might be unexpected. Many companies that senior managers think have a missionary culture are actually filled with mercenary motivations. A manager needs a realistic understanding of the true company culture.

DEFINE PERSONAL VALUES ONE-ON-ONE. Meet one-on-one with each of your direct reports to discuss their core aspirations and values, and how these values fit with those of the company. You don't need to ask employees to publish their individual values on the company intranet or pin those below the employees' office nameplates, but you do need to convert these aspirations and values from implicit hints to explicit points. After all, how can you build a Transformational tour of duty without understanding your employees' objectives?

BUILD TRUST BY OPENING UP. Learning what an employee cares about helps build a relationship of trust. Psychologist Arthur Aron of SUNY Stony Brook discovered that asking participants in an experiment to share their deepest feelings and beliefs for a single hour could generate the same sense of trust and intimacy that typically takes weeks, months, or years to form.[6] Direct questions like "Who's the best coworker you ever worked with?" and "What is your proudest career moment?" help break down emotional distance.

Bear in mind that the underlying power dynamics can make it seem intimidating when you ask direct questions. That's why it's important for you to start by opening up about your own core aspirations and values. Aron's relationship exercises asked *both* parties to share their answers to his deep questions.

Brad Smith applies this principle at Intuit: "We begin every interview by saying, 'Tell me in three to five minutes your life's journey and how it led you to be the person you are today . . . touching on major moments in your life that helped define who you are and your approach to business and leadership, such as dealing with adverse experiences like a bully, the death of a loved one, or major decisions that went wrong.'" What makes this approach work is that the Intuit interviewer goes first, both to set the example and to model vulnerability for the candidate.

More Online: Find interactive exercises for developing mission alignment with an employee at www.theallianceframework.com/alignment.

4

Implementing Transformational Tours of Duty

Tactics and Techniques for Using the Framework

Implementing a tour of duty with strong alignment means leaving behind the rote exchanges of template-driven performance reviews where little of import is said or done. Instead, you need to have frank, open, rigorous conversations. Both manager and employee have an explicit (albeit nonbinding) agreement with shared objectives and realistic expectations. This agreement provides the criteria for regular, *mutual* performance measurement and management. You provide specific feedback and guidance to the employee; just as important, the employee has a context in which to talk about his long-term career goals and whether the company is accommodating them as promised.

Here is a step-by-step guide to implementing Transformational tours of duty, either with your direct reports or throughout your organization. Along these lines, be ready to talk about the employee's career beyond working at your company, if appropriate.

1. Start the Conversation and Define the Mission

Every employee gets hired into a Rotational or Transformational tour. Define an employee's initial tour of duty during the hiring process—or at least start the conversation if the situation is too uncertain to finalize the details of the tour. Establishing a minimum mutual commitment benefits both employer and employee. You ought to know how a Transformational hire will move the needle for the company before extending an offer. Similarly, new employees are much better off knowing how joining the company will allow them to advance their careers.

Even for current employees, defining a tour of duty can provide much-needed clarity and strengthen their relationship with the company. To define a tour of duty, you and your employee need to answer the following questions.

What Is the Overall Objective of the Tour?

The tour of duty you define with your employee should have a clear, detailed, concrete mission objective. Examples include a specific project launch, internal project, or organizational initiative. For example, the objective for Eda Gultekin's initial tour at LinkedIn (see chapter 2) was to investigate and resolve the customer churn issue. The goal is to select a mission objective that helps the company, but also provides an opportunity for the employee to grow.

Based on the mission objective, you should also set the employee's expectations for the length of the tour. Most simply, the tour should last long enough to achieve the objective. In Gultekin's case, her initial tour lasted only six months, but her subsequent tours each lasted a number of years.

The "right" configuration for a tour will also depend on the individual needs of the employee. Employees who value different experiences may want a larger number of short, extremely varied tours. Employees who want more stability may prefer a smaller number of longer, continuous tours, with an eye toward negotiating a Foundational tour.

Finally, the mission objective also needs to help employer and employee align their aspirations and values, as discussed in chapter 3.

What Do the Results of a Successful Tour of Duty Look Like for the Company?

A successful mission objective delivers results for the company for either quantitative or qualitative goals, such as launching a new product line and generating a certain dollar amount in first-year revenues, or achieving thought leadership in a specific market category, as measured by the writings of industry analysts.

At LinkedIn, for example, managers ask, "How will the company be *transformed* by this employee?"

What Do the Results of a Successful Tour of Duty Look Like for the Employee?

A successful tour of duty should move the needle for the employee as well as the company. Success might include developing new knowledge and skills; acquiring functional, technical, or managerial experience to advance the employee's career; and building a personal brand within and outside the company by accomplishing an impressive goal. Usually it won't include an upgrade in job title.

At LinkedIn, managers ask, "How will the employee's career be *transformed* by working here?" All employees are asked to fill out a Transformation Plan to articulate how they hope to transform themselves, the company, and the world.

Pat Wadors, who runs LinkedIn's global talent organization, differentiates between a *Big T* and a *small t* transformation. A Big *T* transformation is something like a promotion or plum assignment. Only about 20 percent of missions result in a Big *T* transformation. That's why the company places as much or more emphasis on the small *t* transformations, which may not seem as flashy but result in concrete increases in the employee's marketability. Examples of small *t* transformations include gaining marketable experience on certain kinds of projects, learning new skills, and earning the endorsement and recommendation of others in the industry. Not coincidentally, the design of the LinkedIn member profile has evolved over the years to enable members to better showcase small *t* transformations.

2. Set Up a System of Regular Checkpoints for Both Sides to Exchange Feedback with Each Other

The traditional corporate approach of performance reviews based on the calendar year makes little sense in the context of a tour of duty. The mission objective, not the calendar, defines a tour of duty. Furthermore, an annual review process doesn't provide nearly enough feedback. You should set up a system of regular checkpoints to assess how the tour of duty is going for both parties (see figure 4-1). These checkpoints could be held at regular intervals (e.g., quarterly) or could be tied to specific milestones in the overall project plan associated with the tour of duty. Either way, the goal is to provide an explicit forum for jointly evaluating progress toward both parties' desired results. This enables course corrections as necessary. Remember, it's a bidirectional conversation: the company talks about the employee's contributions *and* the employee talks about whether the company is helping him meet his career goals.

FIGURE 4-1

Creating and tracking your transformation

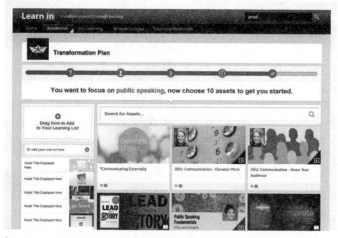

Source: screenshot from LinkedIn employee intranet

3. Before the Tour of Duty Draws to a Close, Begin Defining the Next Tour of Duty

Well before the end of the current active tour, you should set aside time to discuss what your employee would like to do once his tour of duty is complete. Having this conversation in advance can remove the uncertainty associated with completing a tour of duty and even give the employee (and the manager

81

as well) something to look forward to in the future. There are generally two possible outcomes of this conversation.

The Manager and Employee Define a New Tour of Duty within the Company

Part of the commitment an employee makes during an initial tour of duty is to seriously consider your proposal for a second tour of duty. In many ways, a follow-up tour is the ideal outcome for both parties. Both company and employee can leverage past investments. Extending the tour of duty for an employee who launched a product enables that employee to learn how to grow or scale the product, while allowing the company to exploit the initial market success without having to bring a new person up to speed on all that went before.

Follow-up tours can be shorter or longer, depending on the nature of the mission. An experienced employee can make rapid progress on a well-defined mission because he doesn't require much of a ramp-up period. But the increased strength of relationship can also be leveraged in the opposite way. A trusted and trusting employee can tackle more strategic, longer-term missions.

General Electric's management training program for high-potential employees is a classic example of defining interesting, new tours of duty within the company. Promising employees tackle successive Rotational tours of duty in different functional areas, business units, and geographies, which prepares them for the challenges of helping to manage a sprawling industrial conglomerate. No person has ever become CEO of General Electric without completing numerous tours of duty throughout the company.

Before embarking on a new tour of duty, the employee in question should help recruit and train a successor to carry on the previous tour's project. Perhaps the replacement is an even better fit for the next phase of the initiative. Succession planning also provides a more satisfying closure for the employee, who can complete his tour of duty knowing that the product, project, or initiative that he owned for several years of his life is continuing on in good hands.

In the event that no obvious next mission presents itself, you and your employee might find yourselves in purgatory—you both want to continue the relationship, but you're not sure how. In this situation, the best course of action is to extend the current tour, but set up a time to re-examine the possibilities in a matter of months, rather than years.

The Manager and Employee Conclude That the Employee Will Be Pursuing a Tour of Duty at a Different Company

Losing a valued employee is one of a manager's greatest fears. But it happens, and for many valid reasons. No company has ever been able to retain all of its top performers in perpetuity.

You can hardly be expected to welcome this outcome, but even so, a planned exit is better for the company than being blindsided. Discuss a potential departure openly and honestly. As your employee's ally, it's your job to help him choose the right next step. This means helping him assess his options, even if those options include working at other companies. An honest conversation about outside options requires courage from both manager and employee. You need to face the possible departure head on, while your employee needs to feel that you won't penalize him for sharing his true intentions. You earn this "Right of First Conversation" with the trust you build with employees.

Together, you and your employee should negotiate a transition period and draw up a transition checklist. The goal of the transition checklist is to lay out everything that the company needs from the employee to finish the mission, especially the question of who will pick up the project ball going forward. If an employee is able to check all the boxes on the checklist, he should be considered to have completed his tour of duty in good order and remain in good standing with the company after his departure. We'll discuss the details of transitioning people from employees to corporate alumni in chapter 7.

4. Managing for the Unexpected: When There's a Change in the Middle of a Tour

A tour of duty is not a contract—that kind of legalistic approach is the hallmark of free agency and transactional thinking. The alliance is ethical, not legal, and the tour of duty is an informal agreement to respect and honor a key relationship. Managers shouldn't use the moral imperative of a tour of duty to force an employee to stay in an onerous position, especially if the poor fit is the result of flawed management decisions. The goal of the tour of duty is to build trust with honest communication and to create longevity on a voluntary basis, not to lock employees into roles they dislike or lock up companies with ineffective employees.

In the event that either employee or employer wants or needs to end a tour of duty before completion of the mission, the process needs to be collaborative. If an employee gets an amazing offer to work at another company, he should have the option to accept, but he should also feel the obligation to work extremely hard to ensure a smooth succession, and should even delay leaving if necessary to aid in the transition.

Likewise, if a company needs to reorganize or shut down the particular initiative that comprises the employee's tour, you should work extremely hard to make sure the employee can stay on track to achieve the previously agreed-upon professional goals and personal growth objectives. The longer and deeper the relationship has been, the greater the obligation for both sides to preserve that relationship and if necessary work for a smooth and amicable transition.

What Happens If One Party Breaks the Alliance?

If an employee departs the company in the middle of his tour without any investment in a transition, he breaks the employment alliance and has to face the consequences. First and foremost, the employee will take a major hit to his credibility and reputation. He can't betray a key relationship and simply say, "It's just business." Ethics matter. In addition, the employee will also suffer practical consequences. That employee will forgo future benefits, such as distinguished alumni status (more on this in chapter 7) and favorable references.

If the company lays off the employee in the middle of a tour or doesn't fulfill its obligations to provide transformational growth opportunities to the employee, it is also breaking the terms of the alliance. You can't disregard the relationship, then expect an employee to be an ally in the future, whether in terms of speaking well of the company, referring customers and new employees, or anything else. With the advent of social media, the consequences to employers of breaking an alliance are far-reaching. Now that ex-employees can—and do—dish on what it's really like inside a company, an employer (or manager) who makes a habit of breaking alliances is warning both current and prospective employees that it isn't trustworthy. Someday (hopefully soon), we expect an employer or individual professional to be able to simply say, "They broke the alliance," and for the person on the other end of the phone to know what that means.

What Happens If the Employee Gets a New Manager?

If a new manager steps in, it's unfair to the employee to discard the terms of a previously agreed-upon tour, but it's also unfair to the new manager to bind her to her predecessor's plans. The right approach is a respectful transition. The default expectation should be that the new manager will continue the existing tour of duty. However, if she realizes that the mission has to change, she should have the freedom to make the change, while retaining the moral obligation to steer the employee to a successful landing. You can see why it's critical to have a written description of the tour of duty, rather than relying on an undocumented understanding between manager and employee.

What If One Party Is Performing Poorly?

Overall performance impacts the durability of the tour of duty. If the company as a whole starts to fail, it may not be able to hold up its end of the alliance. If the company does not or cannot maintain an environment or role that delivers the promised professional growth opportunities, it is reneging on its commitment to transform the employee's career. Conversely, an employee with poor on-the-job performance is failing to deliver on his commitment to help improve the company's adaptability. But even when performance deteriorates, it's still important to remember that the alliance is a relationship, not a transaction. Ups and downs are inevitable, and both sides should maintain a long-term investment perspective rather than responding in knee-jerk fashion to short-term turbulence. A baseball team would never cut a player simply because he had a bad game. But if the player experienced a month-long slump, the team might very well trade or release him.

What If the Employee Wants to Move into a New Role within the Company?

Even though a lateral move doesn't involve leaving the company, you should follow the same collaborative approach to completing a tour of duty. If an employee can keep his mission on track and arrange an orderly transition, you shouldn't block the change. For example, LinkedIn has a philosophy that a manager won't prevent a lateral move within the organization if the employee has built the structure and process to allow the switch without endangering his current mission. Such a shift respects the employee's wishes, the investment LinkedIn has made in the employee, and the overall relationship.

HAVING THE CONVERSATION
Advice for Managers

The keys to having a successful conversation about tours of duty are to be systematic, consistent, and transparent—which, not coincidentally, are the same principles behind the tour of duty itself.

MOLD THE CONVERSATION TO THE TYPE OF TOUR. Prepare for a more involved conversation if you're implementing a Transformational or Foundational tour, because it involves a personalized, longer-term alliance. In contrast, a Rotational tour is standardized and short-term, which allows you to follow more of a standard template for the conversation.

The style of conversation will also be shaped by when it takes place in the overall arc of the relationship. Having the tour of duty conversation during the initial hiring process is relatively easy. The manager and employee are strangers, and negotiating clearly defined objectives on both sides is natural and expected. Similarly, defining a follow-up tour of duty when the current tour of duty is drawing to a successful close is also relatively easy, as it's a natural transition point. It's trickier to transition current employees from a free agency mind-set to tours of duty. Introducing a new and different approach will require multiple conversations and a steady consistency.

BE SENSITIVE TO POWER IMBALANCES. Usually, the employer has more power than the employee, but the opposite can be true in hot job markets or for employees with highly valuable skills. Either way, a power imbalance creates the fear that the more powerful party will abuse that power to maximize its own benefit. If you have the upper hand, be proactive about demonstrating your commitment to fair dealing. If your employee has the upper hand and tries to assert his power, acknowledge this fact when it comes up, then return the focus of the conversation to reaching a win-win deal.

CHOOSE METRICS THAT ARE LEADING INDICATORS. Metrics such as revenue, page views, customer satisfaction, and the like can play a powerful role in evaluating performance within a tour of duty. In the lifetime employment model, success meant keeping your manager happy. That approach doesn't cut it in the fiercely competitive modern world. The great management theorist Peter Drucker put it best when he wrote, "What gets measured, gets managed." If you carefully manage leading indicators such as mission alignment, an employee's ability to gather network intelligence, or general satisfaction during tours of duty check-ins, you'll successfully manage lagging indicators such as employee retention or engagement.

APPLY MORAL SUASION ETHICALLY. Moral suasion, rather than contractual law, binds the parties to the alliance. But you should only use this force when justified by a violation of the alliance. Too many managers try to guilt employees into staying. Don't make an employee's career choice personal, which can engender resentment even if you convince the employee to stay. Rather, you should appeal to the principles of the alliance.

REGULARLY CHECK IN ON HOW THE TOUR IS EVOLVING. This is not a onetime conversation. Remember that trust is built by consistency over time. Most employees have experienced far too many management fads that came and went without any real staying power. Use action to demonstrate commitment to the alliance, including regular follow-ups, both formal (the checkpoints outlined in the step-by-step directions in this chapter) and informal (whenever a one-on-one opportunity presents itself).

ESTABLISH A BASIS FOR TRUST THROUGH OPEN-NESS AND TRANSPARENCY. It's important to frame the conversation with the kind of vocabulary that conveys the open, bidirectional nature of the relationship. Use words like *trust, transparency,* and *alliance.* Another key way to demonstrate openness is to be willing to discuss scenarios in which the employee might leave the company. This kind of transparency helps build trust and reduces the risk of being blindsided by a departure.

ASSURE YOUR EMPLOYEES THAT YOU'RE NOT ABOUT TO FIRE THEM. Sadly, employees have been conditioned to interpret discussions about their goals and performance as early warning signs of impending dismissal. Emphasize that the point of the alliance is mutual benefit, and that this is being put in place for all employees (or all employees on the team).

Tactical Reminders

BE STRUCTURED. Explaining the tour of duty framework isn't an off-the-cuff conversation. Set aside several hours and schedule a formal meeting on the calendar for the discussion. Book a private office or conference room. Take detailed notes, and encourage the employee to take notes as well. At the end of the conversation, agree on next steps and schedule a follow-up. The final deliverable should be a written Statement of Alliance. (We provide a sample of such a deliverable in appendix A.)

SHARE THE AGENDA IN ADVANCE. This is a collaborative conversation, which means that both you and your employee are better off if you both have ample time to prepare. This shouldn't be a meeting where the manager prepares and the employee has to respond off the cuff. Give the employee time to prepare his own ideas and proposals.

BE AS CONCRETE AND SPECIFIC AS POSSIBLE. The point of the framework is to avoid vagueness around goals and timelines and to get specific. If you want your employee to deploy his individual network, be precise about specific ways he can do so and incorporate those ways into the plan. (We'll discuss networks in much greater depth in chapter 6.) If the employee says he wants to meet certain types of people or accumulate international experiences, spell out how and when that will occur during his tour.

More Online: Learn how to earn the "Right of First Conversation" and develop an expectation of honesty when talking with employees at www.theallianceframework.com/ToD.

5

Employee Network Intelligence

Bringing the World into Your Company

The old lifetime employment model encouraged both managers and employees to look inward. Managers focused on making employees more efficient at fulfilling their job description, while employees focused on enhancing their position within the company hierarchy. But once that model began breaking down, that inward focus became self-defeating self-absorption.

Today, as we've discussed, both company and employee need to look outward toward the overall environment in which they operate, especially when it comes to networks. Companies have to understand the employee's broader place in the industry, while the employee should realize that his professional network is one of the key assets that can boost his long-term career prospects. At the same time, as part of the alliance, the employee ought to tap his own individual network to advance their employer's business, because *who* he knows in the industry can be just as valuable to the company as *what* he knows in terms of skills. Thus, the alliance at work: *growing their professional networks helps employees transform their career; employee networking helps the company transform itself.*

Employee networks are extremely valuable to companies as a source of information. As Bill Gates wrote more than a decade ago, "The most meaningful way to differentiate your company from your competition, the best way to put distance between you and the crowd, is to do an outstanding job with information. How you gather, manage, and use information will determine whether you win or lose."[1]

Most of us utilize a fraction of the information available to us. For example, recall the last time you solved a thorny problem at work. The instinctive response is to . . . schedule a meeting. And assemble all the smart people at the company who might have an answer. But you can't just rely on the information circulating in the brains of your current employees. *There are more smart people outside your company than inside it.* In a healthy ecosystem, this is always true.

Many folks in senior management positions already know this. They frequently reach out to their *own* friends in the industry for information to help them make better decisions on the job. Indeed, it's this instinct that partly explains how they got promoted to a senior position in the first place. But frequently, senior management neglects a broader and more useful resource: the collective knowledge and networks of *all* the company's employees, even the most junior among them.

Think of each employee as an individual scout picking up data from the outside world—from articles, books, and classes, but most important, from other friends inside and outside the industry. Each employee can receive and decipher intelligence from the outside world that helps the company adapt. For example, what's a competitor doing? What are key tech trends? It's the manager's job to recognize and encourage the power of each of these scouts. A more networked workforce generates more valuable intelligence, and when your employees share what they learn from their networks back into your company, they help solve its key business challenges.

In a nutshell, network intelligence that leverages the individual networks of your organization's people is the most effective way for your organization to engage with and learn from the outside world. Even if you choose not to emphasize network intelligence as part of the alliance, your most driven employees are going to build their external professional networks anyway. It's up to you to encourage them to do so for their jobs.

In *The Start-up of You*, we wrote that an individual's career accelerates with the strength of his or her network—we called this principle "I" to the power of "We" (I^{We}). The question for companies and managers is whether you can develop enough trust so that your employees are willing to their use *their* networks on behalf of the *company*. The good news is that high performers want to do this—in our survey of *Harvard Business Review* readers, over three-quarters of respondents said that they used their individual networks to help them on the job.

So don't treat tweeting on the job like an infraction—encourage it! Ask your employees to expense lunches with interesting people. By helping employees invest in their individual networks, you build an environment of trust and reciprocity. And when you ask employees to tap their own networks on behalf of the company, they'll be more likely to respond favorably.

An added bonus is that a proactive network intelligence program helps with recruiting. Entrepreneurs are outwardly focused—they have to be, since they know they don't have the internal resources of incumbent players. Want an entrepreneurial candidate? Facilitating the expansion of his individual network makes you a far more attractive employer.

Despite the benefits of an outward focus, some managers are simply more comfortable sticking to their own familiar corporate turf. They only seek answers from resources they fully control. They tap their own brain and the brains of their immediate colleagues, and no one else's. They might feel nervous about encouraging employees to look outside the firm for information, because such behaviors could inadvertently expose company secrets and strategies to outsiders.

Indeed, an obvious "risk" of making your employees discoverable and externally networked is that they're discoverable by potential employers and their recruiters. This is a legitimate concern. But there's no one-way mirror that allows you to benefit from the outside world without exposing yourself. For many companies, the potential downside of defection is outweighed by the benefits generated by network intelligence. Just ask LinkedIn. It lives this reality more than any other company on Earth: every LinkedIn employee has a public LinkedIn profile that's fully up-to-date. They're highly networked and findable by recruiters. Yes, some employees have left. But far more have helped the company through the connections they made while on the job.

Network intelligence and the associated willingness to seek help from people outside the company is one of the key factors in the success of Silicon Valley. The risks are lower than most people think, and the benefits of looking outward are greater than you might realize.

Network Intelligence Generates Hidden Data, Serendipity, and Opportunity

As we've discussed, the most obvious function of network intelligence is to connect a company with outside information sources. Employee networks act as both a source and a filter for new information.

The second function of network intelligence is its ability to provide access to "hidden data"—knowledge that isn't publicly available. In the pre-internet era, reading secondary sources like business books or attending university courses helped professionals or companies beat the competition. Now, however, Google makes this kind of public information a commodity. To gain an edge, you need to use social networks to tap directly into what's swirling around inside people's brains. And it's this kind of information—up-to-the-second, nuanced—that offers the most significant competitive advantages. You won't find it in the morning edition of the *Wall Street Journal*, or even in a Google search. In a highly networked era, who you know is often more valuable than what you've read.

For example, in the early days of PayPal, its most important rival was Billpoint, a rival payment system that was a joint venture between eBay—PayPal's most important partner—and Wells Fargo Bank. Consider the situation PayPal faced: the vast majority of its business at the time consisted of handling payments for eBay auctions, yet eBay itself owned a competitive payments business (Billpoint) that it was promoting to every single eBay user. To outside observers, the circumstances must have looked grim.

Yet as we know, PayPal triumphed over Billpoint, leading eBay to purchase PayPal for over $1.5 billion.

One of the key factors was PayPal's superior use of network intelligence. Reid led this intelligence-gathering effort for PayPal (he was executive vice president at the time) and asked all the members of the team, from executives to individual engineers, to use their network intelligence to learn about Billpoint's strategy. Billpoint's team, on the other hand, completely ignored the potential for network intelligence to provide insights into PayPal's strategy.

From conversations with other companies that were building on the eBay platform such as Honesty.com and AuctionWatch (now Vendio), PayPal employees learned two key facts. First, the Billpoint team was convinced that the key success factor for an internet payments system was a deep banking relationship to combat fraud. Billpoint's leadership felt that the Wells Fargo relationship represented an overwhelming advantage over PayPal. Second, contrary to Billpoint's belief, the companies on the eBay platform (and their customers) didn't consider a deep banking relationship that relevant. They placed a far greater value on ease of use, especially in e-mail communications. Fraud prevention was a hygiene factor, not a driving force. None of this information was public, but none of it was secret either.

Network intelligence should be tapped ethically; PayPal employees didn't skulk about in costumes, send questions from fake e-mail accounts, or root through Billpoint's garbage bins. They simply confirmed their findings by talking with Billpoint managers and employees and asking them how they viewed the market. Even more amazing? During these direct conversations, the Billpoint people never bothered to ask the same questions of PayPal's people. PayPal's strategy explicitly emphasized network intelligence; Billpoint's did not.

The third function of network intelligence is to generate serendipity, which is a major driver of innovation. Writer Frans Johansson has argued that innovation arises at the intersection of different disciplines and cultures. Most innovation is not sui generis; rather, it consists of the application of existing technology or practices to a new field (such as applying medical IV bag technology to basketball shoes). When employees tap their professional and personal networks, they tend to collect feedback from friends with a wide variety of backgrounds, experiences, and areas of expertise. As Deborah Ancona, Henrik Bresman, and David Caldwell of MIT noted in their paper, "The X-Factor," "When innovation, adaptation, and execution are critical, success is closely related to how the team interacts with outsiders" because successful teams "reach across boundaries to forge dense networks of connection, both inside and outside the organization."[2]

If you're in a broom closet, it's no great accomplishment to be the smartest person in the room. Network intelligence expands "the room" you're in to stadium-sized dimensions, encompassing the vast and diverse global networks of all your employees. This will help you solve problems faster. Better yet, it will strengthen the overall employment alliance. Employees want to be networking, and network intelligence programs and policies help them do just that.

The third function of network intelligence is to help you see opportunities you would otherwise miss. One of the hidden stories behind PayPal's success is the crucial role network intelligence played in discovering the formula for viral growth. Once the team realized that eBay was a major driver of PayPal usage, its members looked to other companies in the eBay ecosystem for inspiration. One of these companies, Honesty.com, had discovered a way to leverage eBay's active sellers to grow. Honesty.com provided an auction counter; if a seller shared his eBay credential with Honesty.com,

Honesty.com could add its counter to every single one of the seller's auctions. This system exposed all of a seller's auction bidders to the auction counter product, prompting other sellers to sign up and begin exposing their buyers to Honesty.com, and so on.

This insight didn't come from Reid or any of the other senior executives; the Honesty.com discovery came from "ordinary" front line employees. Once PayPal implemented its "Pay with PayPal" feature, sellers began adding "Pay with PayPal" to all their auctions, and PayPal's growth took off. Without network intelligence, the PayPal success story might have ended quite differently.

Now let's explore specific ideas for how to implement these sorts of programs.

More Online: Join the conversation and learn how other companies help their employees engage the outside world at www.theallianceframework.com/networkintel.

6

Implementing Network Intelligence Programs

Tactics and Techniques for Investing in Employee Networks

Make the network intelligence flowing into the company via its employees a first-class management concern. Maintain specific programs to strengthen and extend it in order to both attract and retain the best employees, as well as to drive business results. Here is a step-by-step guide to implementing a network intelligence program in your individual team or throughout the organization.

1. Recruit Connected People

Make a candidate's network strength an explicit priority when hiring. It's critical, however, to define network strength correctly. There is a misperception that network strength equals your number of social media followers. Rather than fixating on raw numbers, consider if a candidate is connected to the right people and has the realistic ability to leverage those connections for useful information or to influence others to act.

In the interview process, ask candidates about their strongest professional allies. Find out how they solve problems—do they call experts in their network? Besides recruiting folks who are already steeped in the ways of network intelligence, managers who emphasize network strength send a strong message internally to the organization that this stuff matters.

The need for network assessment is even greater when hiring a senior manager. When Reid interviews a prospective management hire, he always asks, "Who are the key people that you would consider hiring *after* you?" A strong candidate will have people in his network who want to work with him. Reid then often reaches out to those people as a reference check as well.

We're not saying that candidates need to be "net-workers" (in the icky glad-handing sense of the word) or that they must excel at quickly developing rapport with strangers. That skill is a prerequisite for certain roles (e.g., sales), but is less relevant for others. We're simply arguing that, all else being equal, you learn how to measure network strength systematically and then hire people who have strong networks.

2. Teach Employees How to Mine Intelligence from Their Networks via Conversation and Social Media

Many companies, especially public ones, expend their precious energy playing defense, trying to keep their employees from spilling the beans: "Don't talk about impending product launches; don't talk about corporate strategy; ask for permission from the public relations department if anyone asks you about what we're doing as a company." This defensive posture problematically assumes that employees can't tell the difference between *nonpublic* and *secret*.

Too often, the business world conflates all nonpublic information into a single category. Perhaps this is due to the hard line that the finance world draws between "public" and "insider" information. But outside the world of financial exchanges and markets, nonpublic information comes in two very different flavors.

For example, entrepreneurs often contact Chris for his advice on how to price Software-as-a-Service (SaaS) business software. Through his work with PBworks and other start-ups, he has direct operational experience in increasing revenues by introducing new pricing schemes. In the case of PBworks, for example, he was able to increase the size of the company's largest customer from less than $100 to nearly $1 million over the course of four years. Chris's pricing advice rests on "hidden" data that is nonpublic information, but he doesn't reveal any secrets about specific customers or future plans. While there are certainly people who would find this secret information valuable, sharing that information is clearly inappropriate. The point is, employees can engage with their network without ever revealing any secret information.

Encourage your employees to play offense. Direct reports should talk with people in their network about key challenges their group is facing. Equip them with questions to ask their friends, and ask them to report back on what they learn. Here are a few that we like to use with our friends, but that apply to all industries:

- How is a key technology trend (e.g., "Big Data") shaping our industry?

- What are other companies (and competitors) doing that's working or not working?

- What are our customers' sentiments, what is motivating them, and how have they changed?

- Who are the key people in our industry that we should engage with?

- What are the hiring trends in our industry?

- Who are new entrants in the marketplace and which of them are doing interesting things?

To facilitate a good conversation, be capable of answering these questions yourself.

Of course, employees should use their discretion and always maintain their integrity. If an employee is talking to a friend who works at a competitor, it's best to steer the conversation to focus on a *third* competitor that isn't his company or the friend's. Or, when an employee brings information back to the company, he may need to make it anonymous ("I heard from a friend" instead of "I heard from John Doe, director of product at . . . ") or change certain details to protect confidentiality.

Finally, to make sure this information gets back to the company, establish a "push" process for funneling tips or information from employees back to the management team. In other words, a little-visited intranet (or worse, an employee's paper notebook) shouldn't be the sole repository of insights. Knowledge isn't valuable unless shared. Every Monday, Reid's venture capital firm, Greylock Partners, distributes a list of all the *external* people each partner is scheduled to meet with that week. This allows the rest of the partners to trade notes and suggest questions that might generate useful insights or valuable connections. Reid also asks the Greylock Consumer Team to regularly circulate their answers to the question, "Who was the most interesting person you talked to this week?" More informally, the venture capital firm Andreessen Horowitz taps its people's network intelligence in an unusual way: at the beginning of every partner meeting, the firm awards a $100 prize for the best rumor presented, confirmed or not.

3. Roll Out Programs and Policies That Help Employees Build Their Individual Networks

Encourage Employees to Be Active on Social Media and to Make Themselves Discoverable

You should want your employees to be discoverable by the outside world in a *professional* context. They're discoverable anyway, thanks to Google and social networks like Facebook, Twitter, and LinkedIn, so you should incentivize them to craft their presence in a way that's maximally helpful to the company. In 2013, when CEO Reed Hastings identified the top 170 stars at Netflix, he discovered that nine of them weren't on LinkedIn. He asked each of them to sign up for an account because he wanted to make sure that Netflix employees could find the appropriate network nodes within the company.

Push for policies that allow employees to build their personal brands and establish thought leadership. This is not to say that a CEO should order every employee to start tweeting; mandatory brand building will rankle the employee and seem inauthentic to external audiences. Nor should sharing articles about celebrity gossip on Facebook be considered legitimate brand-building work—unless celebrity gossip plays a critical role in the company's business, of course.

Social media engagement can translate into bottom line results. For example, the average HubSpot employee has 6.2 times the number of connections than the average LinkedIn member, and those employees share, comment, or like updates at eight times the average rate. The fact that its employees are growing their own professional networks on LinkedIn pays dividends to HubSpot's "talent brand." The company attracts twice the number of candidates for the job opportunities it posts on LinkedIn than the average LinkedIn customer. It also has over fifty thousand followers of its company page, the majority of whom say they're interested in hearing about job opportunities at HubSpot.

Set Up a "Networking Fund" for Employees

One of the techniques we recommend to entrepreneurial individuals in *The Start-up of You* is to maintain an "interesting person fund"—money earmarked for coffees and meals with interesting people in their network. The corporate equivalent is a "networking fund" for employees. Most companies allow employees to expense business lunches, but few allow them to expense networking lunches. Yet almost all top executives have such lunches all the time, and their company benefits as a result. You should make it not just acceptable but *expected* for your people to do the same—and to report back on what they learned.

HubSpot's Learning Meals program allows all employees to take anyone else out to a meal as long as the employees think they'll learn something. HubSpot's founder and chief technology officer, Dharmesh Shah, developed the practice at his first company, and still employs it today. When he travels to different cities, he always tries to organize a dinner with other entrepreneurs and interesting folks whom he can learn from and who can learn from one another. "My one regret is that we didn't put the Learning Meals policy in place from the start at HubSpot," said Shah. Shah even shares a set of recommendations and best practices for hosting these dinners (pro tips: pick restaurants with good acoustics, limit group size to six to eight, and favor round tables so everyone can see one another).

LinkedIn has a similar program under which employees can expense their lunches with smart people in the industry, as long as they summarize what they learned from the lunch on their expense report—a neat intersection of the alliance with old-school HR operations.

Neither of these programs takes a lot of time and effort; just a single policy and some minimal expense.

Facilitate Speaking Gigs for Your Employees

Give your people time to take on leadership roles and speaking gigs in associations. Employees who are thought leaders outside the company improve the company brand and the employee's own personal brand. For example, Moz, a Seattle-based marketing software start-up has a number of programs to encourage employees to speak. "If you get a speaking spot at an event, Moz will cover the travel and accommodations," Moz founder Rand Fishkin told us. Moz even offers employees the opportunity to create their own speaking gigs. The MozCation program encourages employees ("Mozzers") to travel to exotic locations and host a mini one-day conference for Moz users.

Host Events at Your Company Office

Try to leverage your firm's facilities. Bigger companies, especially, should host conferences and events; these attract outsiders onto the campus and make it easier for current employees to meet and engage with them.

Nor should this practice be limited to formal events that require official support. Simply allowing employees to host clubs and associations is a low-cost way to encourage external networking. We do recommend that any employee who hosts a meeting in the company offices make it open to any other employee who wants to attend (which hopefully helps develop even more new relationships).

At LinkedIn, any employee can use any room, space, or facility on the corporate campus for any external group. For example, groups ranging from LGBT groups to a local Toastmasters club have used LinkedIn facilities to host meetings for their association. LinkedIn also hosts three to four industry events at its offices each month.

4. Have Employees Share What They Learn with the Company

If you're not actively taking what employees learn from their networks and bringing that knowledge back into the company to help solve challenges, it's as if you're flying millions of miles a year without bothering to attach your frequent flyer number to the reservations. The asset is there, but you have to claim it. If an employee takes someone interesting out for coffee or attends a conference, have a plan for "scaling" the learning. Employees can share their lessons learned in forms ranging from a simple e-mail to full-blown presentations.

It's not difficult to make such sessions part of your company's or team's standard operating procedure. Olivier Cardon, the former CEO of British luxury firm Linley, describes how his firm handled this: "Each designer had half a day every week—usually Friday afternoon—to research whatever they felt like as long as it was remotely connected to what the company was doing. Every month, each designer had to present the results of their research to their fellow designers, me, and anyone else in the company who wanted to attend." Not only did this program help build the individual networks of the designers, it also ensured that the insights those designers uncovered would spread throughout the company.

Cardon reports that this program helped Linley retain two skillful but independent-minded designers who otherwise would probably have left the firm.

It also led to unique and innovative products. For example, one of the firm's designers was a skateboard enthusiast and worked with a friend in the skateboard business to research manufacturing techniques. The result was the first product line in the luxury goods business to incorporate skateboard materials for durability and finish.

While Linley made network intelligence a companywide priority, even as an individual manager, you can apply these techniques to smaller groups and teams to reap similar benefits.

Walking the Walk: How LinkedIn Uses Network Intelligence

From the start, Reid built network intelligence into the culture of LinkedIn. Early on, he modeled the behavior he wanted to encourage. For example, he would make sure that he took notes during external meetings and then report his findings back to the team. This "closing the loop" served two purposes. First, it helped LinkedIn's team learn about the company's competitive environment. Reid was friends with Mark Pincus and Jonathan Abrams, the founders of

Tribe and Friendster. As LinkedIn did not compete with either of these other networks, Reid was able to bring back useful information about the social networking industry as a whole. Reid was in close touch with key entrepreneurs and technologists on the trend that became known as Web 2.0. Second, Reid's actions and the time and energy he devoted to reporting back to the team demonstrated the importance he placed on acting as a scout for the company. Other early employees followed his lead, which was a crucial source of hidden data. The network intelligence helped LinkedIn focus on the key issues and quickly integrate other companies' lessons.

As the company has grown, it has created programs to make network intelligence an integral and scalable part of its operations. For example, when employees return from a conference, they're asked to host a brown-bag lunch ("Lunch in Learn") to share with their colleagues what they learned. If an in-person get-together isn't an option or isn't scalable enough, employees can log in to LearnIn, the internal learning portal at the company, and publish their insights on the intranet for all other employees to see. Reid still participates in the process by bringing key industry leaders like Marc Andreessen and Arianna

Huffington onto the corporate campus to share their insights with the company.

HAVING THE CONVERSATION
Advice for Managers

Network intelligence needs to be an integral part of the alliance and the tour of duty conversation. When you define an employee's tour of duty, you should set explicit expectations about how both parties will invest in and benefit from network intelligence. For example, you might tell the employee, "We will provide you with time to build your network, and will pay for you to attend events where you can extend it. In exchange, we ask you to leverage that network as you're working—to deploy your network intelligence to help you and the company accomplish your mission." Here is some detailed advice on how to have this conversation.

MAKE THE CASE FOR WHY NETWORK INTELLI-GENCE IS IMPORTANT FOR EMPLOYER AND EM-PLOYEE. Employees instinctively understand why networking helps improve their career prospects;

your job is to point out how networking is an integral part of a mutually beneficial alliance. Remember the underpinnings of the alliance: *the company helps the employee transform his career; the employee helps the company transform itself and become more adaptable.*

Too many employees are made to feel guilty or conflicted when they attend conferences or networking happy hours. You need to make it clear that the company isn't supporting networks as an employee benefit, but rather as a mutually beneficial asset that helps the company as well.

PERSONALLY EXPLAIN THE COMPANY'S PROGRAMS. Sadly, many corporate policies are honored more in the breach than the observance. As a result, employees may be reluctant to take advantage of things like the ability to expense a networking lunch, even if those benefits are spelled out in the employee handbook. You should encourage your employees to take the company up on these offers by being a role model and doing it yourself, much as Reid did during the early days of LinkedIn.

MODEL PROPER USAGE OF INDIVIDUAL NETWORKS. A critical element of network intelligence is sharing what's learned with colleagues at the office. You should kick off the network intelligence conversation by citing a specific challenge you faced at work and how you tapped your network to help you solve it. This helps establish the norm and provides practical instruction.

ASK EVERY EMPLOYEE TO FURNISH A LIST OF THE SMARTEST PEOPLE HE KNOWS WHO DO NOT WORK AT THE COMPANY. Here's a simple technique to use at the company's or team's next group meeting. Have each employee on the team make a list of the three smartest people he knows. These lists can help the company in many ways, ranging from identifying experts who could be brought in as speakers to educate employees, to identifying potential problem-solving resources. The employee also benefits from this program; he gets the chance to strengthen a valuable relationship by offering potential speaking and consulting opportunities.

More Online: Learn specific tips and techniques that will help your employees use LinkedIn and other social platforms to gather and deploy network intelligence at www.theallianceframework.com/networkintel.

7

Corporate Alumni Networks

The Mutual Benefits of Lifelong Alliance

LinkedIn. Tesla. YouTube. Yelp. Yammer. SpaceX. What do all these companies have in common?

They're not just examples of innovation and massive financial success. All of them were founded by the alumni of a single company: PayPal.

Lifetime employment might be over, but a lifetime relationship remains the ideal, and as the alumni of PayPal know better than anyone, it can be extremely valuable. Unlike the free agency model, the alliance can and should persist even after an employee's final tour of duty. Typically, both company and employee aren't getting as much as they could from a strong corporate alumni relationship. As you'll see, despite evidence of pent-up demand for stronger alumni relationships, few companies have a good strategy for maintaining a relationship with former employees. Conversely, few of the alumni themselves realize how helpful a former employer can be to their career.

Establishing a corporate alumni network, which requires relatively little investment, is the next logical step in maintaining a relationship of mutual trust, mutual investment, and mutual benefit in an era where lifetime employment is no longer the norm.

Both companies and employees benefit from continuing the alliance. When a company is thriving, its alumni look good. For example, when Apple was struggling, no one wanted Apple alumni. Today, Apple alumni are sought after, even those who, like Reid, worked at Apple before Steve Jobs's triumphant return in 1997. Meanwhile, when a company's alumni are thriving professionally, that network becomes a valuable asset that helps the company. For example, much of McKinsey's luster and business comes from its powerful alumni network, which provides network intelligence, candidate referrals, and even sales.

To maximize the benefits of the corporate alumni network, a company should clearly articulate the bidirectional value both parties get from the continuing relationship. Fortunately, this isn't a difficult task. Employees clearly want an alumni relationship. LinkedIn (the service) now hosts over 118,000 corporate alumni groups, including 98 percent of the *Fortune* 500. Yet surprisingly, most of these alumni groups have little to no relationship with their former companies.

In fact, the majority of alumni networks that do exist are run completely independently from the company. A study from the University of Twente in the Netherlands showed that while only 15 percent of the companies surveyed had formal alumni networks, another 67 percent had employees who independently organized informal alumni groups.[1] Think about that—alumni want to connect so badly that they are spending their *own* time and money to set up these networks.

Informal groups can become quite elaborate. The P&G Alumni Network is completely independent from Procter & Gamble. Despite only starting in 2001, today it has over twenty-five thousand members, as well as a charitable foundation and speakers' bureau.[2] These informal alumni networks represent a huge (and largely missed) opportunity for companies. Most such groups focus on helping alumni help each other, rather than on maintaining members' relationships with their former organization. This approach creates some value for alumni, but little for the company.

The value to both parties can be much greater when a company actually contributes to its alumni network. So why don't more businesses do so? Let's start by examining the two industries that do grasp the value of corporate alumni: professional services firms and universities.

It's All about the ROI

Professional services firms are the gold standard of corporate alumni networks. McKinsey & Company has operated an official program since the 1960s, which has grown to over twenty-four thousand members.[3] Bain & Company employs nine full-time people to spearhead corporate alumni initiatives. Six of those full-timers work in the Bain Executive Network, which helps place alumni into executive roles with Bain clients and other companies and provides general career counseling services. The Boston Consulting

Group, PricewaterhouseCoopers, Deloitte, and their peers run similar practices.

Perhaps the only organizations that invest more in their alumni are colleges and universities, which employ armies of staff to print magazines, host reunion events, organize outings, and more. For many college graduates, their alma mater is one of the strongest aspects of their personal and professional identity.

What professional services firms and universities have in common is that their alumni drive direct revenue, making the investment case easy. Professional services alums frequently refer new clients to the firm, or hire the firm themselves when they are in an executive role at a company. College and university alumni donate vast sums of money directly to the university, as well as contribute revenue indirectly through things like ticket and apparel sales.

In most other industries, the benefits of operating an alumni network are uncertain and serendipitous, and so companies ignore the opportunity. When you launch a new product line, it's easy to quantify incremental sales. When you launch an alumni network, the precise return is hard to measure, and might not show up for years. Just as uncertainty doesn't equal risky, unpredictability doesn't equal low value.

If more companies studied corporate alumni networks, they would see that the costs of investing in alumni are much less than they might think, and the returns much greater. That's why creating and maintaining alumni networks is a compelling proposition and key element of the alliance.

Four Reasons to Invest in an Alumni Network

The Alumni Network Helps You Hire Great People

The first way an alumni network helps with hiring is making it easier for "boomerang" employees to return for another tour of duty after an absence from the company. Boomerangs are uniquely valuable because they offer an outsider perspective combined with an insider's knowledge of company process and culture. An ex-employee will be more interested in returning if the company stayed in touch and maintained a relationship in the interim. As the saying goes, Build the well before you get thirsty. For example, the Corporate Executive Board reports that rolling out the CEB

Alumni Network doubled the firm's rehire rate within two years.

Chevron takes things a step further with its Bridges program. Chevron alumni can sign up to be considered for specific contract assignments. It's an obvious win-win. Alumni get consulting opportunities that might turn into full-time gigs; Chevron gets a highly qualified pool of potential consultants whom it knows are a good cultural fit.[4]

Alumni can also refer great candidates. Given the cost of professional recruiters and the value of a vetted job candidate, soliciting alumni referrals ought to be a best practice. For example, companies ranging from consultancy Deloitte to payroll giant ADP offer cash bonuses to corporate alumni who refer successful candidates. Beyond simple referrals, corporate alumni can help with reference checks and judging cultural fit, even when they don't directly source the candidate.

Finally, the very presence of a properly implemented corporate alumni network can help an employer close great candidates. Candidates don't need to guess what impact one or more tours of duty might have; instead, they can simply use alumni as surrogates to get a sense of whether they'd like the job. The fact that McKinsey alumni have gone on to lead hundreds of billion-dollar companies helps illustrate the benefits of joining the firm.[5] Does McKinsey remind prospective employees of this fact? Of course they do.

Recruiting great people is expensive. An alumni network that generates just a few hires a year is easily worth six figures on hiring value alone.

Alumni Provide Useful Intelligence

Alumni are a great source of network intelligence—competitive information, effective business practices, emerging industry trends, and more. Not only do they have knowledge of the outside world that a company's current employees do not, they also understand how the organization works.

Simply conducting regular polls of alumni using standard questions can unearth key nuggets of information, such as how the company is perceived as an employer, competitive intelligence and industry trends, and pointers to potential customers. At LinkedIn, reports and rumors about emerging technologies like WhatsApp are taken more seriously when they come from former employees than from random commentators.

Finally, alumni provide a much-needed outside perspective. Companies find it all too easy to drink their own Kool-Aid; alums can have both the necessary objectivity and the respect and trust of the company to be listened to when they point out uncomfortable truths. For example, an alum who tests the beta version of a new product is more likely to offer honest feedback than a current employee.

Alumni Refer Customers

Alumni can become customers or refer customers, especially when incentivized to do so. Implementing formal incentive programs for alumni can require a bit more paperwork and process—no financial software includes an out-of-the-box "alumni rewards" module. But the value can be enormous, and giving out high-end swag is an easy way to get started.

Business-to-business (B2B) and business-to-consumer (B2C) companies will generally adopt different approaches. A single B2B customer might represent millions in revenue (remember those ex-McKinsey CEOs who hire their old firms?), whereas a single B2C customer might be worth a small number of dollars. B2B firms should incentivize direct customer introductions, while B2C companies should focus on encouraging influencers.

Alumni Are Brand Ambassadors

Your company's brand is no longer fully under your control. Spending money on advertising campaigns can drive awareness, but buzz emerges from grassroots interest, especially on social media. Corporate alumni can help in this regard, especially if they outnumber a firm's current employees. They also have the advantage of being third parties and thus are perceived as more objective. They're not getting a paycheck to tweet. If they promote a product or initiative on social media or respond to the tweets of customers or prospects, alumni have credibility that current employees simply can't duplicate.

In sum, the more a corporate alumni network strengthens the company's brand, the easier it becomes to leverage that network for hiring, network intelligence, and customer referrals.

But the "R," or return, of a corporate alumni network is only half of the ROI value equation. Let's explore the "I"—the investment.

Three Levels of Investment in Alumni Networks

The investment a company makes in its alumni network runs along a continuum from low to high. The level that's right for your company will depend on its specific circumstances.

1. IGNORE. If your worldwide corporate headquarters is also the place where your spouse parks his or her Prius at night, it's probably too early in your start-up's lifespan to start cultivating an alumni network. But once your company's alumni base numbers in the dozens and hundreds, ignoring it means the firm is missing a great opportunity. Remember, an informal group is run for the benefit of its moderators—the company has no control over or impact on the returns to the company.

2. SUPPORT. This level involves creating a direct connection with alumni group organizers to provide informal, largely ad hoc support. This can be as simple as asking, "What can we do for you?" Examples of

inexpensive support include maintaining mailing lists, paying for pizza at alumni meet-ups, and endorsing the independent efforts of alumni. Almost any company should support its alumni, given the minimal cost and the potential returns from maintaining an ongoing relationship. Accenture provides a great example of how a small investment can bring big benefits. The consultancy's LinkedIn group has over thirty-one thousand members who opt in to receive updates and career information from the firm and, more importantly, who opt in to talking with each other.[6] Thanks to engaged alumni, Accenture has saved significant sums on recruiting by hiring more "boomerang" talent.

3. INVEST. This level involves providing formal infrastructure and systematic benefits to alumni. These companies generally run the official alumni group directly; have staff dedicated (full- or part-time) to maintaining the network; offer the alumni benefits such as an employee store discount; and coordinate with the rest of the company employee base to aid in network intelligence gathering from alumni. While this tier of investment has real costs, companies that want to truly incorporate alumni into key processes and initiatives need this kind of rigor to reap the associated benefits.

For example, Harvard Business School recruited Chris to run an alumni association for HBS graduates in the high-tech industry. The school identified the need, sourced a candidate, and then invested in his efforts. This investment included providing the online infrastructure for running the club, as well as inviting club officers to attend the annual conference of all HBS alumni clubs.

eBay adopts the Invest model. For example, they host and sponsor alumni events, which it explicitly models on college reunions. As CEO John Donahoe told us, "We'll organize a dinner of about a hundred people for the 'Class of 2004'—the people who joined in a particular year. We get people to call their peers and get them to come. It's a great opportunity to reflect on shared experiences and to rebond with eBay."

Walking the Walk: The LinkedIn Corporate Alumni Network

Like most start-ups, LinkedIn didn't immediately establish an alumni network. As a high-growth start-up, it had little time to spare for anything other than building the business. And thanks to years of rapid growth, its few alumni were outnumbered by current employees.

As the company matured, however, and the number of alumni grew, it became apparent that establishing a formal alumni network would be a good long-term investment. Given the growth of the company, its management expected the alumni pool to expand rapidly over the following five years. It made sense to set up the alumni network before this expansion took place. As a result, the company shifted from lightly supporting the informal alumni group that emerged organically to truly investing in an official alumni network.

In late 2013, LinkedIn established an official alumni network to continue the alliance with more than one thousand alumni. The company decided to be inclusive—after all, its business model is predicated on the power of networks—which meant that all ex-employees in good standing were invited to join. The alumni network lives as a group on LinkedIn (the service). There, an employee in LinkedIn's HR department posts news about the company (this news is repurposed from an existing corporate communications internal e-mail, and thus requires little incremental effort). The moderator works with operating managers to seed the group with potentially useful questions such as "Has anyone heard anything interesting about the new Google phone?" or "What do people need to be successful in their current jobs?"

On a regular basis (up to once a quarter), all alumni who are part of the LinkedIn group receive an e-mail with a summary of the company's updates, alumni in the news, and a link to a survey that asks questions like "What your favorite new mobile app? Who should become a new participant on our Influencer publishing platform?"

To encourage participation and convey the strength of the alliance, LinkedIn offers a range of gifts to alumni. Every alum receives a free premium subscription to LinkedIn (the service). If they refer customers or employees who are hired, they are thanked with both nice gifts and personal notes.

In addition to the general group, the company maintains an invitation-only network for its most valued and distinguished alumni. This allows LinkedIn and these former employees to invest more in (and get more out of) the alumni relationship than would be possible or desirable for the general pool of employees. The members of the executive team select people into this hand-picked group on the basis of their contributions to the company as employees, contributions to the company as an alumni, or accomplishments in the industry over their careers. To these distinguished alumni, LinkedIn extends special invitations to events on campus, such as judging hackathons or attending fireside chats between Reid and outside guests such as Facebook's Sheryl Sandberg and WordPress creator Matt Mullenweg.

Together, these corporate alumni programs impose little incremental cost on LinkedIn. As noted, much of the content is repurposed from existing initiatives, and the few out-of-pocket costs like gifts for candidate referrals or network intelligence are minimal in comparison with alternatives like paying recruiting fees or hiring consultants and outside analysts.

Your corporate alumni network is a potential profit center, not just a line-item cost. And it's a powerful signal that you embrace the new employment alliance. So make a list of all your ex-employees—if you don't have a corporate alumni network for them, consider them resources that you're leaving fallow. Lifetime employment may be over, but a valuable lifetime relationship with your talent can and should persist.

More Online: Learn how other companies build their alumni networks and join the conversation yourself at www.theallianceframework.com/alumni.

8

Implementing an Alumni Network

Tactics and Techniques
for Setting Up a Corporate
Alumni Network

Here is a step-by-step guide to launching and leveraging a corporate alumni network for your organization, whether for a single department or the entire company.

1. Decide Who You Want to Include in Your Alumni Network

The simplest way to organize an alumni network is to include all ex-employees—stars, corporate middle class, and the most junior employees. Exclude employees where there is pending legal action or the equivalent against that employee or their new company. Exclude employees fired for cause (for instance, sexual harassment or theft). Maybe exclude contractors and interns, depending.

Broad participation can give rise to tricky situations. What if an employee goes to work for a competitor? Or is toxic to the alumni group? Or poaches the company's talent for his new employer? Or bad-mouths the company in the press after leaving? You will want to maintain the ability to "fire" people individually from the alumni network if their behavior is unseemly.

Establishing a "distinguished" alumni group offers a cleaner, longer-term solution to these dilemmas. The company can be more nuanced in who's involved and what benefits are provided. This allows a manager to provide a higher level of service to loyal former stars in exchange for a higher level of engagement. These folks are likely to go on to great things and be the center of their own networks, which could very valuable to the business. In addition, the threat of losing these "distinguished" benefits serves as a stick to discourage bad behavior.

2. Explicitly Define the Expectations and Benefits of the Relationship

The alumni relationship, like the rest of the employment alliance, is reciprocal. To harvest benefits from alumni, your company needs to offer them real benefits in return.

Some of the most common programs for rewarding and engaging alumni include:

Referral bonuses: If hiring great employees is so important, why not make that path easier to follow? Post open positions to an alumni mailing list and offer recruiting bonuses to alumni.

Product discounts and whitelist access: Microsoft alumni receive an employee discount of up to 90 percent at the Microsoft company store.[1] LinkedIn sometimes adds some alumni to a product's beta "whitelist," granting that person early access. These are both benefits to the alum and opportunities to solicit constructive feedback on the products from informed, yet more objective, sources.

Hosted events: Hosting events allows companies to leverage the magic of face-to-face interaction to strengthen the alumni relationship. There's a reason why every college or university holds regular reunions—these are prime drivers behind alumni engagement and, by extension, alumni donations. Implementing an alumni reunion mixer is pretty straightforward. There are also creative options, like inviting alumni to an annual company party or other on-campus events.

Official recognition for select alumni: Companies should consider taking a page from the best practices of consumer-facing businesses such as Amazon, eBay, and Yelp, which recognize Top Reviewers, Power Sellers, and Elite members, respectively, with publicly visible badges. Colleges also employ this practice by offering honors and distinction. A company could officially recognize its distinguished alumni and allow them to talk about their membership in that elite group. To be sure, some companies might feel uncomfortable officially favoring certain alumni; you have to decide whether the benefits outweigh the costs of perceived favoritism, as is true with any public reward or recognition.

Keeping alumni informed: Keeping alumni informed isn't just good for the alumni, it's also good for the company. The better alumni understand the company's current circumstances, the more practical the insights and assistance they can provide. For example, Microsoft provides its alumni with early access to "beta" software. Alumni who find out about unpleasant facts from the press rather than the company itself should rightly see that as a breakdown in the alliance.

3. Establish a Comprehensive Exit Process

Not reinforcing the lifetime relationship with an employee during the exit interview is like setting up a booth at a trade show but failing to collect business cards from the people who stop by—it's a huge missed opportunity. The organization spent significant time and energy building a great relationship—why throw it out? First, at the time of exit, decide if the departing employee has the executive sponsorship to be invited to join the distinguished alumni network. Then, collect from departing employees all the information that the company needs to maintain a long-term relationship. This includes things like contact information, expertise, and what the employee might want to help with in the future. Given the end of lifetime employment, your company shouldn't rely on the ability to leverage your personal relationship with the employee; you should build organizational, as well as personal, connectivity. The company or work group should have a database of the following for all ex-employees: permanent e-mail, phone number, LinkedIn profile, Twitter handle, blog URL, and other similar information.

4. Build Links between Current Employees and Alumni

Once the corporate alumni network is active, value won't flow automatically. Busy alumni may not remember to send in information without some kind of reminder. Current employees might not think to reach out to alumni for insights and help with solving problems.

Senior managers should set up formal programs and processes for tapping alumni intelligence before the need for their contribution arises. These could include alumni advisory councils, topic-specific mailing lists for current employees and distinguished alumni, and regular alumni events where current execs mingle with alumni. Such tools should be a standard part of the problem-solving process within the organization.

The marketing software company HubSpot offers one example of a company that consciously connects with and trusts its alumni. The HubSpot alumni network is an informal group that is managed by former employees but maintains a strong relationship with the company. "A member of the executive team attends every alumni network meeting," HubSpot cofounder and CTO Dharmesh Shah told us, "That executive usually holds a thirty- to forty-minute open Q&A [Ask Me Anything] session, where the alumni can ask any question about the company, including 'What's keeping you up at night?' 'How is the customer retention doing?'" This is confidential information that is not available to the general public.

Companies should also seek to involve alumni in celebrating their big wins. When LinkedIn held its initial public offering (IPO), Reid specifically worked to include alumni in the celebration and acknowledge their contributions. He had personalized bobblehead dolls made in the image of a number of LinkedIn's early supporters—forty-five, all told—most of whom were former employees by the time of the IPO.

HAVING THE CONVERSATION
Advice for Managers

All healthy relationships begin with thinking of how one can help the other party. In all conversations, you should start from the employee's point of view.

There are three times when you need to have a conversation with your direct reports about the alumni network: during their hiring process, while the employee is employed, and when the employee exits and becomes an alumnus. Each time calls for a different conversation.

USE THE ALUMNI NETWORK AS A SELLING POINT DURING THE HIRING PROCESS. Deploy a combination of statistics and stories for maximum impact on recruiting. Remember the promise of Transformational tours: a tour of duty will transform your entire career, and it's the alumni network that helps ensure that promise is realized. It's nice to be able to cite the size, reach, and activity of the corporate alumni network, but to be really persuasive, you should share concrete personal examples of how the alumni network helped *you* on and off the job.

MAKE IT EASY AND OBVIOUS FOR CURRENT EMPLOYEES TO TAP THE ALUMNI NETWORK FOR NETWORK INTELLIGENCE. Because most companies don't have formal alumni networks, few employees will have experience leveraging these networks on the job. As a manager, market your alumni to colleagues in meetings: "Say, couldn't we could ask alumnus John Doe, who's now a leading designer at an ad agency?" Send around impressive alumni's LinkedIn profiles to remind your employees of the assets they can tap.

REINFORCE THE CAREER-LONG NATURE OF THE ALLIANCE UPON EXIT. Emphasize in the exit interview that while the employment relationship may end, the alliance will live on, not just between the two of you, but with the company as well. Despite all the emotions that sometimes surround such a conversation, see it as an opportunity. Because lifetime employment is out, but lifetime alliance is *in*.

More Online: Find practical advice, sample e-mails, and real-world case studies at www.theallianceframework.com/alumni.

Conclusion

Think back to the era of lifetime employment. Although that model lacked the flexibility to adapt to our networked age, it did encourage long-term thinking. During the 1950s and 1960s, we invested heavily in the future and developed the technologies that drove the Information Age.

The free-agency-style era that followed, and in which we're still living, leads us away from long-term investment and to a shortsighted focus on instant gratification. Remember: a business without loyalty is a business without long-term thinking. A business without long-term thinking is a business that's unable to invest in the future. And a business that isn't investing in tomorrow's opportunities and technologies is a company already in the process of dying.

The Alliance creates a model for work that encourages companies and individuals to invest in each other. Imagine a world in which managers and employees have honest conversations about each other's goals and time tables; where managers and team members define jobs that match their values and aspirations; and in which even employees who move on to a different employer maintain an ongoing, mutually beneficial relationship with the company.

It's a world—and a culture of employment—that's already taken shape in Silicon Valley, and we expect its principles will spread to all industries and across the globe. Mutual investment creates massive value for companies and for employees. Even if the effects of the alliance stopped there, it would be a talent framework worth adopting.

But the impact of the alliance extends far beyond company walls.

Improving the microcosm of workplace relationships can have a major impact on society—job by job, team by team, company by company. The alliance may seem like a small thing next to macroeconomic proposals like overhauling the education system or reforming our regulatory regime, but it's a small thing we can all adopt today that will generate big cumulative returns in the years to come.

The trends of nearly half a century are not easily undone. But with *The Alliance*, we hope we have given you a framework that changes how you, your team, your company, and ultimately our entire economy works.

The three of us embarked on a shared tour of duty to write this book because we believe that when the right talent meets the right opportunity in a company with the right philosophies, amazing transformations can happen.

Now it's your turn to build the alliances that will transform your company and career.

—Reid, Ben, and Chris
Palo Alto, California

www.theallianceframework.com

Appendix A

Sample Statement of Alliance

This statement of alliance provides a model for you to use when you're defining a Transformational tour of duty with an employee. Customize the policies and programs (such as the budget for networking) to reflect the specific circumstances of the company and the team you lead. The statement of alliance should also be personalized with individual goals for the individual employee, but for the sake of fairness, the same general policies and principles should apply equally to all the members of the team.

"I" = the manager

"We" = manager and employee

"We the company" = the company

In a larger organization, the senior management and HR leadership of the firm should work to customize the alliance based on the company's needs, but should still allow individual managers the leeway to adapt the alliance to their teams.

To download your own electronic copy of this Statement of Alliance, visit our website at www .theallianceframework.com.

Preamble

- I'm glad to have you on my team.

- I view our relationship as a mutual alliance that needs to help both of us.

- This statement of alliance lets us lay out both our expectations so that we can invest in the relationship and each other with confidence.

- I want you to help transform the company.

- In return, I and the company need to help you improve your market value and transform your career (preferably within this organization).

- While I am not making a commitment to offer lifetime employment, and you are not making a commitment to stay for your entire career, we will act to maintain a long-term alliance, even if the employment relationship ends.

Article 1: Your Tour of Duty

Principles

- Your tour of duty defines what you will do for me and the business; it also defines what the business and I will do for your career.

- While there is no legal obligation on you, me, or the company, and plans can always change, right now we are all committed to completing this tour of duty on the basis of mutual trust. This means that if we're progressing toward our mutual goals, the company won't fire you, and you won't leave.

- As we deepen our mutual investment and commitment, we may someday decide to make a long-term, Foundational commitment to each other.

Expectations

- We the company expect this current tour of duty to encompass the time it takes for you to execute the following mission objective:

  _____

- I expect this tour of duty will last approximately the following amount of time: _____

- Here is what the results of a successful tour of duty look like for the company (product launches, process improvements, sales, etc.):

  _____

- Here is what the results of a successful tour of duty look like for you (knowledge, skills, accomplishments, recognition, etc.):

  _____

- As we approach the end of this tour of duty (approximately 12 months to go), you and I should discuss what you would like to do once the tour of duty is complete, either by defining a new tour of duty at the company or discussing your transition to a different company.

Article 2: Alignment

Principles

- You, I, and the company all have core aspirations and values.

- We will all work together to align as many aspirations and values as we can between the three parties involved, while understanding there will not be 100 percent overlap.

Expectations

- I will lay out my core aspirations and values and what I believe are the company's specific and rigorous core aspirations and values.

- We welcome your feedback and suggestions on those core aspirations and values.

- I would like to learn about your core aspirations and values, even where they differ from mine or those of the company. They are:

_____

- We will work together to set mutual expectations for your career trajectory.

- We will recognize you for both your business accomplishments and your ability to exemplify the company's aspirations and values.

- If gaps exist, we will address them explicitly and proactively, rather than ignoring them and letting them grow and damage our alliance.

Article 3: Network Intelligence

Principles

- Your professional network is a valuable asset, both for you and your career, and for me and the company.

- People, including those outside our company, are a critical source of information and insight for solving business challenges.

- The company and I will give you time to build and groom your network; in exchange, we ask that you use your network to help us achieve your mission objective and make the business successful.

Expectations

- I will be clear about what constitutes nonpublic, nonsecret information you can share with your network.

- While this shouldn't need to be explicit, you should feel free to use company equipment (e.g., your computer or smartphone) and company time for professional social networking so that you are discoverable and active on social media like LinkedIn and Twitter.

- You may expense any event, conference, or club membership up to X dollars, provided you think it will help you build your professional network. For larger amounts, ask me first, and I will try to approve as many of your requests as I can. You are responsible for sharing what you learn with me and your colleagues.

- You may use company facilities to host external groups and events.

Article 4: The Alumni Network

Principles

- Lifetime employment is over for most of us. But a valuable relationship should be lifetime.

- If and when you leave the company, if you're in good standing, we will invite you to our corporate alumni network.

- The alliance between the company and you as an alum will remain consistent with the same principles: mutual trust, mutual investment, mutual benefit.

- As a current employee, feel free to tap the alumni network for help on solving current business challenges.

Expectations

- The company and I commit to keeping you in the loop and up to date on what's happening with the company, including consulting projects or new positions that might interest you.

- When the company or I think there's a way for you to help us, we ask that you give us a fair hearing, though of course you can decline.

- The company will set up tools (e.g., mailing lists, groups, enterprise social networks) to help you tap the knowledge of our employees and corporate alumni.

Appendix B

Mission Alignment Exercise: People We Admire

In our discussion on alignment, we wrote about the importance of understanding the values of your employees, and the technique of asking someone who they admire and why. Here's how each of us completed the exercise—three people we admire, the three traits about each that we most admire, and a rough ordering of how strongly we cherish the traits overall.

Reid

1. Martin Luther King Jr.

A great hero whose vision and courage remains an inspiration for all Americans and indeed the world

- Vision
- Courage
- Compassion

(continued)

2. Marie Curie

A hero of science who demonstrates that you don't need to lead a large organization in order to take fundamental, intelligent risks and blaze a path for people behind you

- Intelligence
- Independent thinking
- Dedication

3. Andrew Carnegie

An industrialist whose evolution into philanthropist has provided a beacon throughout the decades

- Generosity
- Leadership
- Entrepreneurialism

Ranking the traits

1. Compassion
2. Courage
3. Dedication
4. Intelligence
5. Generosity
6. Vision
7. Leadership
8. Entrepreneurialism
9. Independent thinking

Chris

1. Abraham Lincoln

The greatest American who ever lived. He faced greater challenges than any president before or since, and managed to reunite the country.

- Compassion
- Egolessness
- Storytelling

2. Fred Rogers

He may very well have been the nicest man to ever live and impacted millions of children's lives.

- Acceptance
- Authenticity
- Kindness

3. David Packard

Founder of Hewlett-Packard, one of the Godfathers of Silicon Valley and one of the greatest managers of all time

- Initiative
- Trust
- Generosity

Ranking the traits

1. Authenticity
2. Egolessness
3. Initiative
4. Trust
5. Acceptance
6. Kindness
7. Compassion
8. Generosity
9. Storytelling

Ben

1. Benjamin Franklin

A tireless inventor, cofounder of America, and effective diplomat

- Self-improvement
- Entrepreneurialism
- Internationalism

2. David Foster Wallace

A writer with unparalleled ability to explain human nature and the modern world

- Curiosity
- Humor
- Intensity

3. Siddhartha Gautama (the Buddha)

A spiritual leader whose teachings on the meaning of life changed the world

- Equanimity
- Peace
- Discipline

Appendix B

Ranking the traits

1. Curiosity
2. Humor
3. Peace
4. Entrepreneurialism
5. Discipline
6. Intensity
7. Self-improvement
8. Equanimity
9. Internationalism

Appendix C

Getting Started at Your Company

During the writing of this book, we encountered numerous topics that we found fascinating, but that we simply couldn't fit into this book. For example, while we dealt with social media in the context of setting policies around network intelligence, we really wanted the opportunity to explore the topic in greater detail.

We also found that when we shared drafts of the book with the great managers we know, these managers came up with insightful questions and practical concerns that helped improve our arguments and advice. Now that the book is available to the public, we expect you, the reader, to add to this collection of questions and improvements. Perhaps your industry has unique dynamics, and you want to know how the alliance needs to adapt to those dynamics. Perhaps there's a variation on the tour of duty framework that would work best in your company.

That's why we've created TheAllianceFramework. com. This website and the related LinkedIn group will act as a central clearinghouse for additional content, interactive assessments, and even practical worksheets and training guides, to expand our collective understanding of the alliance.

You'll also find information about keynote speaking, training sessions, and webinars.

We invite you to join us at TheAllianceFramework. com, to help us explore these issues and to help you bring the alliance to your organization.

Notes

Chapter 1

1. See http://www.nytimes.com/2001/04/08/business/off-the-shelf-after-the-downsizing-a-downward-spiral.html.

2. John Hagel III, John Seely Brown, and Lang Davidson, *The Power of Pull: How Small Moves, Smartly Made, Can Set Big Things in Motion* (New York: Basic Books, 2010), 12.

3. Harold Meyerson, "The Forty-Year Slump: The State of Work in the Age of Anxiety," *The American Prospect*, November 12, 2013, http://prospect.org/article/40-year-slump.

4. Ibid.

5. Towers Watson 2012 Global Workforce Study, *Engagement at Risk: Driving Strong Performance in a Volatile Global Environment*, July 2012, http://www.towerswatson.com/en-AE/Insights/IC-Types/Survey-Research-Results/2012/07/2012-Towers-Watson-Global-Workforce-Study.

6. Susan Adams, "Trust in Business Falls Off a Cliff," *Forbes*, June 13, 2012, http://www.forbes.com/sites/susanadams/2012/06/13/trust-in-business-falls-off-a-cliff/.

7. Reed Hastings, "Netflix Culture: Freedom & Responsibility," August 1, 2009, SlideShare presentation, http://www.slideshare.net/reed2001/culture-1798664.

8. "Pixar Total Grosses," *Box Office Mojo*, http://boxofficemojo.com/franchises/chart/?id=pixar.htm.

9. David Lazarus, "A Deal Bound to Happen," *SF Gate*, January 25, 2006, http://www.sfgate.com/business/article/A-deal-bound-to-happen-2505936.php.

10. Jack Clark, "How Amazon Exposed Its Guts: The History of AWS's EC2," *ZDNet*, June 7, 2012, http://www.zdnet.com/how-amazon-exposed-its-guts-the-history-of-awss-ec2-3040155310/.

11. Larry Dignan, "Amazon's AWS: $3.8 Billion Revenue in 2013, Says Analyst," *ZDNet*, January 7, 2013, http://www.zdnet.com/amazons-aws-3-8-billion-revenue-in-2013-says-analyst-7000009461/.

Chapter 2

1. "People Operations Rotational Program," https://www.google.com/about/jobs/search/#!t=jo&jid=3430003.

2. "Careers at Facebook: Product Manager Rotational Program," https://www.facebook.com/careers/department?dept=product-management&req=a0IA000000CwBjlMAF.

3. Rachel Emma Silverman and Lauren Weber, "An Inside Job: More Firms Opt to Recruit from Within," *Wall Street Journal*, May 29, 2012, http://online.wsj.com/news/articles/SB10001424052702303395604577434563715828218.

4. Reid Hoffman, "If, Why, and How Founders Should Hire a 'Professional,'" *CEO*, January 21, 2013, http://reidhoffman.org/if-why-and-how-founders-should-hire-a-professional-ceo/.

5. "Rich Corporate Culture at McDonald's Is Built on Collaboration," *Financial Post*, February 4, 2013, http://business.financialpost.com/2013/02/04/rich-corporate-culture-at-mcdonalds-is-built-on-collaboration/.

6. Kim Bhasin, "Jeff Bezos Talks About His Old Job at McDonald's, Where He Had to Clean Gallons of Ketchup off the Floor," *Business Insider*, July 23, 2012, http://www.business

insider.com/jeff-bezos-reflects-on-his-old-job-at-mcdonalds-2012-7.

7. Anne Fulton, "Career Agility: The New Employer-Employee Bargain," blog post, March 21, 2013, http://www.careerengagementgroup.com/blog/2013/03/21/career-agility-the-new-employer-employee-bargain/.

8. Jeffrey Pfeffer, "Business and the Spirit: Management Practices That Sustain Values," Stanford University Graduate School of Business Research Paper Series, no. 1713, October 2001, https://gsbapps.stanford.edu/researchpapers/library/1713.pdf.

Chapter 3

1. Dallas Hanson and Wayne O'Donohue, "William Whyte's 'The Organization Man': A Flawed Central Concept but a Prescient Narrative," September 21, 2009, DOI 10.1688/1861-9908_mrev_2010_01_Hanson, http://www98.griffith.edu.au/dspace/bitstream/handle/10072/36379/68117_1.pdf;jsessionid=17A80215986F988028592EC7D30739DE?sequence=1.

2. John Bell, "Why Mission Statements Suck," June 13, 2011, http://www.ceoafterlife.com/leadership/why-mission-statements-suck-2/.

3. Sharlyn Lauby, "Company Values Create the Foundation for Employee Engagement," HR Bartender (blog), November 6, 2012, http://www.hrbartender.com/2012/employee/company-values-create-the-foundation-for-employee-engagement/.

4. Adam Bryant, "Neil Blumenthal of Warby Parker on a Culture of Communication," New York Times, October 24, 2013, http://www.nytimes.com/2013/10/25/business/neil-blumenthal-of-warby-parker-on-a-culture-of-communication.html.

5. See http://en.wikiquote.org/wiki/Theodore_Roosevelt.

6. The Importance of Connecting with Colleagues," Bloomberg BusinessWeek, June 10, 2010, http://www.businessweek.com/magazine/content/10_25/b4183071373230.htm#p2.

Notes

Chapter 5

1. Bill Gates, *Business @ the Speed of Thought: Using a Digital Nervous System* (New York: Warner Books, 1999), 3.
2. Deborah Ancona, Henrik Bresman, and David Caldwell, "The X-Factor: Six Steps to Leading High-Performing X-Teams," *Organizational Dynamics* 38, no. 3 (2009), 217–224.

Chapter 7

1. Joe Laufer, "Corporate Alumni Programmes: What Universities Can Learn from the Business Experience," November 5, 2009, SlideShare presentation, http://www.slideshare.net/joeinholland/what-universities-can-learn-from-corporate-alumni-programs#btnNext.
2. Emily Glazer, "Leave the Company, but Stay in Touch," *Wall Street Journal*, December 20, 2012, http://blogs.wsj.com/atwork/2012/12/20/leave-the-company-but-stay-in-touch/.
3. See the McKinsey & Company website for more information on its alumni program: http://www.mckinsey.com/alumni.
4. See the Chevron Alumni website for more information, http://alumni.chevron.com/chevron-careers/chevron-bridges-contract-positions.html.
5. As referenced on the "McKinsey & Company: A Community for Life" page, http://www.mckinsey.com/careers/a_place_to_grow/a_community_for_life.
6. "Official Accenture Alumni Network," http://www.linkedin.com/groups/Official-Accenture-Alumni-Network-82182/about.

Chapter 8

1. Benefits of membership in the Microsoft Alumni Network and Microsoft Alumni Foundation are explained at http://www.microsoft.com/about/en/us/alumni/default.aspx.

Index

Index

Index

Acknowledgements

Thanks to our families for their support and for their patience through all the late nights and weekends— Michelle, Jessie, Alisha (and Jason and Marissa). Thank you to Tim Sullivan and his colleagues at Harvard Business Review Press for helping bring this project to life, and to Justin Fox at HBR for encouraging us to publish "Tours of Duty." Lisa DiMona, Brett Bolkowy, Saida Sapieva, Yee Harrison, and Ian Alas on our team offered critical organizational and editorial support.

Jeff Weiner was a key partner in developing the tour of duty ideas. Deep Nishar, Pat Wadors, Mike Gamson, Kevin Scott, Nick Besbeas, Kelly Palmer, and Dan Shapero at LinkedIn made the book much better with their feedback and examples.

John Donahoe, Eric Schmidt, Ken Chenault, Aneel Bhusri, John Lilly, Rich Lesser, Brad Smith, Reed Hastings, Linda Rottenberg, Russ Hagey, Niall

FitzGerald, and Muhtar Kent offered valuable feedback as well.

As always with such great feedback and support, we're responsible for any remaining errors in the book.

About the Authors

REID HOFFMAN is Executive Chairman of LinkedIn Corporation and a partner at Greylock Partners. In 2003 he cofounded LinkedIn, the world's largest professional networking service, in his living room in Mountain View, California. Today, LinkedIn has more than three hundred million members in two hundred countries and territories around the world. In 2009 Reid joined Greylock Partners, a leading Silicon Valley venture capital firm. His investments include Airbnb, Facebook, Flickr, and Zynga. He serves on a number of for-profit and not-for-profit boards, including Kiva.org and Endeavor.

Reid earned a master's degree in philosophy from Oxford University and a bachelor's degree, with distinction, from Stanford University.

BEN CASNOCHA is an award-winning entrepreneur and author from Silicon Valley. He is coauthor with Reid Hoffman of the #1 *New York Times* bestselling book *The Start-up of You: Adapt to the Future, Invest in Yourself, and Transform Your Career.* He spent two years as Reid's chief of staff at LinkedIn and Greylock Partners.

Ben is the founder of Comcate, Inc., a leading e-government software company. PoliticsOnline named him one of the "25 most influential people in the world of internet and politics." *Businessweek* named him "one of America's top young entrepreneurs."

Ben is a frequent keynote speaker on talent management and innovation. He has spoken to hundreds of corporations and associations in more than a dozen countries.

CHRIS YEH is Vice President of Marketing for PBworks, cofounder and general partner of Wasabi Ventures, and has been working with high-tech start-ups since 1995.

As described in *The Start-up of You*, Chris's mission statement is "To help interesting people do interesting things." He has been blogging since 2001, both on his personal blogs and as a guest author for outlets such as TechCrunch, Mashable, and VentureBeat. He has written over two thousand posts on topics ranging from the psychology of entrepreneurship to achieving happiness in Silicon Valley.

Chris earned two bachelor's degrees, with distinction, from Stanford University (Product Design Engineering and Creative Writing) and an MBA from Harvard Business School, where he was named a Baker Scholar.

Adapt to the Future,
Invest in Yourself,
and Transform Your Career

#1 New York Times Bestseller

the start-up of

YOU

Reid Hoffman

cofounder and chairman of **Linked** in.

— and —

Ben Casnocha

ISBN: 978-0-307-88890-7

The Start-Up of You, written by Reid Hoffman and Ben Casnocha, published by Crown Business, is available at a discount when purchasing in quantity for sales promotions or corporate use. Special editions, including personalized covers, excerpts, and corporate imprints can be created when purchasing in large quantities. For more information or to order copies for your team or organizations, please call Premium Sales at (212) 572-2232 or e-mail specialmarkets@randomhouse.com.

The Bluest Blood

AN AMANDA PEPPER MYSTERY

Gillian Roberts

Ballantine Books • New York

With love beyond words to the Appel family:
Julie, Dick, Kevin and Leilani,
and the memory of Darren

The Bluest Blood

One

"**D**OWN these green streets a man must go."

"There are no streets out here. They're lanes and courts and roads and avenues and ways," I answered Mackenzie. "These are upmarket byways. And currently not very green."

We drove through wide suburban not-streets lined with skeletal trees with only the slightest whisper of life. It was March, but spring seemed a rumor, a fever dream. I suspected that last month the groundhog had seen not only his shadow, but also the shadow of death.

Nonetheless, the night felt warm with promise. We were en

1

route to a black-tie gala, not exactly a standard activity for us. A Saturday night of wining, dining, and dancing at a fabled mansion I'd never expected to enter. I smiled in anticipation.

Mackenzie glanced over. "You look like a woman havin' delicious thoughts," he said. "I trust they're about me."

"Absolutely. About how irresistible you are in your tuxedo." He was, and it worried me somewhat. Not the attraction, but how much I loved his non-homicide-detective persona. But I wasn't going to dwell on that tonight, not while the very sight of him gave me so much pleasure.

"Good," he said. "An' though I doubt it's possible, if you ever do tire of thinkin' about me, you can think about yourself, about how radiant you look, because you do. That dress brings out the copper in your hair, makes your eyes so green . . ." He paused. "That dress reminds me of you. I mean you're next to me and it's not like I forgot you—but like maybe I had gone blind till now."

"Many thanks." I understood what he meant. It was one of that handful of nights in a lifetime when I knew he was correct. Not that I was as beautiful as he implied—that was not vision speaking—but that I'd been transformed into something else that I would never have admitted wanting to be.

Lacking formal attire, and unable to fill out my six-foot friend Sasha's collection of "antique" garments, I had rented a bronze silk number in a place that recycled the A-list's discards. The word *gown* didn't do it justice. It had been colored and cut by a fairy godmother with an advanced degree in design, and had turned out to be a magic garment, because when I wore it, there was somebody else in the mirror—somebody I wanted to be, and knew I could be, at least while I wore it. Clothes may make the man, but they remake the woman. Tonight, I wore not only a glimmer of bronze, but a sense of infinite possibility. I could present myself any way I chose, pick the play I starred in.

"Whatever makes you smile that way," Mackenzie went on in the drawl that honey-coated his every word, "I do hope it's not the Roederers. Or their palatial digs." He shook his head. "Because then you'd be a groupie for people who didn't do anything except get themselves born into families that did their thing generations ago. Bein' starstruck over pedigrees seems positively . . . un-American of you."

"Going to their house is one thing," I said. "A vacation trip to Moneyland to see what a zillion dollars and good taste can produce. It isn't the Roederers' money I admire, but what they do with it."

He gave a grudging half nod because to do otherwise would have been ridiculous. The couple merrily sprinkled money around, primarily onto the arts, and not in the time-consuming, semi-anonymous manner of Old Philadelphia. They did not sit upon boards and ruminate. They decided what they liked, then popped cash into the hands of those who could make it happen. Their taste was eclectic, their bounty wide-reaching—and it now included Philly Prep's media center, which I wish were still called the library.

I was the unashamed fan of Edward and Theodora Roederer, known more commonly and less formally as Neddy and Tea (as in the beverage). Mackenzie had grumbled about "cutesy-pie rich people tags"—he who had no names at all. He thought that they'd missed a chance to be still more precious by re-nicknaming Edward "Coffee" or "With lemon." "Then they'd be the complete and perfect 'We're-rich-enough-to-sound-as-stupid-as-we-like' couple's names," he'd commented.

"I'd think you'd be intrigued by their history. You're the buff," I now said. Neddy Roederer's middle name was Franklin. As in Benjamin, revered Founding Father and Inventor of Practically Everything. And Neddy's relative. Probably.

It is historical fact that Ben's only son, William, was born out of wedlock, and although William broke with his father in most ways by becoming a loyalist and settling in England, he followed family tradition by siring his own "natural" son, another William, who wound up serving as Granddad Ben's secretary in France.

According to an *Inquirer* article—yes, I admit, I read whatever I could find about them, which wasn't much because the Roederers shied from publicity—Edward Franklin Roederer claimed (with a wink, the reporter noted, as if he were joking or didn't really care one way or the other) that he was the descendant of the illegitimate son and grandson. The Willies, he called them, those "somewhat shady" Franklins.

Tea, the one reputed to have the fortune, had her own dazzling kin listed in the *Almanach de Gotha*, the who's who of Europe.

"You know what Mark Twain said about your hometown?" Mackenzie asked.

I could tell by his tone that it wasn't going to be complimentary, but as always, I couldn't resist a peek into his cluttered, over-full storage bin of a brain.

"Twain said that in Boston, they asked how much a man knew. In New York, they asked how much he was worth. But in Philadelphia, the question was, who were his parents. Nothing's changed, has it? Neddy Roederer's connection to Franklin turns the blood in his veins cobalt-blue. Which harmonizes perfectly with Tea's green, green cash."

Probably true, but it didn't bother me one bit.

Mackenzie leaned forward and sighed. "Suburbs aren't big on makin' it easy for outsiders to find the way."

"Another way the rich are different from thee and me." The road was indeed dark, with the night sky covered by clouds, a paucity of street lamps, and nothing like an address on the curbs. In fact, nothing like curbs. The straggling March grass of the expansive lawns ended at the road's blacktop. The unwritten message was clear—if we didn't know where we were, we didn't belong here.

I'd have thought Mackenzie was used to unlit spaces, however. He'd been raised outside New Orleans in a place I envisioned drooping with moss, humidity, and snapping creatures—and lit only by fireflies and swamp gas.

We passed an attenuated estate now filled with enormous raw homes: châteaux, haciendas, and nouveau Elizabethan half-timbered concoctions, all barefaced against the elements until their scraggly landscaping filled in. On a hill above them loomed a still larger structure, once the manor house. A sign announced: EVERGREEN ACRES, A RETIREMENT FACILITY.

EverGreen sounded familiar. I'd thought it was a nastily ironic name for its inhabitants, so deeply into their own brown autumns that they had to live there. I checked the directions. "Turn here," I was finally able to say. If homes lined this new road, they were too far back and too far apart to be visible. We drove in a tunnel of night. "It'll be on our left in a while." I said it out loud to reassure myself.

Even in profile, Mackenzie showed the full force of his concentration on the dark and unfamiliar road. "You're being a really good sport about this," I said. Without protest, he'd agreed to accompany me, even though I knew a Philly Prep fund-raiser wasn't his number-one choice of how to spend his leisure time. Nor was it mine—except when it was being held at Glamorgan. In any case, I had no choice. I had been told to come and had been handed a set of tickets. I was going to be the Faculty Poster Girl, because I had helped alert the Roederers, through their son Griffin, a student at our school, to the pressing needs of the library. Besides, it wouldn't have looked good if not a single teacher had attended, but we weren't paid enough to squander a cent—or the hundred dollars each ticket cost—on a gala. Particularly when it meant mingling with the parents of our kids—the trees those apples hadn't fallen far from. "Thanks," I said, patting his gloved hand.

His understanding and willingness gave me hope for our experiment in living together. Maybe we two bullheaded people could manage to find enough crossover points to braid our lives together.

"An' I promise not to belch or pick my nose or forget to use silverware when I eat," he said. "An' never to say things like, 'Oh, you're Farley's mother? The one with the jug ears and no brain? Heard a lot about him.' "

"You're a real twenty-first-century sensitive kind of guy," I said.

"Still, I miss the joys of a quiet night at home." He sighed. "Just you—in that dress—an' me and a fire goin' . . ."

I wished I could believe I was the object of his homebound lust, in or out of my gown, but I doubted it, no matter what he'd say. I knew that what he secretly sighed for was, instead, his new computer. Friends swore this was a phase he'd outgrow, but meantime, Mackenzie yearned only to surf the Net and search the Web and electronically natter about topics of subminimal interest.

What a sexy, interesting man he'd been, pre-Internet. "You know," I said, "watching you watch a computer screen . . . well, it's too *intense* for a steady diet. Too overwhelmingly exciting. I need to come up for air, catch my breath, balance the madness of it all with something drab and boring—like a fabulous party in a mansion."

He chuckled, unfazed. He and his pet computer were above my barbs.

"I think we're close now," I said. "Coming up on our left any minute: fabled Glamorgan."

"Be still, my heart," Mackenzie said.

Glamorgan had been named after a place in Wales, like so many other Main Line sites: Radnor, the township it was in, as well as Bryn Mawr, Bala-Cynwyd, Narberth, Merion, Berwyn. All were remnants of the Welsh Barony, fifty thousand acres granted by William Penn to Quakers from Wales. I don't know what Glamorgan means in Welsh, but when I heard or read mention of the house, it was the *glamour* portion that shimmered and reverberated. And the stardust spilled over to its owners.

"Don't be disappointed," Mackenzie said, as if reading my mind, "if neither they nor their house is what you fantasize. These are the Philadelphia suburbs, after all, where snobbery is so refined they invert it. Old money's hallmark is that it's invisible. You're supposed to look penniless. You know: I'm so secure, I don't have to *prove* anything. If you don't know who I am, you're nobody, so who cares? Plainness is the only Quaker vestige you people have left, and it makes no sense."

I just hate it when he says *you people*, lumping me with the entire population of the Delaware Valley, even if this time, my lump was the incredibly wealthy segment. "Is it possible your standard of decor is based on *you people's* New Orleans bordellos?" I murmured. "The Roederers are anything but drab. The day of the school ceremony, Tea Roederer wore a velvet patchwork suit with high-laced boots. And amber jewelry that must have once belonged to the czarina. And he wears gorgeously cut suits and funny black-rimmed glasses—they aren't drab. Not flashy, but interesting, like they're happy with themselves."

"Goodness me," Mackenzie said. "I've never heard you do fashion commentary before."

"Only because I, too, expected dowdy. And older. They're in their forties, which seems too young for the amount of fun they have."

I peered through the windshield, looking for the silhouette of The House, but all I saw was landscaping and high stone walls.

And a peculiar light fluttering behind a clump of trees on my side of the road. As if there were lanterns on the ground, and all of them with erratic batteries.

But, of course, there were no lanterns. Only that warm, erratic ground light, as if the sun had fallen on the side of the road ahead, illuminating unevenly from below so that naked branches became grotesque silhouettes, grabbing at the air.

The car moved on slowly as Mackenzie studied the left side of the road, looking for the house.

Fire. I tried to say so, but only *fff* emerged because we rounded a small bend, and what I saw pushed all the words and horror out shapelessly, squeezed into a scream.

Mackenzie hit the brakes so hard we skidded, nearly slamming into a massive stone post. "What the hell—" Then he, too, saw. He flung open his car door and raced toward the ragged light, toward what I'd seen—a man hanging from a bare-branched tree, dangling, broken-necked, above a pyre, his trousers, jacket, and hair licked by flames.

There was no saving him. Mackenzie could run and perform heroic measures and be as brave as could be. It would still be too late. It was obvious from where I sat, unable to move at all. The lynched man's eyeglasses had melted, their thick frames twisted into dripping shapes. It was too late.

Once he was close, Mackenzie seemed to understand the futility of intervention. He stared at the dangling body before turning back to the car, walking at a regular pace.

"We should—we have to—the police—fire company—" I said,

when he returned. "Even though he's already—" I fumbled in the glove compartment. "Your cellular—in here?"

"Mandy. Wait." He put his gloved hand on my arm.

I shook my head and pawed at the compartment. I found maps and a small tape recorder, batteries, and a roll of quarters, but no phone. "Where is it?" I asked, more shrilly than intended. Yards away, the dead man twirled in thermal currents. The flames' angry orange reflected on our windshield, colored the planes of Mackenzie's face. "We have to tell the people in the house to call—"

"Look," he said softly. "Carefully."

"I know it's too late and we can't save him, but even so—he has to be treated like—give him human dignity—we can't simply—"

"Look," he said softly. "Please."

I closed my eyes and shook my head. "Once was enough."

"Try. Calmly."

I forced myself. I saw the melted glasses again. And then I realized those were all I saw. No nose, or mouth, or features. Where were his eyes, his ears? Where was his face?

"Now look at the hands," Mackenzie said in the voice of a patient teacher.

Pale semicircles lacking digits. Like a rag doll's. Like the face.

"He—it's not a man, is it?" I whispered. "Never was."

"It's an effigy."

The burning form was stuffing covered with cloth. "Nobody was lynched." It comforted me to say it out loud, make it fact. "There's nobody there."

Mackenzie nodded.

I should have laughed with relief, except that what *was* there—the effigy—had been designed to strike terror, and had succeeded. That nobody had been killed was a comfort, but that somebody had gone to great lengths to inspire fear negated that comfort.

The fire had been set on a gravelly semicircle beside the road. A turnaround, perhaps. Or maybe the site where rubbish was collected, because I spotted a trash can near the pyre.

Trash can. I looked across the road at the granite post we'd nearly hit. It and its twin across the drive anchored a pair of arched wrought-iron gates. And on each column, the word GLA-MORGAN was carved in Gothic relief.

"It's them," I said. "Again. This has their trademark all over it."

"I think so, too. Those zombies."

The group he meant—the Moral Ecologists—had declared war on libraries and reading lists, determined to banish "mental pollu-tants." Our small private school was added to their hit list the day our Roederer Trust grant was announced. This past week, via the Moral Ecologists' placards, bullhorns, and pamphlets littering the school's entryway, I'd been informed that *The Color Purple* "cor-rupted" young minds, that *Slaughterhouse Five* would "promote deviant sexual behavior," and that both *The Diary of Anne Frank* and *The Canterbury Tales* were too sexually explicit for our stu-dents. Our students! It would be funny were it not so frightening.

The Moral Ecologists denied responsibility for the series of book-burning bonfires plaguing the city, but praised whoever had done the "good deed," calling them "civic heroes." The fires were nevertheless accepted as their handiwork, although nobody could prove the connection yet.

With each new fire, I saw visions of men wearing black boots and swastikas, of robotic salutes, the triumph of ignorance. The world hadn't taken those people seriously soon enough, either.

Tea and Neddy Roederer, repeatedly funding libraries, giving dollars like so many slaps in the face of the Moral Ecologists and their attempt to restore the Middle Ages, were their prime and fearless antagonists. I shuddered and realized I was shaking my head, trying to deny them access.

"Look at the effigy's glasses," I said softly. Neddy Roederer's trademark black-framed Buddy Holly glasses. "The trash can." The Moral Ecologists, accusing Neddy of promoting garbage, called him Trashman. "The kindling. All right angles. They're burning books again. Only now, they're also burning Neddy Roederer, right at his front door."

"Not Neddy, an effigy," Mackenzie corrected me. "But how'd they know about tonight? Are we to believe they don't read books, but they do read the social calendar? Not that your school's fund-raiser would be listed in it. How did they know?"

"Maybe it's coincidence. Or PR savvy. They always manage to schedule their events to get the most media attention. Remember the one at Penn the day the freshmen's parents came to visit? For all we know, they've harassed the Roederers for a long time."

"Let's go to your party," Mackenzie said.

I didn't budge. Couldn't. The party was now locked in with this malevolence. The excitement I'd felt seemed nostalgic, part of an earlier, more innocent, time. As if I'd been a child half an hour ago. The fire had burned away the shine and coated everything with ash.

"Nobody got hurt," Mackenzie said. "Remember. Nobody got hurt."

"Yet." I shivered, and it had nothing to do with the damp chill in the air. My thoughts were impaled on the idea of people who needed to intimidate and terrorize, on their lethal mix of hatred and self-righteousness, their potential power, their targets. I looked over at the smoldering books on the gravel, and then back at Mackenzie, resplendent in his tuxedo, and I sighed. "Nobody got hurt—yet," I said. "But they will."

And they were. It generally feels great to be proven right, which I ultimately was. But at no point did it feel great. It never felt anything but horrifying.

Two

To my amazement, the up-close power of Glamorgan dispelled the dark brooding that had overtaken me. I paused at the front door, admiring the house's assurance. It was a monument to entitlement, sitting on its knoll as if it had always owned the site, as if serfs might still live in hovels in the rolling countryside surrounding it, might still tug forelocks to their lord of the manor.

The power of the place almost made the ugliness across the road seem a taunt not worth noticing. Almost.

I don't know what style the long-ago architect considered his sprawling stone handiwork. I knew the place had grown over the years from its origins as a farm before the Revolutionary War. Now, it had a hint of château, a whiff of villa, a dollop of Stately Homes of England. It should have been a dreadful pastiche, but when it had all been stirred and simmered and ivy-covered, an exquisite dwelling emerged. Solidity itself.

Once inside, I had to fight to keep my jaw from dangling. Excess can be stunning when each portion of it is exquisite.

A place like this was probably subversive. The Old World's palaces were the result of gross inequities—rigid class structure and unearned privilege—that drove our forefathers away. What then, to make of New World citizenry living in regal splendor? And nobody screeching, "Off with their heads!"

I stood in the entrance hall inhaling the essence of money. Acres of finely grained marble flooring. A circular table inlaid with a tableau of peacocks and palms formed of semiprecious stones. A screen whose panels of pastel cherubim must have once belonged to the Medicis. An RV-sized chandelier that caught its own light in a thousand crystal facets. An upward sweep of curved and carved staircase.

I could live with this. "I was meant to be raised in the lap of luxury," I told Mackenzie.

"Me, too," he said. "Only problem was, luxury stood up before I arrived."

"If you'll follow me," a man in a morning coat said in Brit-crisp syllables.

"Butlers." Mackenzie's voice was low. "You don't hardly find them these days."

"The majordomo," I corrected him. "The *head* butler." Education compliments of *Masterpiece Theatre*.

Mackenzie raised a single, challenging eyebrow.

"Excuse me," I said to the morning coat. "You are the Roederers' majordomo, are you not?"

"That some kind of putdown?" His accent was suddenly pure Philly, and his tone, offended. "Because I don't appreciate it. Me, I'm a musician. My cousin owns the catering company. I don't have a gig, I work for him. I gotta eat, too." And resuming his unearned hauteur, he turned his back and again we followed.

"Cocktails in the libr'y," he said. "This way." His Philly had Anglo edges again.

"He's a minordomo," Mackenzie said.

We passed several rooms, a series of settings, visual hits of color and texture: burgundy leather, pale silk, dark wood and floral wallpaper, a harp, a globe, flowered chintz, a marble bust on a pedestal.

"I need a phone," Mackenzie said.

"Ask the minidomo." I was busy coveting. I'm not materialistic. If I were, I'd have to be masochistic as well, because my profession cuts me no slack on the "stuff" score. So I don't yearn or fester or covet. Not usually. But there are exceptions to every rule, and this was one of them.

We reached open double doors. "The libr'y," the mock-butler said. "The bar is in here. Another is in the music room."

I nearly swooned.

"Be a sec," Mackenzie said.

"Why?" The word was not out before I remembered why and couldn't believe I had forgotten. Obviously, galloping materialism causes short-term memory loss.

"In case the local police don't know." He moved off, followed by the major dummy.

Without Mackenzie as shield and ally, I was acutely aware that my dress was rented, I hadn't paid my way into this gala, and probably nobody but my principal wanted me here. I made an uncomfortable entrance into the library. Nobody hailed or beckoned. Your basic party nightmare.

I squelched the urge to hide in the powder room. Been there, done that a hundred years ago. At thirty-plus, I had to relinquish adolescent behavior. I tried to look thrilled with my own company and prayed Mackenzie wouldn't be too long.

I'd been in houses that labeled any room containing a book The Library, but this room actually functioned as one. Every inch not otherwise occupied by stained glass casements or the towering Gothic fireplace was filled with floor-to-ceiling shelves, some with etched glass doors, all filled with books. A library ladder on wheels was positioned for easy access around the room.

The firelight caught the luster of leather wing chairs and sofas. It splashed off the polished surface of a library table, the carvings on a delicate writing desk, and sharpened the indigos and rubies of the stained glass windows and the guests' jewels.

I tiptoed over intricately patterned carpets until I noticed what I was doing and forced myself to walk normally, and behave as if I were accustomed to home libraries as large as an entire home, to furnishings made of precious and probably endangered resources. All the while, I was sure somebody was about to lift an eyebrow and say, "What are *you* doing here?"

I accepted a champagne flute from a smiling server, eager to quell my dry mouth and jumpy nerves, but I only sipped. Elegantly packaged parents eyed me sideways. You look familiar, their expressions said, but from where? They normally paid me as much attention as they might any other appliance they'd purchased. To many of them, and to my regret, I was an upper-tier servant, hired to fill their children's days and minds. A function with a face, forgettable. Tonight, I was out of costume and context, and thereby unrecognizable.

It was easier for me to know who they were, even though they, too, looked remade. I was used to faces red from embarrassment at teacher conferences, or redder still from the elements, carrying forgotten medications, lunch money, or assignments. Philly Prep was a service that was supposed to free them, and they were always impatient to get out of the place. Maybe they were afraid they'd be told their offspring had turned out to be just like them.

Tonight they, too, were in disguise, transformed by gloss and cummerbunds. Or maybe this was their natural costume, because they seemed at ease.

Mackenzie, having completed his good-citizen run, returned. "They knew," he said. "They've gotten about fifteen calls. They are out there now—no sirens, no fuss."

I considered the other people milling around, many of whom must have placed calls, none of whom seemed to be discussing the outrage across the lane, and I understood why. It was so ugly, so appalling, that mentioning it would be like dragging something dead and rotting into the party, a gross breach of etiquette. Still, it felt strange, as if we were all playing blindman's bluff with a fearsome phantom in the room with us.

Mackenzie and I hovered on the periphery until a flinty woman with whom I'd had a bitter to-do about her son's grade waved with an attitude that suggested papal dispensation. Or lack of recognition. In either case, she was our first friendly face, and we needed all the socialization we could squeeze out of this crowd.

She moved closer, and Mackenzie and I introduced ourselves. Even knowing who I was, she remained civil. The evening held promise.

We swapped many oohs and several ahs about the house and the hors d'oeuvres, but even while supposedly speaking to me, she didn't look my way. She looked Mackenzie's way. She hadn't floated over to socialize, but to seduce. Happily, she wasn't good at it, and I made an excuse about meeting someone in the music room and aimed my man and myself toward the doorway. There is a limit to precisely how accommodating I have to be to parents.

En route to the exit, we perused the bookshelves. It's automatic with both of us. But at least half my attention was still on the woman's arrogance and talons, so it was Mackenzie, not I, who registered how extremely rare were the contents of the glass-enclosed case near us. "Unless they're facsimiles, which I do not believe would be the case," he murmured, "these are priceless. Look here, Corneille's *The Cid*, early sixteen-hundreds. Vaughan's *Poems*, Izaak Walton's *Life of Donne*—the first professional biography," he whispered. "Whole shelf is seventeenth-century."

I squeezed in next to him and looked at the bindings, the gilded titles on their spines. "You were wrong about this house not living up to my fantasies," I whispered back. "My fantasies were too impoverished to live up to this house."

"Miss Pepper, isn't it?"

My sophisticated response was to bang—loudly—my head against the cabinet's glass door, startled as I was by Neddy Roederer's voice. Had the etched glass been of a lower quality, I would have required stitches. As it was, only my ego was lacerated.

I'd met him the week before at the library ceremony honoring the Roederer Trust gift, a collection of art history and photography books, plus an annual bequest. "Mr. Roederer," I croaked in a humiliated voice.

It wasn't odd that I remembered him, but it was head-bangingly shocking that he remembered me. *Me!* I couldn't have been more irrationally dazzled had he been the original, certified Prince Charming.

Which he was not. He was a tall, rangy man with forgettable features, dark-rimmed glasses, and a shock of black hair, all of which bore an unfortunate resemblance to the effigy across the way.

"Did you think I'd forget you?" he asked with a warm smile. "Who else inspired the newspaper staff to write about the library's needs? Or to have our son, Griffin, shoot the photos for the article? You're the reason we became involved." He gestured at the roomful of people. "So I suppose you're the reason for tonight as well."

I held my breath. I felt like Harriet Beecher Stowe must have when Lincoln called her the little lady who started the Civil War. Fortunately, I had no idea how apt that comparison was.

"For which aid, assistance, and prodding, I'm quite grateful," he said.

"We were admiring your collection," Mackenzie said, saving me from having to formulate words while I remained flabbergasted. "You seem particularly fond of seventeenth century English works."

"An interesting time for literature, don't you think, Mr. . . ."

I found my voice, or most of it, and began introductions, feeling less ept with each stammered approach to the mystery of Mackenzie's C. K. What the hell. "This is Caleb," I said. "Caleb Mackenzie."

Mackenzie winked at me. That wasn't his name, either, then.

Roederer shook Mackenzie's hand with boyish, semiawkward charm. "Restoration works intrigue me," he said. "Perhaps you'd enjoy one of my favorites, an interesting edition of *Pilgrim's*

Progress, although not the original, not the first. This edition wasn't printed until 1690, but it's quite beautiful."

He bent to insert a tiny key in the lock. "Climate is controlled in these cabinets," he added. "But doesn't hurt the books to breathe real air once in a while."

I backed off, afraid to be near a priceless object after my unfortunate encounter with the cabinet door. I was sure I'd tip my champagne onto its pages, or have a sneezing fit.

A thick-featured man with a shelf of eyebrows had been watching our threesome, and as Edward Franklin Roederer retrieved his book, the observer moved closer, craning his neck to see the title.

Roederer seemed amused and pleased by the other man's curiosity. "All bibliophiles welcome," he said. "*Pilgrim's Progress*, 1690 edition, beautifully illustrated. Come, look."

The man seemed taken aback, as if he'd expected a different response. "You like old books, too, eh?" He made his words half inquiry, half sneer.

Roederer's smile became tentative, but he nodded. "A passion of mine for some time now. And do you share it, Mr. . . ." He stopped to study the man, who said nothing. "We've met before, haven't we? You look familiar. But I seem to need assistance remembering where it was." He extended his free hand. "Edward Roederer. Everyone calls me Neddy, I'm afraid. And unfortunately, my memory for faces far exceeds my ability to recall names."

The other man waited longer than was civil before proffering his hand, all the while peering at his host. Then, as they shook hands, he apparently had done enough reconnoitering to respond. "Didn't think we'd met in person," he said, "but you look familiar, too. I mean I know who you are, but I thought only by reputation. Still and all, I know your face. Probably from the paper, eh?"

Roederer's smile turned quizzical.

The Roederers' pictures were seldom, if ever, in the paper. Even at the dedication, they declined to be photographed. Too many crazies, they'd explained. I thought of the fire across the way and agreed.

"Are you perhaps Canadian?" Roederer asked. Good breeding showed. He continued to play gracious host to a boor who didn't care a whit about *Pilgrim's Progress*, didn't glance at it once he'd established its title, and hadn't introduced himself when asked.

"Born, raised, and educated in Toronto. How'd you know? You Canadian, too?"

Neddy Roederer laughed and shook his head. "Not specially anything, I'm afraid. Born in France, schooled in Holland and Hong Kong. Lived all over even before meeting Tea and her wanderlust. But since then, even more. Horrified our families by being footloose. We did try Canada once, but it was too cold, so we moved on to Bali. Or maybe South Africa. Can't remember. We're nomads."

My kind of nomads. Forget yurts—they bedded down in the most substantial and rooted of dwellings.

"The *eh* made me ask," Roederer said with a smile.

The man shook his head. "Never hear myself say it, but the wife tells me I do it all the time." He gestured behind him, although he didn't turn his head to verify if "the wife" was there.

She was, apparently. A reasonably attractive woman in an unreasonably unattractive dress. Her garment, a putty silk with the life drained out of it, was designed to disappear into the background, but at this event, its deliberate drabness stood out. Her hair, loose and long, was a faded brown-gray mix; her face bare of makeup; her ears, neck, and wrists free of jewelry. She watched the man's back like a trained dog awaiting its next command.

"The wife's not Canadian," the man said. "From Jersey originally. Lived up there long enough, though. Still, she notices it. I don't."

"Forgive me, I didn't catch your name," Roederer persisted. As if anyone had offered it. He couldn't possibly have any real interest in the man, nor any expectation of ever seeing him again socially. But his graciousness seemed ingrained, and he stood patiently, his lips in a welcoming smile.

"Spiers." The voice was flat and resolute. I thought he was talking about weapons, until he spelled his surname. "Reverend Harvey Spiers."

The drab woman watching the reverend put her thumbnail in her mouth and absentmindedly chewed on it. There were deep creases between her eyebrows.

I couldn't think of a student named Spiers. A newcomer or future enrollee's parent? A friend of one of our parents?

I sensed more than heard the softest possible exclamation from Mackenzie. He glanced at me as if I'd understand. His expression registered recognition, but no pleasure. I looked back at the Reverend Spiers, wondering why he'd produced this reaction.

And more. A shudder of revulsion distorted Neddy Roederer's well-bred features. "*The* Reverend Spiers?" he asked.

"Believe so." The other man made a mock bow. "I believe I am the only one with that name and position in the area."

"Reverend Spiers of the Moral Ecologists?"

Of course. That's who it was. The party setting had thrown me off. This was the last place I'd have expected to see this man.

Roederer's voice had risen on a cresting wave of incredulity until it cracked, which I now well understood. The Moral Ecologists had reviled him, labeled him Trashman and, I was certain, burned him in effigy outside his front door. And Neddy knew. He had undoubtedly been the first to call the police.

"You—" Roederer said. "You and that woman—"

Spiers bowed his head as if humbly acknowledging achievement. "You refer to Mother Vivien, I assume. My right hand."

Plus other appendages, too, from what I heard. Mother Vivien had founded the Moral Ecologists, although she'd been eclipsed and supposedly seduced by the reverend. I'd seen her hard face and waist-length tresses on TV. Heard her shrill claims and demands. She seemed the least benevolent Mother since Medea.

"Alas, she's not here tonight," Spiers said. Behind him, "the wife" scowled.

"May I say . . ." Roederer's Adam's apple bobbed up and down as he swallowed. "I'm . . . I never expected you to come to my

19

home, Reverend," he finally managed. "I thought our interests and . . . and circles . . . were at opposite ends of . . ." He seemed too stunned and enervated to manufacture more words.

Tea Roederer materialized, as if summoned. I hadn't seen her approach, and she was a lot of woman to have missed. As tall as her husband, and as athletic and fit. They'd both been fished out of the same rich person's Olympic-sized gene pool. Theodora Roederer was the sort of strong-featured woman called handsome as opposed to pretty, but she didn't have the hunched self-effacing posture of women who try to minimize their height or plainness. After all, there was no one she needed to please, no cultural ideal she needed to meet. She was married to a descendant of Ben himself, was a zillionaire member of one of the world's name-brand families. Why would she want to be anything except herself?

Harvey Spiers' smile was tightly strung. "We came because the wife was eager to dress up, celebrate, be worldly for once. We don't generally have the time or inclination to be frivolous."

The Wife looked in anything but a party mood, but I had a new appreciation for why, perhaps, her expression was so unrelentingly tense.

Spiers put his hands out, palms up, in a traditional gesture of mock male-helplessness. "I do as she says." He winked at Mackenzie. Guy to guy. Loathsome.

"Neddy?" Tea Roederer asked tentatively. Her outfit tonight was again anything but Main-Line dowdy. She wore a silver gown beaded with jet that seemed handed down from a wealthy flapper. It gave her a rakish air with overtones of smoky speakeasies, as did her silky black hair, also old-fashioned, with bangs to the eyebrows and the bob that was a mark of rebellion back in the Twenties.

A student who was a good friend of the Roederers' son had told me that Tea always wore a wig, and indeed devoted an entire room of the mansion to this strange affectation of hers. Rows of mannequin heads, he said, each wearing a different style and length. I supposed it was an expensive way to never have a bad hair day, and quicker than an in-house stylist.

"Dearest?" she asked. Perhaps because of her costume, and his, the Roederers made me think of Scott and Zelda Fitzgerald. Of course, Neddy and Tea's idea of fun was less self-centered and alcoholic. Plus, they had more to spend.

"Neddy, dearest?" she said again.

"Forgive me," he said. "Introductions are due. May I present Miss Pepper."

"We've met—at the library," she said, with a gracious nod.

I'd noticed the oddities of her speech the other day, too, including the way she said *liberary*. Her English was not noticeably accented, but perhaps the occasional mispronunciation was due to her multilingual background. Or perhaps it was another larky upper-class whim, like the wig.

"And this is Mr. Mackenzie and . . ." Neddy paused. "The Reverend Harvey Spiers."

Tea's face blanched so that freckles across both cheeks became obvious. She drew herself up and I could almost see breeding kick into overdrive. "Welcome to our home," she said. However, she nodded only toward Mackenzie and me.

Spiers chuckled, wallowing in their discomfort.

"Fact is," Reverend Spiers said, "this event is for my son's school. We do what we can."

"Your son's at Philly Prep?" I spoke too brightly, hoping to redirect and defuse the conversation. "I teach English there. Do I know him?"

He squinted. "You the one does the school paper?"

"I'm its advisor."

"I thought I'd heard your name. Jake's so wrapped up in that column he writes for you, I worry. Makes his computer obsession worse. People shouldn't worship machines, spend too much time with them."

"Your son's name is Jake?" There was only one boy by that name in the school. But his last name was Ulrich.

"Stepson, technically," Harvey Spiers said. "However, since his father is in Canada and never sees him, and since I am raising the boy, I sometimes forget that in the eyes of the law, and of nomenclature, I am not considered his actual father."

"I didn't mean to suggest . . ." Good thing I hadn't tried for a career in the diplomatic corps. I tried to make amends. "Jake's a wonderful young man." He was, but he was also a young man I worried about more with each passing day. He was increasingly edgy, defensive, and morose as if something awful were over-taking him. I looked at Harvey Spiers and thought I might be seeing the awful thing possessing Jake.

"Jake Ulrich?" Neddy Roederer asked. "He's a good friend of Griffin's. I hadn't realized he was your . . ."

Jake was indeed tight with Griffin Roederer, bound by com-puter nerdhood and low-grade depression. It was confusing and sometimes annoying to converse with either of them, but they understood one another.

But how uncomfortable for Jake. To visit here so often that he knew about Tea Roederer's wigs, and all the while keeping his family identity a secret. Not that I didn't understand why he wouldn't volunteer his stepfather's name in this house.

Griffin was our newspaper's photographer, a boy who needed a filter between himself and the world. He spoke via computer and saw through a camera lens, but he was also talented, and an asset to *The Ink Wire*. The paper was another bond between the boys because Jake wrote a monthly column about life aboard a computer.

"I read Jake's work, too," Neddy said. "We both do."

Tea nodded, her eyes fixed on Spiers.

"We're impressed with your son's ability to explain esoteric ideas," Neddy said. "I'm afraid we aren't nearly as computer lit-erate, and while we prefer ancient communication methods, such as these books, Jake's articles convinced me that the machine has remarkable research possibilities. His report on that conference that deals with unsolved crimes was revelatory."

"Don't like him involved with that machine, is all," the rev-erend said.

Neddy Roederer cleared his throat. "Indeed. Well, I'm afraid I've been rude to Mr. Mackenzie. He and I were about to discuss this volume and now we must, but I fear you'd find it tedious. Book preservation doesn't seem a special interest of yours."

Mackenzie seemed ready to draw a gun he wasn't carrying.

"Books," the Reverend Spiers said. "Books are such an incendiary topic."

At which point, all pretense of civility was put on hold. As was my breath. I waited, expecting anything.

And in the taut silence, heard the crystalline tinkling of bells. Many of them. A summons to dinner, and none too soon. We smiled at each other with relief, and after a bit of casual conversation, we dispersed, leaving the subjects of books and fires to die for lack of oxygen.

The feel of Mackenzie's tuxedo sleeve reminded me that I was at a party in my bronze gown, that this was my one chance to visit and enjoy Wonderland. I tried to focus on my date, looking so resplendent I nearly had to avert my eyes. I told him so as we walked back into the great central hallway, and I forced everybody else out of my mind.

"A little too museum-quality for me," Mackenzie whispered, as we once again passed the series of perfect rooms. "I'd like to see their *real* house. The rooms with the books they read. The ones with family photos and half-done projects and a good sound system and TV."

"Not me. I know about that kind of room and life. I don't know about this one." I chose to believe that the Roederers lived a perfect life in perfect surroundings. And with those thoughts, I slid back into my fantasies and walked into a room that made the library seem a cramped antechamber. The ballroom's domed ceiling was frescoed. And under the frolicking gods and goddesses were tables laden with hothouse roses, surrounded by gilded chairs. A string quartet played music to dine by. Definitely not the homey spot Mackenzie sought.

I wondered if the Roederers would like Griffin to be privately tutored. At their home. By me.

Why not? Griffin could use extra help, catch-up time. According to the rumors about him, he'd been the child of a young woman who couldn't get a grip on him or on her life. He'd spent a Dickensian childhood in foster homes, until he ran away at age twelve and became a featured news story somewhere in New

England, where the childless, nomadic Roederers had found themselves—and him. They gave the tough and scared street boy who called himself Grief an incredible new life and the new name of Griffin.

Maybe they were now ready to balance their family with a daughter. Say one in her early thirties, close enough to their ages so we could be pals.

My parents would understand. Lord knew my mother spent half her life and energy looking for ways to make me "safe." She thought the route was through marriage, but how about through a fortune, instead? She wanted the best for me, and this was as close to the best as I was likely to get.

Or if not adoption, maybe I could become their ward. My ninth graders were reading *Jane Eyre*, so the wards of the wealthy were on my mind. Mr. Rochester had one. Why not Mr. Roederer?

"I can't get over Spiers," Mackenzie said softly.

I didn't want to hear. I was having my Cinderella moment, was not at all ready for the pumpkin and the mice again.

"Burnin' the effigy of your host, then tauntin' him," Mackenzie whispered. "What a piece of work."

Too late. Mackenzie was living in the present, and all too willing to share it with me. My fantasies dissolved, the walls around us thinned to transparency, and the outside world became visible. The palatial splendor surrounding me was suddenly as fragile as the gilded, spindly chairs.

Beyond this point lay monsters. I had been there and seen them.

I deeded enchanted evenings to old musicals and Cinderella.

Sometimes I simply cannot stand reality.

Three

MONDAY morning is never the emotional highlight of my week, but this one felt particularly daunting. I arrived at school early enough, but the Moral Ecologists arrived still earlier, in time for a grim greeting to the students.

They were arranged in a line down the pavement with blowzy, hard-faced Mother Vivien keeping them in order like a drill sergeant in a muumuu. Several carried placards in the shape of books. The slogan on them was the same as the protestors chanted: "Don't pollute minds!"

It would be funny if it weren't appalling. There they were by virtue of guaranteed freedom of speech, using that freedom to deny it to others.

"Don't pollute minds! Don't pollute minds!"

With what? Ideas, history, the graces of language? I envisioned their unpolluted minds—empty pools you could see straight through, with never an original thought rippling the waters.

"Shame on you, child molester!" Mother Vivien screamed, as I walked up the entry stairs. "You teach trash! Force it on young victims!"

They weren't making my job a whole lot easier. Reluctant scholars would be thrilled to be redefined as victims. Vivien's hatchet face, topped by baby curls, looked desperate to find her way to a headline.

I opted not to grant her wish, so I didn't exercise my guaranteed freedom of speech.

By the time I was in the building I was in a foul mood, which wasn't helped by an encounter with Alex Fry in the faculty lounge. One coffee with cynicism. I liked a dash of wry now and then, but Alex made me afraid I'd someday agree with him.

"Know what I think?" he said. I did. He had one central belief from which all others flowed, and it was that as teachers, we were locked in a hopeless undertaking, our every action both futile and meaningless. Alex taught math, because, he said, he preferred numbers to people. He kept his job because he muted his negativity when Havermeyer was around, and also because it was difficult to find math teachers. People whose minds work that way have more lucrative options.

More unsettling than Alex's philosophy was his conviction that I harbored a secret passion for him. "Let's go burn those books," he said. "Get them off our backs before Open House, which will reduce the odds of Havermeyer having a stroke." He shrugged. "Who'd care? The kids surely wouldn't. Otherwise, the media'll swarm around, bye-bye parking spaces, the parents will bitch . . ."

"Alex, I'm not giving up until I find a principle you believe in."

He was sitting in a deep, worn upholstered chair, and he now shook the morning paper out, preparatory to reading it. "The principal I believe is Havermeyer. I also believe that he is crazed about the upcoming Open House," he said from behind the paper. "And furthermore, I believe in getting him off our backs."

"I agree."

"Then run away with me," he said, still masked by the news-paper. "Let's flee this holding tank and find a place with no kids. No parents. No Havermeyer."

Running away was tempting. Particularly alluring was the No Parents segment, even though I was deliberately misinterpreting Alex. He meant our students' parents. I meant my own, although in this case, I could run but not hide. I took my coffee, waved goodbye, and headed for my classroom.

My loving, overbearing parent, the phoning one, had called this morning, early enough to serve as a premature alarm clock. I'd awakened with a jolt and answered with a pounding heart, thinking there must be an emergency.

She made an increasing number of these off-hours calls. My mother was playing footsie with long-distance providers. Let me be blunt: She'd become a phone service slut, accepting checks and perks for going with one, then the other, playing both sides of the street, showing neither loyalty nor fidelity. If they had the money, she had the time.

She considered these dividends a special phone fund, and she called more often, still using the cheapest calling hours and always, even with the best intentions, nagging. Most often about my unmarried, unstable state.

This particular dawn, I picked up the phone and heard—barely—a croaky whisper. Trust my mother to use bonus time even if she couldn't speak. "What's wrong?" I asked. "Laryngitis? Maybe you should write instead of calling. Sounds painful."

Mackenzie groaned and rolled to the furthest extreme of the bed, putting his pillow over his head. He is alternately amused and irritated by my mother's incursions into our life. This, under-standably, was one of his less appreciative moments.

"Is he there?" she whispered.

"He?"

"Shh! Yes or no."

"Yes." When had C. K. lost even his initials and become *he*? Why did she sound furtive? My mother's so-called normal behavior is not to be confused with the statistical norm, but this was truly aberrant. "Hold on," I said, glancing at Mackenzie. "I'll get the portable." I padded across to the kitchen wall, got the phone, padded back, hung up the receiver by the bed, and made my way to the sofa, where I sat, shivering—and belatedly realizing that in a loft without full walls, relocating a conversation doesn't make much difference. "Now, what is this?" I whispered.

"I read an article," she said in a breathy rush.

I approve of reading. Encourage and endorse it. Except in the case of my mother and newspapers. In fact, if the Moral Ecologists censored her reading, I'd be tempted to look the other way. According to her, ink on newsprint produced sacred text—although she paid scant attention to what was generally considered sacred text. I had pointed out the newspaper's daily corrections and retractions, hoping that would lessen her gullibility, but she felt that proved the paper's dedication to total honesty. And may I add that her choice of newspapers is eclectic, often including the variety that features newsflashes about Elvis fathering Michael Jackson's alien ten-foot-tall love child.

"I want you to hire a detective," she said.

"Why on earth? What's wrong?"

"I'm not saying anything necessarily is."

"But a detec—"

"Don't *say* it—you'll put him on guard!"

Him. The pronoun trying to catch a night's sleep. "Mom," I said, "I have no idea what you're—" I went in search of something to wrap around me. "Are you in trouble?"

"There are people, detectives. You hire them to find information—"

"I know that." I pulled the cloth off the oak table, wrapped it around me, and resettled onto the sofa.

"This is a special kind who finds out about . . . you know."

"I most certainly do not!" It's a real strain to disagree in a whisper.

I heard her sigh. I was *supposed* to hear her sigh. "Look," she said, "you meet somebody, and what do you really know about him? Exactly nothing. A girl could get hurt."

"We're talking about me?"

"Believe me," she said, "it's dangerous out there."

"Are we talking about him?"

"Yes!"

I took a deep breath. "He *is* a detective."

"*His* specialty is people who are already dead. You're alive— what's that worth to you? Besides, Mrs. Simmerling's niece—"

Second only to newsprint, the adventures of her acquaintances and their relatives were Bea Pepper's source of irrefutable wisdom. I prayed to be spared another Boca Raton homily, but the Lord put me on hold.

"—her fiancé turned out to have been engaged twice before, and both girls died suspiciously. Deborah could have become suspicious-corpse-number-three. This is a new kind of detective. A romantic detective."

Wrong. The pronoun in my bed—that was a romantic detective, but I wasn't wasting predawn breath on syntax. I counted to ten. It did no good. "Listen, Ma, you know and I know that . . . *he*"—I lowered my voice again—"goes after murderers. He isn't one!"

"He has enough time to do both. Or something else bad. It doesn't have to be killing somebody."

"Goody. Not that this isn't fascinating, but . . ." I couldn't believe I was sitting in the dark wearing a tablecloth discussing Mackenzie's possible murderous past.

"What do you really know about him? You met, and blammo, a *relationship* and you're living together. Like that."

"Not even in the *blammo* ballpark. It was more than a year before I moved in here." Foolishly, I had thought she'd get off my case now that I lived with Mackenzie. But, bottom line, I was still single and she was still out there, the Avenging Mother.

"Mom, do you have coffee before you make these calls? Or do you just bound out of bed, at the ready?" She'd told me that the older she got, the less sleep she needed. And Bea awake was Bea on the phone. I was doomed.

"The man won't even tell you his own name! What does that say about him?"

How could I answer? The missing name had become a shaggy-dog joke between us, a game I enjoyed. I thought of him as Seekay, and liked the slightly Asian overtones of the name.

"Have you met his family?"

Her round. "I was invited," I said. "I couldn't go." The Mackenzie family had scheduled their reunion during finals week, when I couldn't possibly take off from work. Not if I wanted work to return to. A zillion Mackenzie relatives couldn't reschedule for the convenience of one female with no legal ties to them. Nothing to hold against C. K., was it?

"His family could be anything," she said.

"What would it matter? I'm sure Princess Di thought she was getting a fine family along with Charles, and look how that—"

"The good news," my mother said, "is that I know of a young man who *is* that kind of detective."

"Don't tell me. He's related to somebody you know."

She ignored me. "It's done all the time nowadays. No shame attached. Part of the modern age, what with diseases and financial problems—"

"Anybody after my money would be too *stupid* to be dangerous."

"I'm sure he's got nothing to hide, but wouldn't it be more comfortable to know that? You're my daughter." As if I might have forgotten. As if I would tolerate this ungodly hour and topic if she weren't my mother. "I can't bear the idea that you might get hurt. Think about it. I'd loan you the money."

I said something sufficiently noncommittal to allow the conversation to end. And then I sat on the sofa, watching the skylight brighten as my mood darkened. It wasn't her well-intentioned meddling. It was her reminder of the dark potential that could be anywhere, the unknown, the dangerous, the secretive and lethal.

And now that she'd mentioned it, how much did I know about Mackenzie?

Or about anything?

So that's where I was before Monday began, and my encounter

with the Moral Ecologists' misplaced enthusiasms pounded me deeper into the ground. I went up to my room and took the only avenue of revenge at my disposal, the literary high road. I rummaged through the bookcase and found what I wanted, then filled an entire segment of the board with it, writing in multicolored chalk. *Think about Censorship,* I wrote. *What's "Safe" or "Good" and Who Decides? Here's how Mark Twain responded to news that his books had been banned in Brooklyn:*

> I wrote *Tom Sawyer* and *Huck Finn* for adults exclusively, and it always distresses me when I find that boys and girls have been allowed access to them. The mind that becomes soiled in youth can never again be washed clean. I know this by my own experience, and to this day I cherish an unappeasable bitterness against the unfaithful guardians of my young life who not only permitted but compelled me to read an unexpurgated Bible through before I was fifteen years old. None can do that and draw a clean, sweet breath again this side of the grave. . . . Most honestly do I wish that I could say a softening word or two in defense of Huck's character . . . but really, in my opinion, it is no better than those of Solomon, David and the rest of the sacred brotherhood. If there is an unexpurgated Bible in the Children's Department, won't you please remove Tom and Huck from that questionable companionship?

I wrote *Do Not Erase* at the top and then realized that Jake Ulrich was behind me.

There was something inherently touching about Jake, a boy-tangle of uncontrolled growth—physically and mentally. Outside, he was tall and broad-shouldered, possibly destined to achieve hunkhood someday, but en route, he was a lad conspicuously endowed with an Adam's apple, too many elbows and knees, and a mouthful of braces.

Today, his spirits seemed more dampened than usual, his expression more cloudy. Even his large frame seemed slightly bent.

He loomed in my doorway, one hand touching the top of it.

He nodded toward the board, acknowledging the Twain quote. "Sorry you met him," he said without preamble. "I thought I could keep him my secret. I hate having you know—hate having anybody know."

"Come in," I said gently. "Sit down. Let's talk."

He nodded and entered, but didn't settle. He prowled the room, touching the backs of chairs, almost ritually. "He's out there, you know," he said after a while. "They're all out there now." He touched more chair backs, went to the window, but didn't look out. "He's not my father. He's my mother's husband. You've got to understand that."

"I do." I nodded for extra emphasis. "He made that clear, too."

"Why was he at the stupid fund-raiser, given how he feels about the Roederers? I'm sick they know about me now. And you, too. I feel . . . marked."

What could I say to ease the ugliness of living with that obnoxious public enemy? Being a teen was hard enough. Add to it the strain of active loathing, and life becomes unbearable. "He seemed proud of you," I offered, although I couldn't manage much enthusiasm.

"I don't think so. Besides, what if? Who cares what a crazy man thinks? He has this *thing*, this one stupid thing about dangerous books, and he's *gross* about it. He knows stupid people will listen to him. It's all about power. He hates computers, too. He's sure I'm only interested in finding pornography on it. Why are parents so weird about everything new? Even Griffin's—they bought him a computer, but they hate when he uses it! He scanned and digitalized some things and they went ballistic."

I shook my head. "You've lost me."

"Changed pictures," Jake explained. "He made the Mona Lisa scowl. It was funny, but they freaked. Said the computer would destroy art."

"It does make everything suspect. We can't believe our own eyes anymore."

He nodded dismissively. "Seeing is believing" was obviously an old-fashioned adage he had no time for. "I should have come in and kidnapped him. Locked him in the basement."

"What are we talking about now?"

"Him. Harvey. Saturday night. Before anybody found out. The Roederers didn't know." He looked devastated.

"You were there?"

He shrugged. "I hang there when I can. Griffin's cool and his parents don't pester us. We do our thing, they do theirs. Now I don't know if they'll let me be there anymore, and I can't stay home. Harvey doesn't go anywhere except to preach, or start one of those fires he says he has nothing to do with, or be with his, with that—"

I shouldn't have intercepted his train of thought, but when he mentioned fires, I couldn't help myself. "What do you mean by 'start fires'?" Jake had been there Saturday night. Surely he'd noticed something through the upstairs windows.

He shrugged again. "Maybe not literally. He and Vivien, they *decide* a fire. That's what they call it, deciding. I've heard them. Well, *they* don't do it. What they do is fight. And also . . ." He shook his head, dropped that tack. "I heard them fighting about which one of them would get to be the boss and decide."

"When?" Maybe there'd be a provable link between the group and the recent fire.

"Whenever. She thinks he's stolen her place, and she's right. But it's as much her fault, whatever happened between them. She let him take over because she . . . they were . . ."

"Who starts the fires?"

"There's all those followers, drones. Why?"

Because it made it worse. Harvey Spiers could have been and undoubtedly was responsible for kindling Saturday night's bonfire, but there'd be no way of proving the connection.

"My real father isn't anything like him," Jake said.

"But Jake, he does provide a home for you."

"So would my father, if Harvey would stop making it an international incident. Harvey acts like my dad's the Devil, saying I'll turn out like him if he doesn't shape me up. Like my father's bad. My father *tried* to get me. There were court orders and injunctions and all that kind of thing."

"And your mother . . . what does she say about this?" It was difficult to imagine the putty woman generating enough energy to formulate opinions.

"She gets angry with me." Jake looked heartbreakingly young and permanently incredulous at his mother's choice of targets. "She cries. See, she and Harvey, they have their own problems and . . ." The flood of words dried up.

I now understood more of what bound Jake the intellectual and Griffin the street-smart kid together. They were princes in exile. Jake's kingdom was across international lines with his M.I.A. father. And even though it would appear that Griffin had been rescued from bleakness into a happy ending, I'd heard him grouse about being "used" by "them" as if the Roederers had purchased him on a whim as an interesting accessory. He'd brainwashed Jake on this point, too, so that despite Jake's expressed fondness for the Roederers, he'd join Griffin in claiming that the adoption was just to make the Roederers "look good," that he was their "show kid." And, for all his tough veneer, Griffin possessed vaguely articulated beliefs that somewhere, in an inaccessible Eden, his real and loving family had straightened out and now yearned for him.

Two lost boys who felt at home only on a computer.

"It pisses me off," Jake said, "because he's ruined her life, too." He was still talking about his mother. "Not just the crap he preaches, but . . . the other stuff." Jake looked as if he were struggling with a decision to reveal or hide something else. "Like with her," he blurted out.

"Your mother?"

He inhaled jaggedly and shook his head. "*Her*. Mother Vivien. She and Harvey . . . the *Reverend* Harvey . . . everybody knows about them. Even if it's over, it's disgusting!"

The workday hadn't begun and I was tired of what made the world spin.

"My mother knows, and all she does is cry about it. And then Harvey tells her she's crazy."

Whenever he spoke, I saw the flash of his braces, as if to underline his malleability. More than his teeth were being pushed into, or out of, alignment. He seemed so young and vulnerable. He needed reassurance and a hug. But a female teacher does not hug adolescent male students unless she wants not only to further confuse them but also to face a sexual harassment suit. So I made sympathetic noises, hoping Jake regained his equilibrium before my first-period class barreled in.

"When I realized he was there, I felt crazy. I had to get out, like I couldn't breathe that air. So Griffin took me for a ride in Mrs. R.'s Jag. It was seriously fantastic."

I exhaled. From despair to "seriously fantastic" in less than a breath. Nothing like wheels, or even the memory of them, to anesthetize a young man's pain. "But Griffin has his own car," I said. The junker was infamous, resembling camouflage with its dulled-out gray patchwork and rust stains.

Jake shrugged. "They check his mileage but not their own. Besides, their cars never need gas. Grif always forgets that stuff, runs out a hundred miles away. Easier to take one of theirs."

It didn't sound like the most ethical solution, and I would have said so, but I suddenly became aware that Caroline Finney was at the open door. Our Latin teacher was a whisper of a woman, her skin aged into crumply silk. She smiled, put her finger to her lips so I wouldn't interrupt my conversation, and mimed writing on a board, then pointed at the chalk pieces resting on the board's ledge, her eyebrows raised. I nodded. Taking mine would spare her the pain of begging Helga, the Office Witch, who guarded supplies as if they were endangered species.

She tiptoed to the board, then stopped to read the Twain quote.

Jake, his back to her, seemed oblivious to Caroline. "What does your Dad think of your writing?" I asked him quietly.

"I e-mailed the column to him," Jake said. "He's a newspaper-man, you know. Used to do crime reporting."

Nowadays he covered real estate. I suspected that to Jake, this reportorial fall from glamour was his father's only flaw.

Jake's latest column hawked a Web site that (fruitlessly, I thought) discussed unsolved crimes. Every subject from Lizzie Borden to the missing Russian princess's whereabouts. I'd enjoyed the column, especially lesser-known cases with alliterative nick-names worthy of Dick Tracy. "The Two-Headed Homer," a pyramid scam that began with cabbages. "The Devil's Dishpan," in which a woman had been drowned in her kitchen sink. "Gretchen of the Green Feet," a headless corpse, female, found nude and frozen in a lake, remarkable for the odd color of her soles. "The Cheshire Cat," in which a pale and pudgy balding man (Jake included his photo in the article) embezzled millions and dis-appeared into thin air. "The Recycled Romeo," who married seven times, extracted all the money from each wife, misplaced three of them, and was still missing. If only his intended had talked to my mom and hired a detective.

Jake thought it would give his schoolmates a sense of the pos-sibilities of the Web, and he was probably right. Even Neddy Roederer had said the column made him realize the computer's potential as a research tool.

Jake planned to discuss a different Web site each issue. Next month's dealt with sports.

"My dad must be away," Jake said. "Not picking up messages."

Behind him, Caroline nodded her appreciation of Twain's biting commentary, then carefully considered the chalk. I could almost hear her mentally gauge my total stash and estimate what amount would be fair and proper to commandeer. Caroline was nothing if not civilized.

"After all," Jake said, "Dad's a journalist. He'd be interested." It sounded a lot like a plea.

E-mail traveled by computer. Why hadn't Jake's father both-ered to respond? Did the man have any idea how unhappy his son was? How much he wanted and needed him? Did he care? Or was it a matter of out of sight, out of mind?

If only missing and fantasized parents would reappear long enough to cure their children of illusion. A reality-based wound could heal. Chronic yearning merely festered.

In the brief silence, we heard the chanting outside. "Don't pol-lute minds!"

Jake walked over to look out the window. "The books from

the Roederers piss him off, especially the art books, especially the Appleby photos."

These were a collection by the controversial Rocco Appleby, whose body of work included bodies, and not always perfect, Grecian-godlike ones, but instead, acutely human ones.

"Look what he's doing!" Jake waved in the general direction of the street. Apparently Harvey hadn't been able to let Mother Vivien hog the spotlight. "Why do people listen to him? He's . . . sick, twisted. He's what's polluted." His voice had flattened out, as if all the emotion were worn off his words. Its calm, musing tone made his words chilling. "You read every day about people getting killed. Good people. Little kids who never hurt anybody. But never people like him, even though they hurt other people. And he *likes* doing that. But monsters like him—they're never touched. Why is that?"

Caroline looked at me, her eyebrows raised.

"I think about it," Jake said in that frighteningly calm voice. "How if something happened to him, I could be with my real father, and my mother would stop going crazy, and Mother Vivien—well, she could go to hell."

"Jake," I said sharply.

"No point in daydreams, is there?" he said.

Caroline waved and left, her hands filled with chalk, and the room filling with first-period students. *Jane Eyre* time. Another saga of a sad child.

"Thanks for listening," Jake said. "Guess I needed to blow off steam."

I nodded, and he, too, left.

I sat at my desk, heart pounding, well aware that whatever portion he'd blown off wasn't enough. He was still full of that steam and I couldn't blame him at all. And the bottom line was that I'd been of no help to him.

From outside, I heard the rhythmic chants. "Don't pollute minds!" Over and over, the *-lute* sound pierced the windows.

I wondered what that did to Jake's nerves, stretched as they were against his red-hot resentment. I had worried about him for a while now, tried to be the friend he needed. Now, that wasn't nearly enough. I saw him in my mind, a flailing figure in the dark sea, going down for the third time.

I made a note to arrange a conference with his mother and the school counselor. *ASAP*, I wrote. I underlined it.

As if that resolved anything.

Four

BETSY Spiers had been so phlegmatic Saturday night, and so unsure of herself on the phone, I thought she'd wobble when she walked. When I'd called to suggest a conference, her voice quavered, then grew shrill as she stammered out a string of half sentences. "Oh, no, is anything . . . ? Has Jake, has something . . . ? I could never forgive myself if—"

Like a leaf that quakes so hard it creates its own windstorm and blows itself off the tree. She didn't leave air-time between questions, as if the last thing she wanted was an answer. What if she paused long enough for me to say that yes, her son was having serious problems?

Given her level of incipient hysteria, it was heroic of her not only to agree to come in, but to urge that our conference be the next day, Tuesday, after school. Most likely, her motive was to get the terror over with, but that still constituted a form of bravery.

Particularly since, as it worked out, she had to cross her husband's gang to gain entry. There were still more picketers, their numbers fueled by the interest the media had shown in Monday's demonstration. As city schools went, we were exceptionally photogenic, housed as we were in the nineteenth-century beer baron's mansion across from the Square, and this was true even on a grumpy gray day when the air was chilly and the light so flat nothing had color. Plus, we were new—that is, news. The public schools had long been under siege, but we were private, small, elitist, the administration basically one pathetic man and a board who okayed whatever he said. We were an easy target and easier, too, to summarize in a news bite.

"I—I lied," Betsy said. "I told Harvey I was coming here to help the cause. That I was going to talk with you about curriculum choices." Tears welled up. "Vivien called me a liar and a traitor. *Her.*"

We sat in the school counselor's office concluding the Jake-excluded portion of our meeting. He'd not been pleased by this format. "What am I, a pariah?" He shrugged. "Just kidding. Don't get me wrong, but I don't like being talked about behind my back."

"It's more likely a chance to let your mother talk about herself," I'd answered. "You've said she's unhappy, and doesn't seem to understand how you feel about your living conditions, so she needs private time."

He shrugged and said he'd watch the protestors while he waited. Given that the source of his miseries was the leader of the protestors, or, more accurately, the two leaders, I was surprised. Given the weather, I was even more surprised, but Jake and the picketers were obviously of heartier stock than I.

This infinite winter was becoming the stuff of seasonal legend. This is the sort of thing that makes us loathe Floridians and Californians—anyone who hasn't recently slammed his coccyx on the ice, or remortgaged his house to pay the heating bill, or ripped his hands putting chains on his car.

It was not a year or a day when anyone sane would voluntarily carry a sign up and down a pavement, which is why the less-than-sane were hard at it.

The Moral Ecologists had apparently decided on permanent residency. They had permits, they had pickets, they had student hecklers, and they were attracting gapers who felt in need of a complaint, any complaint. Some of the less clearheaded parents had heard that something bad was being forced on their kids— and they, too, hovered outside or phoned the school demanding conferences. Our principal, Maurice Havermeyer, was in a record-breaking foul mood.

Maybe Alex Fry had been right. If we'd burned the books—all our books—these people would have gone away and Havermeyer's level of anxiety would be nearly bearable.

But we hadn't, and at the end of this week loomed Philly Prep's annual Open House, the yearly big deal when we preen like birds in mating season and try to attract yet another fresh-man class.

Competition between private schools may be bloodless, but it is nevertheless serious. To headmasters and admissions commit-tees, this time of year is the equivalent of the Miss America pageant, and nobody wants to be Miss Congeniality, or even First Runner-up.

Havermeyer's nervousness index could be calculated by the number and inanity of the directives he stuffed into our mail-boxes, conveying that it was imperative to shine, become what we only dreamed of being, eradicate our warts, be sure our knowl-edge was encyclopedic—and deliver it with the pacing and style of a stand-up comic.

Also, we were to change the personalities of most of our stu-dents, raise their IQs, and lower their apathy. Above all, we were to attract, to emit scholastic pheromones, bookish musk.

Problem was, he didn't know, nor did we, precisely how to do it. That increased the per diem memo flow. As did the fact that ten percent fewer souls had applied to date than had a year ago. There were rational reasons for this: The economy stunk, the city kept losing employers and revenue, and Philly Prep wasn't much to write home about in the first place. But Maurice Havermeyer didn't care about socioeconomics. He knew how to point his finger in only one direction—at the easiest scapegoat. In this case, his woes were caused by some unidentifiable but lethal deficiency on the part of the staff.

With pug-faced Harvey Spiers and Mother Vivien of the golden tresses hurling their invectives and demanding that every last "tainted title" be removed, beginning with the photography collection that included the unclothed human body, there went Havermeyer's vestigial sanity.

Betsy Spiers had a tentative voice and she didn't try to project it. "It isn't that he's hard on Jake," she said of her husband. "It's that he cares." Then she burst into tears. "No, he doesn't! He doesn't at all! Not about me, either! Not the way he should!"

Her voice changed, took on an aluminum coating and a cutting edge. "Jake *goads* Harvey, and there I am, caught in the middle, and that hideous Vivien, tugging at his loyalties, undermining his leadership, when *he* was the one who brought the group up from obscurity!" Rachel Leary, Jake's counselor, kept her expression impassive and handed Betsy the box of tissues.

She pulled out a handful and blew her nose. "Harvey's beliefs are biblical. He's spiritual. Jake doesn't understand." She pulled out another tissue and shredded it for a while, then looked up at us and shook her head. "When I met him, he was ordinary. An insurance clerk, not a reverend. That's what I liked. My first husband couldn't stand being ordinary. Always expected to become a star, the Woodward-and-Bernstein of Canada. Ambition made him thoughtless, a bad husband, never around to help me. His ego, you know . . . didn't care about anybody but himself. What was I supposed to do?"

We'd gotten so far off the track we couldn't even hear the trains anymore. We'd already been deflected from talk of family counseling. Psychology, it seemed, didn't fit Harvey's religious beliefs. He counseled people, and the Lord counseled him. End of story.

After half an hour of dead ends and evasions, Rachel and I had switched to Plan B: finding out whether Jake could take a breather from the local tension and spend time with his natural father. And here we were, stonewalled again by Ms. Helplessness.

"Harvey was humble. Considerate. He paid attention."

The sexiest thing a man could do, as well as the easiest, even though many of them found it daunting. I wondered if more men would give it a whirl if they realized that even a pudding-faced clod like Harvey Spiers became irresistible simply by paying attention.

"Then we moved here and it changed. He changed. Thought only about himself, about what he wanted, needed, had to have. Got involved with . . . that group. And with her. Her fault, I'm sure. Hate the sin, not the sinner, I know—but she is an evil woman. I'm so unlucky with men. Why does this keep happening to me?" Her voice was on the upswing again, much like a firehouse siren.

She should have hired a "romantic detective" before marrying either one of them. I'd get my mother on her case. And off mine.

My determined parent had made a second phone solicitation for detectivation during dinner last night, interrupting a far more serious discussion.

There'd been another book and effigy burning, this time within city limits, near Masterman School, where rigorous academic standards presumably meant the inclusion of "pollutants" in the curriculum.

The shadow of the night at Glamorgan still hung over me, and I couldn't believe that nothing could be proven about who was setting the fires. I knew these weren't homicides and so weren't Mackenzie's business, but apparently, they weren't clearly anybody's first order of business.

"Arson's the malicious burning of somebody's property," Mackenzie explained, before my mom called. We were eating takeout Chinese. I had forgotten to buy food. I'd make up for it later this week, prepare a feast—unfortunately of the farewell variety, because Mackenzie had to leave town to retrieve a prisoner. "Even though somebody owns the empty lots where they set these fires," he said, "or the right-of-way across from the Roederers', the fires don't destroy the property. An' nobody's ever claimed the books that burned, nor has anybody tried to collect insurance for them or for the lots. So even though there's apparently malice involved, it isn't the highest priority crime, and it's murky. Not a hate crime. And nobody's ever there by the time it gets noticed. See what I mean?"

"Maybe the antiterrorism people have to claim it, then," I said as the phone rang and my mother launched into her rent-a-detective-to-spy-on-him pitch.

I looked at the good guy across from me, thought about the real problems of the world, and as gently as possible—and as obliquely, because I didn't want Mackenzie to know precisely how my mother can hog-tie me in her would-be safety net—I told her to please never again mention the subject. Not ever.

The voice of Jake's mother, not mine, pulled me back to the present. "He wanted the easy life," she was saying of her current husband. "The American way. He thought this minister stuff—" She looked wildly from Rachel Leary to me. "Not that he doesn't believe in it, but he didn't go to a seminary or anything. One day, an insurance clerk and the next day, the call and he's a reverend. But people accepted it right away. They send him money, and the more extreme he is, the more money they donate to his cause." She managed a feeble laugh. "His *cause*! His only cause is Harvey Spiers! Not me, that's for sure, because if he cared, would he be out there in public humiliating me with that . . . with that *floozy*! But what can I do? He says I'm his wife until death, and he's a minister. I couldn't leave. What would I do?"

Rachel cleared her throat and leaned forward. "There's a note on Jake's file that says you're paying his tuition, and that Mr. Spiers is to be kept under the impression that Jake is here on a scholarship."

Betsy nodded. "Harvey wouldn't want the money spent on . . . he has so many other important causes that . . ." She didn't bother to finish the sentence. Instead, she studied her nails. Then she looked up. "I'm *trying*, do you understand? Do you see how much pressure I'm under?"

"The thing is—you have an independent income."

She shrugged. "Not enough to live decently on my own. I have no choice!" She wept again. "I'm so unlucky," she said, dabbing at her eyes.

"Mrs. Spiers, we'll help as much as we can with your domestic problems. But I'm Jake's teacher and Ms. Leary is his counselor, and we're concerned about finding a solution for him, too."

"Don't you think I'm worried sick myself?" she whispered. "To get a call like that from you? My blood pressure sky-rocketed. I thought I was having a heart attack."

"We promised Jake we'd be brief, and we haven't yet dealt with his depression, or what we can do to help it." Rachel spoke softly, but firmly.

Betsy Spiers looked confused, as if processing who Jake might be, what problems he could possibly have, and most of all, why she should be concerned about them.

Rachel cleared her throat and spoke again. "He wants to return to Canada."

"I know."

"And?"

"I can't. I'm married. I live here, now. I made *promises*."

The woman had mirrors for eyes.

I tried again to redirect her attention. "We were considering Jake's prospects. Jake's ability to live with his father. And while I know it would be difficult to be separated from your son, maybe it's worth a try, given his unhappiness."

Her eyes widened and she clutched the tissue to her chest. "Oh, no!" she said, with more emphasis than I'd heard thus far. "Not possible. Not at all." Once again, tears welled from her eyes.

I braced myself for reasons why it was not possible—heartlessness or depravity or other disqualifying traits on the part of Loren Ulrich.

"I couldn't bear it!" Betsy said. "I need Jake."

"But he—" Rachel began.

"Oh, no." Betsy Spiers' voice had gained strength and altitude again. "I'm not a strong woman, I'm in an unfamiliar city, I have no friends. If Jake weren't with me . . . No! He can't. Did you tell him he could? You have no right to do that, you know. He's still a minor."

She was an iron-willed woman, for all the putty and fluff stuck on as disguise, and she controlled by means of hysteria.

"And Loren," she went on. "He's probably with somebody else, having another child for all I know, leaving that wife and baby alone, too, and I wouldn't send any—"

To my relief, even though it further complicated the dynamics, the door was knocked upon and opened in one motion, and Jake entered. "He caved," he said flatly.

Betsy stood up. "Harvey?" she asked. "Gave in? Went away?"

"Yes and no." Jake lounged against the door in what I was sure he considered the insouciant, sophisticated pose of He Who Knows. In reality, he looked like an awkwardly hinged set of adolescent parts. I still wished I could give him a hug.

"What do you mean, Jake?" Rachel asked quietly. "What's yes and no?"

"Yes is that Harvey's gone," he said. "He went away."

Hooray! Havermeyer would relax, we'd return to the ordinary level of insanity that preceded Open House, and—

"Because Havermeyer caved. Said he'd remove the books and is doing so right now. For all I know, he's giving them to Harvey to burn. Can we write an article about it for the paper? Or an editorial? Or both?"

We could headline the story OUR PRINCIPAL: A MAN OF NO PRINCIPLE.

It was, indeed, quiet outside. But inside, it crackled with tension. Jake looked from his mother to me, back again, and then his glance flitted to Rachel Leary, who took the plunge. "Your mother doesn't seem to think your leaving Philadelphia is feasible."

"Mom!" Jake said. "I thought for sure . . ." His voice cracked. "You know how much . . ." He swallowed, hard.

So there it was, one boy's options needlessly narrowed, his

hopes dashed. Less than an eye blink in the cosmic scheme, which is not to say it didn't matter.

"It doesn't make sense, Jake," his mother whined. "Your father's undependable. He forgets about you all the time."

Jake winced. I looked away.

"—and he's not—not a *good*, a *moral* man, he'd be a bad influence on—"

"Not good! Like Harvey's good! Or moral! My God, he's so immoral his own followers hate him—his *partner*—"

"Vivien isn't his partner, she's—"

"She started—oh, who cares. Forget Vivien. He's the one who's immoral. I *heard* him. That wasn't the way a good man talks. Those were threats."

"Jake," I said. "This probably isn't the place for whatever you're talking about." My mind and energy were mostly out in space trying to absorb the idea that a school principal had agreed to remove good, even classic, works because a fanatic said so. But a part was here, increasingly worried about this boy-man, who was having the air crushed out of him.

Betsy, who wasn't concerned about the future of the world, or anything except herself, seized my message and ran with it. *"Jake!"* she said in her fire-engine siren tone, "she's *right*. What we talk about in our home is *private*!"

But Jake was two steps beyond propriety. He wheeled toward me. "He said some guy was a *pervert* and he—Harvey—would make him pay for pretending to be what Harvey calls normal." He turned back to his mother. "That's blackmail. You call that good and moral? Is that who I have to live with? Is that what I'm supposed to become?"

"You're deliberately misunderstanding. Again." Betsy sighed.

"He said!"

"He said pray. He meant prayer, repentance."

"Pay, not pray. People don't pray through the nose!"

"You might want to get us back on track here," Rachel said softly. "See if we can find a—"

Betsy Spiers ignored the counselor. "He was talking about a

hypocrite, a person pretending to be what he is not. That's the immorality and the problem that needed to be addressed, but you do that all the time. You deliberately misunderstand Harvey and you cause trouble, and you never consider what you're doing to me." She dabbed at her eyes again.

Poor-Li'l-Me's give women a bad name, and leave me with a bad taste. I wanted to remind her that not every happening on the planet was a chapter in the epic saga *How Betsy Was Victimized*, that she had a vulnerable, stranded son begging for attention.

"Don't preach to me about *good*," Jake said. "My father doesn't burn books or blackmail people or run around—why can't I *talk* to him, okay? Or visit."

"It's too far, Jakey," she said in a new, wheedling voice. "A foreign country . . . he might kidnap you, and I'd never get you back."

"It's Canada, for God's sake! I'm taller than he is! I'm not a baby!"

She sat immobile. I'd bet she had been one of those kids who held her breath and turned blue until she got what she wanted.

"It'd be all right for Mr. Ulrich to visit Jake here, wouldn't it?" Rachel Leary's voice was like a therapeutic tool, a sort of trowel smoothing down rough emotions. "When it fits both their schedules," she added, heading Betsy off at the pass.

"Loren won't want to." Betsy pursed her lips. "If he'd wanted to, he'd have done so, long ago."

"For Christ's sake—"

"You stop using the Lord's name in—"

"—he didn't know our address! You wouldn't let me write to him. If I hadn't gotten onto e-mail, I wouldn't have ever—"

"Why are you doing this to us?" Betsy asked Rachel and me. "Why did you drag me here to create a situation, make trouble. Do you see what you've done? Why?"

"But if Mr. Ulrich does want to?" Rachel persisted. "Jake, if he does, if he can, would you like that?"

He nodded. It wasn't a solution, but it was something.

"This is a ploy," Betsy said. "You think Loren will sweet-talk me into giving up my son, don't you? Take him out of the only stable environment he's ever known."

"Stable!' The veins on Jake's neck showed. "Like where animals live! Why are you pretending to be so blind, when I *heard* you fighting with him about her? Is it stable when Harvey says he can't control Vivien? If she throws him out before he can—"

"*He's* the organization. Nobody'd let her—"

"—then he won't have a job and that won't be stable, will it? Or what if he splits from you instead and makes Vivien his partner, will that be stable? Even now, when he's blackmailing somebody, or when you fight every night, and cry, is that stable?"

Sing hey for the family values, for which Harvey Spiers so loudly proselytized.

"Eavesdropping is a sin!" Betsy snapped. "Why do you hate us so much? Why won't you call him Dad, the way he asked? He provides the roof over your head! I get one last chance at happiness and look what you do to it! What did I do to deserve treatment like this?" She was winding up like a tornado, and we were supposed to flee.

"Mrs. Spiers," I said, "I want to thank you for coming here so promptly. And thank you, too, for agreeing to Mr. Ulrich's visiting his son. That was selfless and generous, and I'm sure it means a great deal to Jake, as it would to any boy who'd been separated from his natural father."

I wondered whether she heard me. Or whether her mind was on what life might be like without her son around and with only worthless, cheating, lying, hypocritical Harvey Spiers. Who might dump her and opt for Mother Viv and fifteen minutes of fame.

I wondered to what lengths an hysterical Poor-Li'l-Me might go to save whatever it was she thought she had.

Five

If Havermeyer had thought to restore peace by capitulating to the Moral Ecologists, he was dead wrong. If he'd imagined he was clearing the way for a serene Open House, he was wronger still.

What he did was generate Philly Prep's first demonstration of moral outrage. I'll bet most of our students think the First Amendment is a rock group, and even if it were explained, would be hard-pressed to care about censorship when they don't place any particular value on reading in the first place.

So their reaction may have had nothing to do with the forfeited books. It might have been that the weather on Wednesday morning was benign and welcoming, close to a miracle. A thin wash of spring-colored sunshine made the out-of-doors infinitely preferable to winter-weary classrooms.

For whatever reason, by the end of homeroom, word of Havermeyer's appalling decision and a plan of action had spread by interclass tom-tom, and when the bell rang for first period, the troops, as one, headed for the pavement. Teachers followed, exhorting halfheartedly, as if by rote. Nobody was happy about what Havermeyer had done.

Maybe he'd hear the voices of his students. Maybe he'd even listen. Learn something.

"Moral Ecologists suck!" a boy near me shouted, but it was almost a tongue twister. It was in competition with other instant slogans as well. In fact, a pundits' power struggle was in progress, slogans hurled one against another, creativity playing with words and ideas.

"Don't break my art!"

"Don't ban books. Ban Moral Ecologists!"

"We have a right to see bare buns!" Some ideas were less lofty than others.

"What kind of school won't let us read?"

"Don't check us out of the library!"

If they'd known they were working at literary craft, framing ideas in words that were clever, articulate, and succinct, they'd have applied the brakes. But they didn't even suspect.

Creativity aside, the result was chaos. Too many words, too many people, and too little walkway created a dangerous situation. Students overflowed off the pavement, treating face-offs with commuter traffic as a game. Brakes squealed, and teachers dispersed along the student body's perimeters, as if ready to have cars smite us in lieu of our charges. We were all inspired to new heights of nobility.

Across the street, on the fringe of the Square, Moral Ecologists stood in clumps like an infestation we hadn't properly exterminated, observing what they had wrought with grim satisfaction. Only one of them looked uncertain or ashamed, a man in a Russian-style fur hat who seemed unwilling to meet my glance. He turned away and faced the Square. Good, I thought. One down.

51

The "don't cave" chant slowly gained ground, winning by virtue of brevity. "Don't cave, don't cave, don't cave, Dr. H.!" had a jaunty, if futile, air.

Havermeyer was nowhere to be seen.

Fifteen minutes later, the effort to push too many students back to safety on too little pavement would have appealed only to Sisyphus. Our arms were no match for adolescent energy, yet it didn't seem ethical to abandon our charges to becoming traffic fatalities. We needed a plan.

Eventually, through negotiations with class leaders, an intricate but workable strategy was agreed upon: Beginning with seniors, each grade would strike for one period, repeating the rotation throughout the day. There were no real complaints.

With fresh troops arriving each period, and fresh vocal cords, the "don't cave" chant became our loud new background music, as attractive as the sound of fingernails scraping down the blackboard.

Meantime, Sally Turner, the librarian, had a hissy fit that grew too large for the building. She called a local news radio show, the ACLU, and the teacher's union; labeled Havermeyer's actions "an abomination"; and said she refused to part with a single book, especially the Rocco Appleby photographs the Moral Ecologists had singled out as "pure filth."

We were inundated by Minicams and microphones. Helga, the Office Witch, burst into tears—her only documented sympathetic act—as she tried and failed to intimidate the press. Reporters were tougher than teachers. The students reveled in their new roles as political activists and media darlings.

Late in the day, I, too, was seduced by the promise of fame via a sound bite on freedom of speech, book burning, and censorship. While I tried to be both honest and noninflammatory, students cheered and waved at the camera, and Havermeyer himself appeared.

He did his bit as well, huffing unintelligibly about "the matrix of academia and the populace" and "proactive responses to the bifurcation of aesthetics and ethics." The reporter looked cross-eyed with confusion. Then Dr. H. switched to a riff about "living lessons in democracy," spouting inanities in praise of freedom of expression—the very idea he'd violated. He was so ravaged by the hissing and shouting behind him, so clammy and sweaty on this sunny but cool day, he looked and sounded like a man who required the Heimlich maneuver.

Or tutoring in physics—the old action-reaction, cause-and-effect thing. He didn't understand about putting your money and your mouth in the same place, about how if you preach integrity and freedom of speech you shouldn't negate it all in a few shameful seconds. He seemed so confounded and befuddled, I actually felt a twinge of compassion.

Then, off camera, he herded me aside and said he found the Twain quote on my board "inflammatory" and suggested it be erased.

The smidgen of concern I'd felt disappeared. The quote remained.

Our principal's interview was followed by one with Edie Friedman, gym teacher and perpetual yearner for romance. "I think it's *great* that today's kids really *care*," she said, flashing a smile at the camera—or possibly the cameraman. "Plus," she said with a wink, "they're getting exercise! You know, *walking* has been proven to be the very best exercise possible!"

Next was Potter Standish. I suspected the Moral Ecologists of pushing him forward to make us look bad. However, the chemistry teacher and secret drinker managed to out-Havermeyer Havermeyer in the unintelligibility sweepstakes. Something about "numinous acceleration," if I heard correctly.

The last interview I stayed for was with a student, Melissa Daley. Not the brightest specimen, but one of the cutest, and she thought it was "like, *interesting* to do this, you know? A change of pace, kind of." She looked blank and frightened when they asked which of the removed books she wished she could read. They filmed her doe-in-the-headlights gape for much too long, and I could only hope they edited out a whole lot of it later on.

And then they were finished with us. At least they hadn't

interviewed Alex Fry. God knows what outrageous things he'd have said.

We had acquired a fringe of people with no idea what was going on, but who wanted in on it. If it was good enough for a television crew, it was more than good enough for them.

Tawdry of me to feel such glee at the way Havermeyer's decision had backfired, but I couldn't help myself. It felt like maybe this one time, the forces of good might actually triumph.

Maurice Havermeyer, Ph.D., did not share my delight. Throughout the day, like a horrified slow learner, he'd gone to his office window, stared at the protestors in wordless misery, then retreated. Then he'd reappear, repeating the intent observation as if hoping his earlier impressions had been a hallucination. But there they'd be again, and there they intended to remain until the books were returned (or summer vacation appeared, whichever came first) whether or not prospective applicants would have to pass through their midst to enter the building. If, of course, anybody still wanted to apply to Philly Prep, knowing what kind of principal it had.

At one point during the day, I'd been in the outer office gathering mail and messages, when a shell-shocked Maurice Havermeyer walked out of his inner sanctum. "This is terrible," he said. "This has to stop."

That was when I really worried about the state of his mind. He'd spoken in unadorned, intelligible sentences, forgetting to modify, embellish, and obfuscate. He'd spoken so clearly and succinctly, I knew he was on his way to a breakdown.

Near the end of my sidewalk time, as I was about to return to my classroom, a shiny-bright TV-type tapped my shoulder. "We're taping a roundtable on this issue today at four-thirty," she said. "We want a faculty member and we liked your segment. We'd like you to be part of it."

I was flattered, but said, "No, thanks."

"You're popular with the students. They also suggested you."

Even more flattering, but tonight was promised to Mackenzie and Mandy. A cohabitation special. Candlelight, music, good wine, and aged steaks. Eat, drink, and be merry, for tomorrow the cop goes to Kansas to retrieve a baddie. He'd said for one night only, but I'd seen how many books he'd packed—"in case"—and I wasn't holding my breath.

"Please," the TV woman said. "We need you."

I smiled, but shook my head. Too often, C. K. and I were like little figures that emerge periodically on a big clock. Animated, determined, and on the move, we nonetheless never got anywhere or bridged the space between us. Sometimes now, both locked in our separate concerns, we didn't seem together even when we were in the same place, and we barely ever used home as home base. This dinner was one attempt to change that.

"It'll take an hour at most," she said. "Four-thirty to five-thirty, that's all."

"Thanks, but—"

"Look." The TV lady's tone announced she was coming in for the kill. "With all due respect, do you want your principal, the one who removed the books, to be the only representative of your school? Of educators?"

I sighed. "How late did you say we'd be?" Maybe Mackenzie could meet me at the station. Maybe steak was a bad idea. He was, after all, on his way to beef-land. And no maybes about it—he'd be proud of my standing up for our constitutional rights. Right?

ONCE, after being out in a small motorboat all day, I could still feel the motion of the waves even on dry land. That's how it was when the teaching day was done, pictures still playing through my mind, sounds echoing in the empty school. I made two phone calls—one to Mackenzie, rearranging our evening, and one to my friend Sasha, to see if she wanted to play when Mackenzie was in Kansas.

"Not with you," she said. "I have found male perfection."

"Again? Who is it this week?"

"This is different. This is Dr. Wonderful. An M.D. who works for a foundation in India."

This was indeed different. Sasha tended toward the fringes of acceptability. Her men were more likely to be social outcasts than to have social consciences.

"Did I mention handsome? He's gorgeous. And sexy? Flawless. My reward for all the bad apples. The handsome prince after all the frogs I've kissed. Perfect."

Perfect Pete, she called him. Dr. Wonderful. And he wanted to be with her every possible moment until he had to go back to India. Nauseating, like an eighth grader. "A simple yes or no would have sufficed," I said. "But . . . good luck and have fun."

"Fun," she said. "I have never before—"

I hung up. After I got in my car, I sat there, motor running, while I agonized over whether I should go home and change before my TV debut, redo my hair and face, or stay with the pale green sweater I had on, a comfortable favorite, and fresh lipstick.

I put a tape on and let the Three Tenors go off the decibel meter. Their dulcet tones entered every one of my pores. It didn't help me reach a decision about anything, but it made me not care. Aural sex will do that every time.

I put the car into reverse, looked around, and saw Jake Ulrich wave from the corner. I waved back. He slowly, slowly lowered his hand. The pace and timing of the wave made it less a friendly salute, more the motion of a drowning victim's hand above the water. I looked back. He still dawdled at the end of the parking area. And Griffin was with him.

I pulled out of my slot fighting to override intuition, but I lost the round, and turned off the ignition. "Hey," I said, getting out of the car. "What's up?"

Griffin, his usual taciturn self, said nothing, but ducked his head deeper into his long overcoat. I think that meant everything was going satisfactorily.

Jake looked fidgety, wired. Yesterday, his stepfather had bullied his school into acquiescence, and today, Jake had led his schoolmates in protest against that very triumph.

"Today was cool," Jake said. "Felt good having everybody agree on something. We're planning the piece for the paper. Remember? You said we could."

Griffin nodded. He often had a gleam in his eye that made me suspect a private but rich vein of humor. Maybe someday he'd want to share it.

I didn't remember giving the go-ahead, but why not? This was the happiest, most energized Jake I'd seen in months of taking his emotional temperature and worrying over the results.

"I want to trace everything that happened, back to the time the grant was announced, then the ceremony, and what all happened. Get quotes, opinions and all, real investigative journalism. What do you think? Griffin's been taking photos, too."

Again, Griffin did his head-duck, indicating agreement. "A lot," he said.

"Plus we could get some of the news footage, do you think?"

I hadn't needed to stop my car or to worry. Jake was fine.

"Nothing like this ever happened at Philly Prep, I'll bet," Jake said. "It's like the Sixties. Maybe we could have a sit-in tomorrow."

"Better still," I said, "time it for Open House. That'd be terrific. A great first impression."

Griffin's eyes gleamed even more.

"I was being facetious," I said. "Don't you dare!"

He grinned. I was sure there was an interesting person in there and I wondered why he kept him hidden, even now, when he lived in comfort and safety.

"There'll be picketing," Jake said. "Prospective students deserve to know what the place is really like."

"Sounds great."

They gave each other high fives. "I told that TV lady I was writing it," Jake said. "She invited me to be on this show they're taping. She said I'll be the voice of the student body. Cool, huh?"

"You have a great future as a reporter," I said. "But is going public this way—your stepfather's on the panel. Is that going to create—"

"You think I care?" His features turned stony. He cared too much. It must be so hard being Jake, containing those cataclysmic emotions.

"Sorry." That was his family and his decision. "Could it be that before fame hits, you could use a ride to the TV station?"

Jake's lack of wheels was a topic he lamented, over and over. It was also another bond with Griffin Roederer who, of course, had his wreck of auto mobility parked across the street.

"Well," Jake said. "I guess I . . ."

Griffin said, "See you there, man. Give you moral support. I have things to do first." Sometimes his voice sounded as rusty as his car, as if he needed to oil it between sentences.

But the obvious thing was that he'd been expecting to drive Jake.

"I'd appreciate a lift," Jake said to me.

There was, then, still an untouched agenda. Something he needed to talk about en route.

As soon as we were on our way, Jake opened and shut his mouth, but said only, "So."

"Something up?"

"I'm, ah . . . I'm glad you gave me a ride. Because . . . see, I feel bad about stuff I said. Yesterday. At the meeting. Miss Leary, you, and my mom?"

"I remember," I murmured, intrigued by how emotion segmented his sentences. "Showing your honest feelings isn't a reason to feel bad."

He shrugged. "She—my mom—said I didn't love her and that's why I want to leave. And he—Harvey—he's berserk. Worse than ever. Bragging how he made Havermeyer 'bow down'—I swear, that's what he said. And then, talking about . . . more, about . . ."

I waited. The sentences were lengthening, growing more complex. He was gaining control of whatever it was.

"He hit her. I wasn't there, but there were red marks on her face when I came into the kitchen."

"That's a real problem. Does your mother talk about it? Has she done anything to protect herself?" Dear God. Yet another pathological stone added to what the kid already carried. "This can't all be on your shoulders."

His eyebrows converged as he wrinkled his brow in obvious confusion.

"The abuse," I said. "Isn't that what you're getting at?"

He shook his head. "I mean, sure, I try to stop him, but I can't make her leave or do anything. It wasn't only that, though. There was the thing he said. Remember?"

"Remind me."

I heard him swallow. "Harvey had this guy he was going to blackmail. The one who was secretly gay?"

Ah, yes. Harvey, the amoral moral enforcer, although I hadn't known his victim's so-called crime. But why was this relevant?

"The thing is—I know who he was talking about. I knew yesterday, too." He darted a glance at me, then looked away again. "I didn't say anything, and I feel bad about it."

I kept quiet. Sometimes a speaker needs a soliloquy. My role seemed to be the skull that Hamlet held, a symbol toward which Jake could direct his to-be-or-not-to-be.

"He's always been nice to me, and now, nice to the school."

He. A nice-to-Jake he. That narrowed the field. Combined with nice-to-the-school, it could mean only Neddy Roederer.

"So to know Harvey wants to blackmail him, or thinks he can, or whatever—I don't know what to do." I felt his gaze like a tug on the sleeve, asking for a response this time. I kept my eyes on the road ahead as long as I could, glad of the need to drive safely.

"Help me out on this," I said, when my comprehension refused to untangle. "How do you know your stepfather was talking about Mr. Roederer—if I've followed you correctly."

"He called him the Trashman. He said he finally knew why he'd recognized the Trashman at the party. Placed him. Remembered him from Canada. He said he met him at a New Year's party and that he—Neddy—lived with another man back then. Harvey knew the other man, too. And he saw them hug and kiss at midnight. He said Mr. Roederer wasn't any big social deal then, either. He was a nobody, Harvey said. No talk about Benjamin Franklin, no mansion. A nobody. Who had a 'no-good man' on the side. And then Harvey got really angry and said that now the Trashman was everybody's darling. A leader of society, up for a political commission, some appointment. He wanted to know what people would say when they knew the truth about him. What his *wife* would say."

Jake sounded as if he could have cried out of frustration. "I don't know what to do, who to tell. For sure, I couldn't tell Griffin."

I felt pressure in my chest and realized I'd been holding my breath. "I don't get it," I said softly. "Who cares about Neddy Roederer's private life? Suppose it's true, suppose he's bisexual, or homosexual. So what? Mr. Roederer's life or history shouldn't matter to anyone else. And I doubt that a single part of it is true, anyway. Mr. Roederer said he and his wife were in Canada only briefly. He and his wife. Where was she if he was out on New Year's with a man? Your—Harvey met somebody else."

"Harvey wants to stop him from using his money to pollute minds. Like with the books he gave our school. Those pictures of naked men. He says Mr. Roederer's a pervert."

Now I saw the warped logic, and it exhausted me. I was too weak to battle the manic, unceasing energy of a fanatic. It was too difficult ducking, let alone deflecting, Harvey Spiers' fury.

"He said what he knows would land Mr. Roederer in jail."

"Well, that much is ridiculous. Even if he had the right man, even if it were true, people do *not* go to jail for their sexual preferences these days. This is Philadelphia. This is the Nineties."

No jail, but an accusation, a flutter of prurient public interest, embarrassment to Neddy and Tea Roederer. And then, when he'd done as much damage as he could, Spiers would turn his attention and wrath elsewhere. And the Roederers, if they were nearly as wise as they seemed, would relocate as far away as possible and start over. Speaking selfishly, the bottom line would be that our schools would no longer receive the gifts we desperately needed. And Griffin and Jake would each lose his best and possibly only good friend. What an equitable service the Moral Ecologists provided. Everybody lost.

"Should I do something? What? I don't know what to do."

And neither did I. I know I'm supposed to have answers to issues beyond whether a semicolon is required in a given sentence. But I was flat out of solutions, even, perhaps, about semicolons. "Can I think about this overnight?"

He shrugged. He didn't look happy about leaving the issue in limbo, but he didn't have any other options, and neither did I.

"Let's talk about your article, instead," I said. "And what points you plan to make during the roundtable."

For the rest of the ride, I listened. And prayed, silently, for a visit from the goddess of inspired responses to impossible situations. There just had to be one in the pantheon. Or at least on the Internet. Maybe it was that Dot Com who was evoked in every online address. So I prayed to her.

Six

THE greenroom wasn't. It was cream-colored and minimal, and there were too many of us crammed into it, perched uncomfortably on furniture that looked like a dental office's rejects, or hovering around a small table holding a half-filled coffeepot, Styrofoam cups, and a plate of doughnuts. Oh, the unbearable glamour of it all. When was reality going to edge even close to my fantasies?

I was nervous about being in front of a TV camera as a spokesperson for "educators." Was I speaking for teachers everywhere? The idea gave me palpitations.

I wished I could think of a way to pass the time. I didn't want to drink coffee, for fear of having to be excused while on the air. I didn't want the doughnuts, which looked stale. I tried to concentrate on the TV that quietly played the station's current broadcast, but it happened to be a discussion of whether the gross national product was up or down, or subject to interpretation, and I couldn't concentrate enough to comprehend its significance. Didn't care, either.

Bored and agitated. A bad combo. How to fill the waiting time?

A squabble was not what I'd had in mind. "You might as well know now," Neddy Roederer said to my headmaster. "We're withdrawing Griffin from Philly Prep. Immediately. I intend to discuss our reasons on the air."

"Oh, no!" Havermeyer looked shocked, as if biting the hand that fed him—and his library—wasn't supposed to matter. I glanced at Jake, who was standing next to Griffin. This was old news to both of them, it appeared, but Jake looked devastated and Griffin smoldered with rage.

"We need," Havermeyer said, "to talk about—"

"There's nothing to discuss. Griffin needs a coherent moral structure, not a demonstration of spinelessness. We've already contacted several boarding schools." Next to him, his wife looked subdued in a severe suit as dark as her hair. Today's costume was meant to signify grimness and determination. It succeeded. She nodded agreement with each point her husband made.

"But Griffin has done so well at Philly Prep."

If Havermeyer had any sensitivity, he would have realized the futility of arguing. The fact that oh-so-private Neddy Roederer was willing to talk on TV about this issue meant he was passionately concerned. The wrongheaded administrator who had driven him and his wife to this point wasn't about to change their minds.

"Griffin will do as well elsewhere," Neddy said. "Our decision was made the instant you made yours about removing books. You allowed us no other choice."

Tea nodded again. Her hair, long today, shifted and resettled like a shaken bolt of silk.

Nobody asked Griffin's opinion. I hoped it had been asked earlier. He leaned against the wall as if it were holding him up.

"The grant, of course, is hereby rescinded."

Tea nodded twice.

Havermeyer looked apoplectic, visions of bankrolls flying out of his hands. He was going to need makeup or cosmetic surgery before he'd be presentable on camera.

"Pretty high and mighty, aren't you?"

Jake winced at the gravelly voice. I checked the wall clock, wishing they'd start our taping immediately. People were reasonably polite to one another on-air.

Harvey Spiers stood near the coffee table, arms folded, thick features squeezed into a sneer. "You're a fine one to squawk about *coherent morals*. From what perverted perspective do you get outraged when somebody does the right thing and protects the nation's young?"

"Please." Jake put up a hand like a traffic cop. "We're supposed to have the discussion inside, when they tell us to."

"This isn't for the TV public, is it, Reverend Spiers?" Roederer asked. "This is a private vendetta you have with me, although I have no idea why."

"Don't be silly," Betsy Spiers said softly. "There's nothing personal about whatever Harvey has to say. He has principles, that's all." She was again in vague colors tending toward mud, and she sat in a corner, clutching a coffee cup. She wasn't a panelist, she had explained to everyone who entered. Only "here for Harvey." And, I suspected, to monitor her husband's brassy partner/lover/competitor, Mother Vivien.

"You're a corrupt presence, Mr. Roederer," Mother Vivien said. "Your money's empowered you to spread filth." She wore a flowing dress of emerald green, and her little-girl curls cascaded over her shoulders and down her back. I could not believe she honestly thought the combination of a mask of makeup and those incongruous baby curls was attractive. I could, however, imagine her opting, for better or for worse, to regain the ground she'd lost to Harvey by sheer attention-getting, and for starters, she'd look like nobody else. She'd succeeded with at least part of that.

"I can speak for myself," Harvey said.

Mother Vivien pursed her lips. Betsy Spiers allowed herself a small smile.

"You know perfectly well why I don't like you," Spiers told Roederer. "I knew you when you were slumming."

"Please!" Jake said. "This is really—"

"And soon," Spiers went on, "the world will know as well. Your money and position don't blind me. I don't care about worldly things. Rich or poor—"

"Sin is an abomination to the Lord," Mother Vivien said.

Harvey wheeled toward her. "We agreed *I* would speak. Are you going to pull this trick on the air, too?"

Her voice was strained and piercing. "We agreed? *We* did? Or was it another of your *pronouncements*? Should I be mute so you can continue the illusion that *you* alone *are* the Moral Ecologists? Confuse people again about our leadership, about whose vision this really is, just as we grow stronger? I'll talk whenever I want to!"

I didn't think it was love or sex between them, at least not anymore. Each wanted something the other couldn't bestow, like power, celebrity, or money. Maybe all three.

"Don't be spiteful, Vivien." Betsy Spiers had put her coffee cup on the floor, and sitting forward, she watched eagerly, her chin propped on her hand, a tight smile on her lips. Her husband's heart apparently didn't belong to the other woman, or if it did, they were having serious heart trouble, and she was delighted. If they would come to blows, she'd be deliriously happy.

"Just a minute here," Neddy Roederer said. "We haven't finished our—"

"Let it be," his wife said.

"I'll talk whenever I have something to say!" Vivien shouted at no one in particular. "Nobody dictates to me!" She glared at Harvey.

The door opened. All sounds were temporarily hushed, all grievances put on hold. I expected a station official, ready to boot us out, but I was wrong again. A woman in her forties wearing a pinstriped suit, carrying a briefcase, said, "Hi. I'm Kara Adams. For the panel on censorship, right? I'm from the ACLU."

Instantly, the din resumed. I heard a welcome from Tea Roederer, "damned liberal blah-blahs" from Spiers, and a burst of something louder still from Vivien. I glanced away, up at the monitor. "Look!" I said. "It's us! We're on the news!"

On the TV, Edward Franklin Roederer delivered stirring lines on the dangers of capitulating to fanaticism.

The ACLU woman applauded. Mother Vivien hissed.

When Harvey was on screen, Vivien had a few caustic things to say about his attention-grabbing proclivities. "Listen, Harvey," she said. "One and only one of us is going on the air." Harvey said fine, if she wanted it that way, he'd be the one. He hadn't read the rules of how such exchanges were supposed to go.

I tuned them out and watched the screen. I thought I looked a little moonfaced, but Jake, in a stage whisper, said I'd been "great." Griffin didn't even glance at the TV.

The news shifted focus to the follow-up of a story about a twenty-nine-year-old woman who'd been reported the day before to have been abducted from Plymouth Meeting Mall by a stranger. It now appeared that no strangers had been involved. Her fiancé, a man with a long history of violence, was charged with her murder.

Maybe this story wouldn't make its way south to fan my mother's paranoia. Florida grew a bumper crop of their own murders and didn't need to import ours. I hoped.

The door opened again, and a cute girl in a tiny skirt and a name tag that said HEATHER beamed at us. "Those of you on the roundtable, would you follow me now?" she said. "We'll start taping in five minutes, okay?"

There was a bit of elbowing between Harvey Spiers and Mother Vivien, but his elbow won. We left the room to Betsy, Vivien, and the volcanic Griffin. I wished I could have had a camera trained on them.

MACKENZIE MET ME at the sushi restaurant, full of questions. He'd already ordered, which was fine with me. I was ravenous.

"It wasn't that bad," I said. "Which isn't to say it was good." I filled him in on the day's events, up to and including my small-screen debut. It had not turned out to be as entertaining as the greenroom performances. There were too many people and ideas in too little time: the law's position, the ACLU's, the Moral Ecologists'; my riff, more or less echoed by Jake, on the value of classic literature and on teaching students to think for themselves, which was to say, become adults; Havermeyer's pathetic attempt to turn expediency into policy; the Roederers' position on art and aesthetics and the need for stretching the envelope and the mind.

The best that can be said was that it concluded without bloodshed.

"They're airing it Saturday morning," I said. "Dawn. One of those times nobody watches TV. I'll tape it if you're still in Kansas." Of course, he'd still be there. Unwrapping a prisoner of two states' red tape would take forever. "Or I'll borrow Jake's copy. He asked for one to send his father."

"Can't he program his VCR?"

"I think asking for it, explaining how his dad's a newspaperman up in Toronto made it clear, politely, that he's not Harvey's kid. Or maybe they don't have a VCR in that dismal Spiers household. But let's not talk about them. What's up with you?"

"Nothing much." It was only unusual cases that Mackenzie talked about willingly or with enthusiasm. Mostly, he'd explained, homicide detection involved either quick solutions, thanks to stupid criminals, or tedious inspections, slow piecings together of fragments, and in both instances, a lot of needless, brutal, impulsive, and meaningless destruction. Besides, so much evidence was based on bodily fluids that it was seldom dinnertable talk. "Ah, but," he said. "There was the Stupid Crime of the Day. Or maybe week."

The waitress brought us trays laden with gorgeous bundles of fish and rice. One of the many pluses of a Japanese restaurant is that the servers don't recite specials, feel the need to tell us their names, or pop over intrusively and repeatedly, as if convinced we need them in our conversational circle.

While Mackenzie paused to find a piece of paper and write something on it, I snagged a piece of smoked salmon.

"This one's an English teacher's dream," he said. "A guy goes into a bank off Broad Street and hands the teller a note that reads like this." He handed me the piece of paper.

This is stikup. Give me yer muny kwik or I shut you with my gun.

"So," Mackenzie continued, "the teller figures this isn't exactly a genius in front of him, and he says no problem, he'll hand over the money, except that the robber has to sign for it because that's the bank's policy on robberies."

"And he did?"

Mackenzie nodded. "Signed his name and address, took the money, and was arrested maybe an hour later."

"The moral is, work on your spelling."

Perhaps because she is a fine speller, Mackenzie said, "I just remembered—your mother called."

"Why?"

"Does she need a reason? The rates drop, and the woman phones. This time, she wondered if you'd seen something on the news about a woman up here who was killed by her fiancé. She'd like you to call her, too."

I nodded.

"Any kind of tension between the two of you?"

I shrugged. "Not really. You know how my mother is."

"She said I should ask whether you were thinking it over. What's *it*? Are you?"

My mother was out of her mind, playing games, laying clues in front of a homicide detective. His work might be tedious, but he was good at it.

I don't as a rule approve of lying, but I couldn't bring myself to tell him the truth. Partly, I feared, because my mother had touched a sore spot. There were indeed lots of things I didn't know about the man I lived with, beginning with his first name, as she'd pointed out. "You know how they are about my living in the city," I muttered. "There's a condo near them she wants me to buy."

The trouble with trusting one another is that it makes it too easy to lie.

"Uh-huh," he said. "They think the solution is for you to move to Florida, is that it?"

And that's the trouble with intelligence. Mackenzie didn't believe my lie for a second. I liked him for that.

But I was determined to make the evening work, despite the long-distance doubt my mother had planted. "Think about it," she'd said, and willingly or not, I had. And kept doing so.

While it seemed appalling to hire a P.I., it didn't seem offensive to sleuth on my own. The investigation of each other was a long and honorable tradition called courtship. "So, um, how many brothers and sisters do you have?" I asked, apropos of nothing, after I'd downed a piece of unagi. I knew stories about scads of Mackenzies, swamps-full, but it suddenly seemed suspicious that C. K. had never produced a precise head count. Genealogical charts, birth and marriage stats. Photos, Social Security numbers.

"Depends whether you include Alicia and Junior Bear, the second cousins once removed who came to us when their folks went to work down in Guatemala and stayed seven years, or Carl Henry, after his folks died in a small-plane crash," he said. "Or the foster boy, Micah. He was with us four-five years. Or Sallymarie, my mother's youngest sister—she's nearer our ages than Mom's, and she moved in along with Grandma after Grandpa died. Then again, you wouldn't count her. She's my aunt."

His family was a mob scene in a Hollywood spectacular without the togas and horses. People swirling, appearing, disappearing. "How did you all find room in one house?" I asked.

"*You*-all? You tryin' to talk Southern now?"

"I'm talking *all*, I'm talking hordes." Maybe he'd grown up in a plantation mansion, a Tara.

"Bunk beds, four to a room. Dorm style, any which way. Depending on the current population, people slept on roll-aways in the dining room, and on the dining room table as needed. On the couch, on the porch swing. Floor, two chairs. Whatever worked. It wasn't a flophouse or a shanty, but it wasn't *Architectural Digest*, either." He grinned. "We managed. Somebody needed space, we found it. My mother is—" I watched him search for the right word. "—a most resilient woman."

My mother seemed his mother's shadow self, so unresiliently

nervous about possibility, she wanted to hire a detective to control my fate. "But who were all of you? Aside from the cousins and wards and those who wandered through."

"Why the sudden interest?"

"It's not sudden. I get your stories mixed up, and then I'm not sure I know all that much about you." At least some of that was true.

"Don' think of myself as a secretive type," he murmured.

"Nor do I. So who is there, as in siblings?"

He ticked off names, looking mildly bemused. "Lessee . . . my brothers Porter, Nick, Madison, and Noah—and my sisters Phoebe, Bunny, and Lutie."

"There were eight of you," I said. Had I known that? "Not counting the floaters."

"You look surprised. Surely I've provided this data before."

"Have you? In any case, it is an awesome amount. Just imagine my mother with all those people to fuss over."

"Numbers of that magnitude dilute fussin' till you can't hardly recognize it."

"Nice names they all have," I said, even though I thought Bunny belonged in the nickname category, a bit too precious should she want to be the first female president of the U.S., say. "Why'd they reduce you to initials?"

He smiled and shrugged.

"What do they call you when you're all at the homestead together?"

He looked around, then leaned over the small table, so close I was tempted to kiss him—but then I'd miss the answer. At long last. "They call me C. K.," he whispered. "Don't tell." He sat back, chewed sushi, drank sake, then smiled again. "Have we finished that odd drill?"

I sighed and nodded.

"Then are you ready to tell me what your mother really wants? Surely it wasn't an accounting of who all slept at the Mackenzies'."

What the hell. "It's too ridiculous. The niece of a lady in her complex almost married a rotter, so she's into hiring a detective to ferret out your secrets."

"My secrets? Ah—the murdered woman in the news. Or maybe she means those bodies I stashed in the basement. Tell her it was a bad day. They got on my nerves. It won't happen again if you don't annoy me."

"That's why I didn't want to tell. It's mortifying. Besides, you don't have secrets."

He extracted his charge card from his wallet. "Didn't say that." His voice was soft, lulling. "Everybody has secrets. And isn't that nice, too. Keeps the mystery alive."

"You mean your name?"

"That, too," he said.

I found his response disquieting. I like mysteries, but not unsolved ones, so I pestered and pouted and finally, after we'd both made our way home in our separate cars, and after we were back up in the loft and I continued to dither, he put his index finger up in mock scholarly-lecturer fashion.

"I have a relevant tale to tell," he said. "Of the literary variety. You know the sad tale of Peter Schlemiel?"

"You're making him up the way my father used to make up homilies about kids who'd met with disaster because they didn't look both ways before crossing."

"Amanda, *Peter Schlemiel* is an ancient fable, and the subject of Adelbert von Chamisso's most famous work. Those Northern schools . . ."

I hate it when he takes to *my* field and bests me at it. I had never heard of either Peter Schlemiel or Adelbert von Chamisso. And neither, I was willing to bet, had most normal people.

"Peter Schlemiel sold his shadow," Mackenzie said. "A useless thing, we'd say—to a mysterious stranger."

"The Devil?"

Mackenzie shrugged. "If you like. In return for this easy trade, he got never-ending riches. But the thing is, without his shadow, he frightened everyone, so they all rejected him and he couldn't find friendship or love."

"And the point is?"

"We *need* our dark sides, our shadow selves. Without that, we're two-dimensional freaks. Inhuman."

"And you?" I asked. "What is your shadow side?"

He ran his fingers through his salt-and-pepper hair, looked worried, and paced. "Hell," he finally said, "you'd find out, so it might as well be now."

The air around us hissed my mother's warnings—see? See?

"In fifth grade, I shoplifted three packs of baseball cards. And got caught. My record was sealed because of my age, but my parents considered me a criminal and kept my butt on the line for a long while." He winked a river-blue eye. "And now you know."

I did. I *knew* this man even if I didn't have all his stats, and I knew him to be good. The rest was details.

My mother should have had lots more children, the way C. K.'s mother had, to divvy up the worrying and hovering until they reached a normal level for each offspring. Or better still, to have had—and still have—a life of her own aside from the totally domesticated, other-centered one she led. Problem is that nothing much ever happened to her, so she invented demons—"What *if* her boyfriend turns out to be a mass murderer, hmm?"—then shooed them away in order to generate excitement.

I wouldn't be as foolish as my mother. I'd enjoy what I had, completely. All was well, and it was a good evening in a good world.

This is what's meant by "Ignorance is bliss."

Seven

A T a ridiculously early hour we arose, Mackenzie to leave for the Midwest, I to see him off. The sun wasn't yet up, but TV never sleeps, so I clicked it on for a forecast, though I couldn't say why. No predictions except news of the imminent Apocalypse would change the miserable days ahead. Mackenzie would leave town, the kids would protest, Havermeyer would have small strokes, and tomorrow's dawn would bring prospective applicants to stare at me as I taught. Nonetheless, I puttered about, listening for the jolly nonsense spiel of the weatherman while I made coffee.

Meantime, I worked myself into a *Lovers Bid Farewell!* mood. I saw the letters in white on a black backdrop in a silent film. My man was flying off while I waved my hankie and wept, discreetly.

I enjoyed wallowing in the image, although my socks and fuzzy bedroom slippers, the aroma of the coffee, Mackenzie's absentminded whistle-and-hum as he tossed toiletries into his suitcase, the chatter of the TV, and the tangle of my morning hair made it a difficult fantasy to sustain. We needed a train platform, steam billowing, possibly a fine rain as well.

Mackenzie's biggest fan did not require props. Macavity the cat knew something was different about the morning routine, and to an archconservative feline, different means bad. Mackenzie sat down to drink coffee and Macavity plunked himself on the chair next to him. Over the oak table's surface, the cat stared without blinking at his now-suspicious idol.

"If looks could kill," Mackenzie said. " 'Pussycat sits on a chair/Implacably with acid stare. . . .' "

"Tell me you made that up," I said. "Please."

"Can't. It's from a poem by Edward Horn. Seemed appropriate."

By a remarkable act of will, I said nothing. Not about that and not about the idea that if he were going to spout poetry before dawn, it should be about my eyes, not a cat's. But smart-ass reactions to literary show-offs did not fit the goodbye-at-the-railroad-station scenario. I went to brush my hair. Which is what I was doing when Mackenzie kissed the tip of my nose and said he had to get moving. I had offered to drive him to the airport, but he wanted his car there. It wasn't a farewell fraught with glamour, waving goodbye at an elevator door. And in the background, the weatherman admitted this wasn't going to be the best of all possible days, which I already knew without studying meteorology.

It was too early to go to school, but too late to go back to bed. So while the news team recited traffic reports, I made much of washing our coffee cups and deciding what I would have for my solitary dinner, and then I gave up and began dressing. Given that pleasant yesterday had apparently been a tease, and March was reverting to the "winds doth blow" mode, I decided on a light blue turtleneck under my blazer. Almost the color of Mackenzie's eyes. When he was gone, I felt at loose ends and slightly deserted, which was ridiculous, but true. I didn't like the sensation of being incomplete when by myself. Not at all. Living with someone was getting to me, and not in altogether favorable ways.

My mind once again circled the pros and cons of cohabitation, a subject that deserved a better hour and fully activated brain cells. On about my third mental trip around the issue, I realized that the anchor's voice had dropped into a solemnly alarmed register, the timbre that signals a Big Story. And Big Stories are always bad news.

"There's been a tragic end to a conflict we've been monitoring." His co-anchor erased her smile and nodded gravely. "Just yesterday," he continued, "this station was preparing a special in-depth Roundtable Report—"

Tragic. Roundtable. Yesterday. A hammer banged my ear. From inside.

"—to be broadcast Saturday as part of our ongoing—"

I took several deep breaths. That did nothing except produce hyperventilation.

"This morning, police are left wondering whether a conflict over freedom of speech may have escalated all the way to homicide."

I had been edging toward the set while he spoke. Now I sat down on the sofa and waited. One of us, one of the people in the greenroom—was dead. Murdered.

"This is the sight that greeted police late last night." The clip showed a flaming bundle, the twin of the effigy outside Glamorgan. The anchor's voice rode over the image. " . . . at first seemed another 'guerrilla bonfire' as the Moral Ecologists call these staged events, even while disclaiming personal responsibility for . . ."

They'd killed this time, crossed the line and murdered someone. It had seemed inevitable the night of the Roederers' party, and yet now, it seemed inconceivable that anyone would kill over the right to speak freely.

"But what Radnor Township police found late last evening was not an effigy but a body—"

75

Radnor, where the Roederers lived? They killed one of the Roederers? *Killed* to punish them for perceived immorality?

Neddy. I thought of the Trashman effigy the night of the party, of the raging hatred Harvey Spiers had breathed in the green-room the day before. The man was like a dog with its fangs in Roederer's calf. And now, in his throat. I felt ill, fearful that I had unwittingly started a ball rolling toward Neddy Roederer's murder by involving him in our library's future, which in turn led to the fund-raiser, which produced the first face-to-face between those two men.

"—wrapped in layers of cloth in order, police theorize, to resemble the symbolic bodies burned as protests. But this was not symbolic. Inside the wrapper was a human being." He paused, listening, I suspected, to the voice in his earpiece. Something else had happened. His eyes widened before he resumed his neutral face.

"Radnor Township police have just now released the identity of the victim," he said. "He is the Reverend Harvey Spiers, leader of and spokesperson for the Moral Ecologists, the same protest group that has lately . . ."

I found myself looking around the room, as if some other presence would validate that I'd misheard. Harvey Spiers?

Burned as if in effigy? Hoist with his own petard? But why? By whom?

"Preliminary autopsy results indicate that the victim was dead by strangulation before he was immolated, but at this time, police are unwilling to comment on motives or suspects, nor have any charges been made."

"You think the Roederers could have had anything to do with . . ." I was talking to an enormous but empty room, except for the cat, who apparently had no opinion.

Besides I didn't think the Roederers had anything to do with it. They weren't the type—elegant madcap stranglers?—and they didn't need to resort to violence. They could move away if they were uncomfortable. Another gift of wealth.

". . . further details as they are released. And now, in another fire story, but with a more positive note," the female anchor said, "people are cheering a valiant cat named Scarlett who yesterday returned to a burning building five times, each time to save one of her kittens. At last report, Mama was singed but with a good prognosis, and her kittens were safe and sound."

The screen was filled with a shot of a bandaged and seared cat. Heartrending, although the segue had been in the worst taste. But even with burned flesh as the link, this was an "up" sort of story. A demagogue had been strangled, then strung up and burned, but we weren't to think about it for a second longer.

I saluted the heroic cat, but I felt bad. Very. Even Harvey Spiers deserved a full moment of reflection. I turned off the set and slumped onto the sofa, still holding my pantyhose.

Harvey Spiers loomed over me, charred and smoking. I was amazed by his mortality and by the ironic method of his murder, and wondered what it meant to the other people who'd been in the greenroom.

Could Jake now go back to Canada if he still wanted to?

Would this protect the Widow Spiers and her funds so that she could more easily spend them on her son and a better life?

Would Mother Vivien exult in having lost her competitor and threat?

Without the reverend on his case, would Havermeyer relent about the books, and would that end the demonstrations?

Would Neddy Roederer let Griffin remain at Philly Prep and restore the grant? Would Jake stay in favor with the family, keep his closest friend?

Every possibility that had come into my mind was positive. A whole lot of people would be happier because Spiers was dead, and no one would be truly sorrowful.

Which was the saddest epitaph I could imagine. He'd lived in vain.

It also meant, no matter how I felt about them or their characters, any of the above could have killed him.

Sadder still.

DESPITE THE EDGE of rawness in the wind, the pavement in front of school was, as always lately, a solid mass of humanity. But

77

today the decibel level was lower. Then I saw the reason. Haver-meyer and the Roederers stood on the front steps. The Roederers looked ravaged, although their clothing was happy enough. Tea wore a green velvet coat and matching hat, like a feminine Robin Hood. And Neddy's topcoat looked woven of heather. But their tightly controlled expressions and body language didn't match their ensembles. I wondered why they were here, given their righteous anger with the school. Havermeyer himself looked as wrung out as a puffy-faced, self-important poppet could. Was all of this to do with the death of Harvey Spiers?

My headmaster repeated a request for silence three times be-fore most of the talk subsided. This was the first time since my innocent first day at the school that I actually wanted to hear what he had to say. Mostly, to figure out why the Roederers were with him. Besides, I had no real choice. The door directly behind the trio was the only route into the school on this side of the building. I could push them aside and enter, or make a fuss get-ting around the crowd and to the back door. Or I could listen.

Havermeyer cleared his throat half a dozen times. "I wish first of all to say something that is not related to the announcement I had prepared. Boys and girls, a terrible thing has happened. Jake Ulrich's stepfather, Harvey Spiers, whom some of you have come to . . . know . . . of late, was the victim of a foul and fatal crime last night, and on behalf of all of his son's classmates and faculty, we wish to extend our condolences to his family."

I noticed the careful wording. More coherent than was usual for my principal, but quite skillful in skirting any false expression of loss or grief and expressing only sympathy for the victim's family.

There was a buzz of whispers as those who'd flicked on the morning news shared details about the manner in which the deceased had reached that state.

Havermeyer looked in extreme distress, and the Roederers appeared to vibrate with barely controlled rage or fatigue, or a combination of the two. They said something to the headmaster and his alarm visibly escalated as he shook his head. I thought I lip-read him asking them to "Stay, please stay."

It took Havermeyer four more requests until the noise again subsided. "I wish this morning," he said, "to publicly acknowledge that with the best of intentions, in an attempt to ameliorate a degenerating, inflammatory, and, I thought, potentially damaging, possibly dangerous, situation, I nonetheless unintentionally made a conceivably grave error."

His audience blankly sifted through his syllables. Somebody abstracted the message and said in a stage whisper, "Hey! He's apologizing!" This was greeted with applause.

Were we supposed to believe this announcement had nothing to do with the one that preceded it?

The Roederers seemed uninterested in both Harvey Spiers' death and Havermeyer's mea culpa. Neddy Roederer appeared absorbed in his own thoughts, his head tilted away from the crowd, as if listening to inner voices. Tea looked exhausted, with dark circles beneath her somewhat puffy eyes, and peeved— perhaps by being coerced into this ceremony, the purpose of which still confused me.

Havermeyer raised, then lowered, his arms. The applause died down. "I have therefore," he continued, "returned to our library the collection that was part of what is known as the Roederer Grant—"

Sakes alive. I thought they'd rescinded it. How desperate was this man? Would he *kill* to keep his school attractive to applicants, get his tiny empire out of jeopardy?

The thing was, I couldn't imagine Maurice Havermeyer doing anything as direct and to the point as murder. It was his nature to fuddle, fester, circle, hem and haw. To bore somebody to death. But to assert himself definitively—and a deliberate, premeditated murder is surely an assertion—seemed emotionally impossible.

At the news that the books were being returned, the students applauded again, but Havermeyer plowed on resolutely. It wasn't like him to minimize whatever rare burst of adulation came his way. Therefore, it seemed that despite his verbosity, he hadn't yet made his point, and I suspected that it would have nothing to do with the First Amendment.

"—and this action therefore negates the necessity for further

79

public demonstrations, as they are now without foundation and cause."

And there we had the point. The students directly in front of me looked at each other in search of interpretation, and then turned to me. "He means go back to class," I translated. "There's nothing left to protest."

How quickly we'd disposed of Harvey Spiers, though his after-image still swung above me, hovering low and casting chilly shadows.

The students moved toward the building as slowly as possible. Havermeyer gestured toward the door. The Roederers gave tight shakes of the head. With a few unanswered parting words—I was certain they were begging words—Havermeyer reentered his fiefdom. The Roederers stepped down from the entryway to make way for the students. I found it peculiar that they had come in from the suburbs for the announcement, but would not deign to enter the building.

I looked across the street at the Square, but the Moral Ecologists, presumably in mourning, were not standing across the way like ghouls. Except for one, the round one in the Russian hat, he who'd turned his back to me the day before. Now, seeing me watch him, he ducked behind a tree. My inner alarm bell went off—why was he here? Was he a Moral Ecologist at all? We'd have to check out anyone acting so strangely, lurking near a school.

The Roederers nodded at me so I paused. "I'm glad he changed his mind," I said, hoping they'd tell me whether they, too, had changed their minds.

Tea didn't seem eager for small talk. Her smile was the bare minimum required for civility. Her nod had probably been meant to suffice.

"Things have gone entirely too far." Neddy peered at me intently, as if I would understand his meaning, but I wasn't sure I did. "This has gotten out of hand."

"The demonstration?" I asked.

"Edward," Tea said. "Really." She looked at him, then at me. I felt put in my place—not somebody to whom confidences should be made. Not their peer.

"But not anymore," I answered him. "Now that the books will be returned—"

"All the same," Neddy said. "In the wake of the death of that . . ." He shook his head, as if unwilling to put the shape of the man's name in his mouth.

"Reverend Spiers?" I asked, and when he nodded, so did I. "Awful. But I can't believe that was why Dr. Havermeyer—"

"So much fuss. Your Dr. Havermeyer stirred things up. A TV special. Escalated everything, that show, going public with grievances, putting antagonists face to face. Things spin on, intensify . . ."

"Edward," Tea said again. I didn't blame her. He was falling apart. She looked at me. "We came in to take care of the loose ends of Griffin's transfer, pick up his records, because we're off to visit schools the next few days. We didn't realize we'd be ambushed and involved in his announcement. Neddy is quite shaken by it. But rather than say things have gone too far, I would say it's a matter of too little, too late."

Neddy looked at her with the same alarm I felt. Was she dismissing Spiers' murder as insignificant and belated?

She looked from one to the other of us. "The *book* thing," she said. "Frankly, I'm sick of the whole library issue, of the pressures on all the libraries and the curriculum by ignorant people. We tried to do a good thing . . ."

I always forgot her odd pronunciation, the occasional rough edges, the way she added a syllable and made the word *liberary*, or dropped one and turned *tried to* into *tryda*. I wondered again who had taught her English, or whether this was an affectation, slightly Bertie Wooster, like Lord Peter Wimsey's *ain't*.

But this wasn't the time to ponder linguistic quirks. I had enough on my plate getting ready for tomorrow's critical visitors, particularly since almost half my classes hadn't met—except on the pavement—for two days, and they were sure to capitalize on that with bluster. I was positive there'd be general amnesia as to what their last assignment had been.

Feeble but mean-spirited flurries began. I bade farewell to the Roederers, and turned to face the day.

Instead, I faced Griffin Roederer barreling into me. I fell down onto the pavement. "Sorry," he said, helping me up. "I came down the steps too fast, slippery patch there. I didn't mean—"

His father rushed over and took my arm. I felt like a behemoth as they tried to right me.

"Jeez," Griffin said. He blushed a painful-looking cerise. "I guess I wasn't looking. I'm so—you okay?"

I nodded and brushed the front of my coat. Only my pride had been bruised.

"Griffin!" his mother said, and after another burst of apologies, he went over to her.

Neddy Roederer still held my arm. "I'm fine," I assured him. "Truly. Thanks."

He didn't release his grip. "Miss Pepper," he said, his voice so low, it was almost inaudible. "Do you think Caleb could spare me a minute?"

"Who?"

"Your friend, the police officer."

Oh, mercy. Caleb Mackenzie, indeed. "Yes?" I asked.

"Would you know how I could get in touch with him?" He spoke still more rapidly. "Privately. I need information, professional advice, and seeing you reminded me of him. Do you know his phone number, or where he lives?"

The phone was listed under my last name. Having his number go public was the last thing Mackenzie would want, but I couldn't see the harm in this. "Want me to write it down?" I said, scrabbling in my purse.

"Just tell me," Neddy Roederer whispered. "Now. I have a good memory for numbers." He leaned close as I spoke.

Tea advanced on us, looking at me oddly. I'd been having a tête-à-tête with her husband and it was not seemly. "Sorry to interrupt the two of you, but we need to talk, Neddy."

"Were you able to hear me?" I asked him.

"Yes." His tone was sharp as he turned away from me, toward

his wife. He lost his gloss under stress. Havermeyer, Griffin, all too much.

"Goodbye, then," I said.

He looked surprised that I was still there.

What was that about? An aristocratic dismissal, or a sign of mental illness, something more egalitarian and strange?

The bell rang. No time. Like the Scarletts—cat and O'Hara—I'd think about this tomorrow.

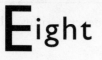ight

"I T is when the gods hate a man with uncommon abhor-
rence that they drive him into the profession of a school-
master." Alex Fry grinned.

Too apt to be acceptable. I shook my head and poured myself a
cup of disgusting coffee.

"Hey," he said, "I thought you'd like it. Been saving it for you
'cause it's literary. I didn't make it up. Seneca did, two thousand
years ago. That is what is known as the wisdom of the ages."

Four minutes until homeroom began. I sat down in a wing
chair I was sure had been salvaged from a vacant lot. "Did Seneca
teach math?" I asked.

"Seneca taught Nero. Until Nero grew tired of him and ordered the teacher to take his own life. At least our students don't demand that we commit suicide. We do it of our own free will here, and that's what I love about this country."

I shook my head again. Alex does that to me, gives me a mild palsy. I finished my coffee, and as he again proposed that we run away together, and detailed how we'd fill our time, I excused myself.

"Jake!" I said, when I saw him in the hallway. "I thought—I didn't expect to see you here to—"

"She said I didn't understand her grief." He walked upstairs with me. "She just about accused me of having ruined her life, and of killing Harvey, so I left. Maybe I'll go home later. Maybe not."

I unlocked my door and ushered him in.

He looked dazed. The shadow of Harvey was on him, too.

"I'm sorry," I said, as I entered. "Sorry," I repeated as I emptied my briefcase and readied the room. "I know you didn't care for him, but his death is nonetheless traumatic to your mother and your life."

I could have been whistling, or pressing my nose into the board for all he noticed. "That thing I told you?" he asked.

"Which thing?" I meanwhile checked that I had paper. This wasn't the morning to beg Helga for supplies. To my relief, I was safe.

"Yesterday. About"—he leaned close—"Harvey. And the Trash-man. What he was going to do, you know? Blackmail?" Jake, standing still, looked as if he were spinning with tension.

I felt some of it myself. Of course. Yesterday. The question I'd deferred, and now . . .

"Do I have to—should I—" He took a deep breath. "Harvey's *dead*. Do the police have to know? Should they? My mother—she's—as soon as the police left, she goes, 'Don't tell, don't tell.' She didn't say about what, but I knew. But if it made somebody murder him, wouldn't she want the police to know?"

The tendons of his neck stood out. He was tall and broad-shouldered, but he looked brittle.

"She's ashamed." He paced the room as he spoke. "She wants his memory kept clean. That's how she puts it. Says there's no reason to stir up a fuss. What should I do?"

"Did the reverend follow through with his threats?" I asked. "The talk and bluster may not have gone any further. Did he say anything to Neddy Roederer?"

Jake shrugged. "There was the business at the TV station yesterday. That was harsh."

Yes, but also inconclusive. More suggestive than concrete. "It felt like generic name-calling, to tell the truth," I said. "What about after?"

He shook his head slowly. "I took my mom home, dropped her off. She let me have the car. Harvey went to a meeting. With Mother Vivien. My mom told me Harvey was getting rid of Vivien, kicking her out of the group. Said she was the past and he was the future."

Showed how much anybody knows. He was the one who became history that night.

"It could have been Vivien, don't you see?" Jake said. "She has a temper. She knows how the burnings work. She could do it— she could get people to light the fire, do the dirty work once she wrapped the body up and got it to hang. They'd think it was another dummy, a heavy one, wouldn't they?"

"You've given this a lot of thought," I said. All to direct suspicion away from his mother, who sounded like a woman with no alibi and a whole lot of anger about her husband's behavior. It wouldn't serve her claims of being the happiest of brides if the police knew that in addition to his beating her and having a flagrant affair, Harvey was dragging his wife into something she found as repugnant as blackmail. And did we have any outside source to verify that Harvey and his honey were splitting up?

"What should I do?" Jake asked again.

"I need to think about it." Déjà vu all over again. I'd asked for time yesterday as well, and for the same question. Only now, one of the people involved was dead.

Was it worth it to raise an issue that was irrelevant—unless, of course, Neddy Roederer had found it so relevant he resorted to murder? But if he hadn't, this would needlessly smear his name, create suspicion where it didn't belong.

I needed Mackenzie's sane approach. He didn't dither over moral issues. He looked, he saw, he comprehended.

I missed him with all the poignancy of that old-movie heroine on the train platform. Except they don't make movies about a heroine yearning for her man's ability to make speedy ethical calls. Oh, I missed him other ways, too.

But whatever I wanted of Mackenzie was far away, and I was here with Jake, all elbows and ears, and visibly disappointed with my evasiveness. As well he might be. Still, with a flare of resentment, I wished he'd stop coming to *me* for Big Answers. The flare subsided. I was available, nonhysterical, and his friend. It wasn't so much that he'd chosen me as that he had no options.

"I am honestly afraid to rush into a decision on this," I said. "If you tell, then your mother's going to be miserable and so will the Roederers, and most likely to no purpose. What if we wait a few hours and see what the police come up with before we decide." Let the killer be Mother Vivien and let her be caught, tried, and convicted by sundown, I silently begged. And while you're at it, disband the group, let no one succeed her as leader.

Jake looked as if he had plenty to say in response to my nonanswer, none of it complimentary. But living with his mother and stepfather had undoubtedly trained him to stifle his thoughts, and he did so now. "Am I still writing the article, then?" he asked, his tone bitter. "The one about this whole business? The grant and the picketing and everything? Griffin has the photos, even though they're sending him away. It'll be his last article. So can we at least do it?"

All his bottled-up disappointment leaked into that *at least*, and I deserved it. I also needed to ignore it. "If you still want to," I said. "It could be awkward for you."

"Everything's awkward for me! I don't know—"

We were interrupted by Edie Friedman, calling, "Yoo-hoo!" Nobody outside of comic books, except Edie, says that. With her springy step, and the set of her shoulders, she had been born to be a gym teacher. Probably arrived on this planet with a whistle on a string around her neck. "Did you catch the news?" she asked. "Last night?" She glanced at Jake without recognition. Sports tend to break down according to sex, and Edie favors coaching girls, particularly after the courts decided that forcing students to shower after gym violated their privacy and was an infringement of their civil rights.

The boys had taken this ruling to heart, and thereafter had not taken to the showers. Edie had avoided any close contact with them since. I wish I could do the same.

I, too, am for civil rights. That's what the ruckus with the Moral Ecologists was about. But all the same, I feel—as does Edie—that a teacher's civil rights should be considered as a part of the whole. I invite the Supreme Court to visit my classroom on a hot day after modest young men finished gym and refrained from washing. Those judges would reverse their decision on the spot. If they could breathe deeply enough to speak.

"I saw you," I said.

She smiled. That's what she'd needed to establish. She'd been on TV and she'd been seen. Then she made a face of mock-disgust and waved away my words, as if I'd said something flattering instead of simple fact. "I looked like a tank! TV adds so much weight, I could have died when I saw myself!"

My turn to wave away her words. "Don't be—" but she was already bouncing off on her expensive running shoes. It was comforting to know that some things never change, and Edie was one of them. Her thrill at having been on the air was in no way tarnished by the murder of the man who'd caused the demonstration. The important thing was how she looked.

Think of the Edies throughout history, missing the point as they worried whether they'd worn the right toga while Rome burned, fretted over frayed gloves for the Boston Tea Party, or brooded about whether their bonnets were giving them hat hair at Gettysburg.

Jake sighed heroically. I turned back to him.

"Does your father know what happened?" I asked. "And do you think your mother might move back up there now?"

"She said no," he answered me. "First thing this morning—she screamed it, really. Said she was staying where Harvey was going to be buried." He shook his head, bewildered by her, as was I.

"And your father?"

"I e-mailed him. I'm sure I'll hear soon."

"Keep him posted." It was something for me to say, for him to do, not something to hope would yield results. "Let him know your mother could use emotional support."

His nod belonged to a person much older than the boy reporter he'd been all year. "Maybe I shouldn't write that story. It'd be biased. How did everything fall apart all at once? Even Griffin's being sent away—"

"His parents don't seem willing to change their minds about pulling him out. I thought, given the reversal of policy . . ."

"It wasn't ever about that. That was an excuse. Griffin and them, they don't . . . they aren't . . . they make each other miserable."

"You said the Roederers were nice people. That they didn't hassle the two of you."

"They don't. And they are. But they don't get along with Griffin. Not on purpose, just . . . because. You know, he came to live with them when he was pretty old. He isn't really adopted. They couldn't. His mother would see him just enough, every few years, so the law said he couldn't be adopted away. So there were a lot of foster homes. The Roederers knew all that, but if he does anything—normal things—they act like they got a bad seed and they do something rotten back. Like this, like sending him to boarding school. Might as well be reform school. Why does he have to go away, even if they want him out of here? It's like he just didn't work out, so too bad, get rid of him, but not so people notice. Maybe so they can move again, like this round's over, game finished, give back the toys. Maybe Philadelphia and Griffin bore them now."

"You make the Roederers sound much meaner than you have in the past," I said.

He shrugged. "They're changing. Everything annoys them. Yesterday, at the TV station, they acted like I was committing a crime, getting out of line when I asked for the tape for my dad, did you see? Like anything you do that isn't according to their plan is wrong. And this is mean, what they're doing, isn't it? Sending him away? Like he hasn't been in enough weird places already?" He shrugged again. "They're strung out—Harvey made them that way—and they need a quieter kid. They don't like to pay much attention, you know? Lots of times, the only way we know they're home is if Margaret tells us."

"Who?"

"The housekeeper. She's there, and the maids or the cook, but mostly that's all. Like they got him and then they didn't know what to do with him."

Jake sounded terminally glum. Poor kid had too much to carry. I would have suggested that he reconsider going home, but I was afraid Betsy's bullheaded hysteria would be the proverbial straw on Jake's back. I checked my watch. I didn't have a first-period class today. My ninth graders were off with their general science class on a trip to the College of Physicians and Surgeons. More precisely, to the Mutter Medical Museum, where they'd been promised such sights as Grover Cleveland's cancerous jawbone, skeletons of a giant and a dwarf, a collection of swallowed objects extracted from people's stomachs, and the liver shared by Chang and Eng Bunker, the nineteenth-century Siamese twins. The science teacher had given me a list so that I could use this trip as a writing exercise. Yech. Their teacher, drumming up enthusiasm for a "Scientific Philadelphia" trek, had mentioned the Mutter in passing, and had sparked such interest that he felt obliged to take them there. Who knew what might jump-start a future research scientist? I myself had become intrigued when the teacher told me that Cleveland's jawbone had been replaced by a rubber one in a secret operation aboard a ship. The press never knew. I imagined what the paparazzi and tabloid shows would have made of that today.

In any case, I had a free period in which to plan and catch up—and worry about how my missing class would be tomorrow, while we were being observed. But Jake was not free. It was time for him to get going.

I pointed at my watch. "Why don't we make our decisions during journalism class? If you decide to stick around." That gave me till the end of the day, although I don't know what I hoped for in the interim. A search of the Internet for www.the-answers-to-everything?

There was no hope or expectation in Jake's nod, and his stride as he left was aged and defeated. I had to come up with something. And in fact, I already knew what it would be. I should have said it right away. As irrelevant as it might be and as damaging as it could be, Jake had to tell because it might turn out not to be irrelevant at all.

That's what Mackenzie would have said. He was becoming my conscience, my Jiminy Cricket. Was that normal? Healthy? Sane?

I walked down to the office to belatedly pick up my mail. There were, sooner than expected, flyers full of warnings and admonitions from Dr. H. No references to the recent strike were to be made! No class writing while being observed! Three Important Ideas: Activity! Energy! A Positive Impression of Philly Prep!

One for my eyes only: Miss Pepper—the inflammatory statement by Mark Twain is still on your board!!

I chucked the flyers. I refused to associate with that many exclamation points. As I walked toward the faculty room for another cup of coffee, I felt a whisper of a touch on my shoulder, and I half turned to face the Latin teacher, Caroline Finney. "My dear," she said, "isn't it terrible?"

Apprehension chilled me. It was not like Caroline to risk being late for class for the sake of gossipy commiseration.

"Were you as troubled as I when you heard the news about Reverend Spiers?" she asked in a quiet tone.

I couldn't answer that, as she knew, so I waited.

"Because of Jake," she said even more quietly.

I turned her words over, looked at them from the other side. "You mean because Reverend Spiers was his stepfather?"

She raised her eyebrows.

I plowed on. "I'm worried where he'll go now. His mother seems incapable of functioning on her own, and his father—"

Caroline tilted her head and regarded me with piercing blue eyes. I felt like one of her students, suddenly transparent, all my mental potholes visible. "No, dear," she said. "I mean because of what he . . . Amanda, I'm afraid that if you haven't already done so, I'm going to notify the police."

I'd just had this conversation with Jake, but she didn't know about Spiers' threatened blackmail. "Why?"

"About Jake, dear. Perhaps even if you have already done so. To corroborate, you know."

"Why would I have?"

"Ah," she said. "So you haven't. Pity. I'm a bit intimidated by them, you see, and given that you have familiarity with them, I had hoped . . ."

"Please, Caroline, I need you to explain." I thought of Jake, of the world that kept closing in on him, and a fear as painful as strep rose in my throat.

She inhaled, shook her head, and exhaled. "I was there, you know. In your room borrowing chalk while he was talking."

I got it. But I didn't want it, so I refused acceptance, as if being obtuse and stubborn would stonewall Caroline Finney, when nothing I knew of ever had.

"He said he wished Harvey Spiers was dead."

"No, not really. Whatever he said was talk. You know adolescents, what they say versus what they mean. You can't possibly think—"

"He said that better people were killed all the time, even children, that he could go back to Canada if his stepfather were dead, that his life would be better—as would his mother's. Whatever the specific words, the boy was full of rage."

"He was understandably upset. He's a teenager—he exaggerates. Hyperbole, bluster, not—"

"My dear," she said gently, "I see you're nearly distraught by the thought, and I understand. I, too, am agitated about it. It's a moral dilemma. I'm also fond of Jake and, in truth, I was not at all fond of his stepfather."

"He's had such a rough time," I said. But in my head, a whirl-wind deafening me, was the image of Jake hoisting his loathsome stepfather, the man who had him in a bear trap, who was costing him everything he held dear. Hoisting the man up over a bon-fire—and nothing that said *impossible, inconceivable.*

92

"Amanda," Caroline said, "we are a school full of the products of less than optimum parenting. Having not had children of my own, I try to keep my observations on this subject to myself. But whichever direction you'd point, you'd find a child who is neglected in some serious way. Except economically."

Griffin. Jake. Half a dozen others. And that without any conscious effort at thinking. Lousy parents, selfish parents, childish parents. You couldn't use that as an excuse around here, only as a fact of life. The exceptions were the newsworthy ones.

"If this were only about bad parenting, not murder," Caroline said.

Oh, Jake, I thought, and his name cut through me.

"I have heard," Caroline was saying, "many children make foolhardy statements, but this was different. Jake's attitude—his lack of emotion chilled me. I had a dreadful moment thinking I should do something, except I had no idea what it should be, so I talked myself out of it, told myself it was old-lady nonsense, but of course, now I'm consumed with guilt at having said and done nothing at all, and I can no longer ignore the force of those words." She looked heartsick. *"Principiis obsta; sero medicina paratur cum mala per longas convaluere moras."*

I shook my head. It had been too long since Latin I.

"Ovid," she said. "It means 'fight the disease at the start—once the symptoms develop, medicine comes too late, losing effect from delay.' I've known that wise quotation for decades. Why didn't I act on it, then?"

"He's a gentle person," I said. "His words were harsh, but he couldn't murder, Caroline. He simply could not!"

She looked even sadder, her crepe-paper skin pleated and fine around her eyes and mouth. "That decision should be left to people who do that sort of work. Meanwhile . . . I'm afraid all logic points that way. This crime required brawn and heft along with hate. Someone had to lift that body, to construct and tug on a pulley with the rope."

"Jake's all sudden growth. He's big, but he isn't that strong. Honestly." I sounded pathetic.

"He's not yet filled all the way out. That isn't the same as weak," Caroline said. "He plays soccer. He and Griffin lift weights, go biking. He told me. He is not weak."

And then I felt light-headed, wondering whether Jake's visit this morning had been honest, or an attempt to implicate Neddy Roederer, or Mother Vivien—or his own mother—anybody else, and to use me for that purpose.

How had I so quickly come to distrust the person I'd most wanted to protect? I fought a quick and urgent need to cry.

The bell rang. "I'm sorry to have upset you," Caroline said, "but I do understand. You are a person who cares about your charges, and I admire that. Unfortunately, we can't let that blind us. Times like these, situations like these, shouldn't exist. It's almost unbearable, isn't it, when doing the right thing feels dreadfully wrong?" Her voice trailed off as she turned and left.

She was wrong about one thing. The situation didn't feel almost unbearable at all. There was nothing *almost* about this.

This was, well and truly, horribly and thoroughly, unbearable.

Nine

I could barely face Jake in after-school journalism class. I grabbed a few pages out of the pile of article drafts and began proofing one, almost convincing myself I was occupied with the work of checking stories rather than buying a few more minutes and praying for inspiration. Jake wasn't going to burst into a room full of his peers and demand my instant and full attention, but sooner or later, I had to answer him.

He came in silently with Griffin, both their faces hollow-looking shells, their minds and emotions missing in action, off-limits to me. I'm sure the concept of aliens assuming human form started with an adult who had to deal with teenagers.

Given that both their situations involved humiliation by over-visible parents, and generated avid and unwholesome interest wherever they went, I understood their withdrawal. They sat near one another, presumably involved in preparing their big story; except that each time I glanced their way, they were whispering to one another. Nodding, head-shaking, shoulder-poking, debating. They looked like coconspirators. Two boys furious with their parents. One parent down.

I wished I had somebody to whisper to. I wished someone would whisper wisdom back.

What was I going to say?

The universe opted to keep its opinions to itself. I returned to the printout on the desk in front of me.

... no more than seven inches of soapy water, face down. The Web site shows photos of the suspects as well, with computerized aging, and they're a whole lot more interesting than those Have You Seen Me? flyers that come in the mail. This is more like *Unsolved Mysteries* on TV, except that since a Web site doesn't have to create a whole drama around it the way TV does, they can list a whole lot more crimes and be even more interesting.

Too many *more*s. I red-circled the last two and considered the rest. Not that I was their copyeditor, but I didn't see any harm in working with a student's writing style while I had him captive. The drowned woman felt overfamiliar.

... for example, the case of Chester Katt, whose name and the fact that he disappeared with millions of dollars (which probably left him smiling) has him nicknamed the Cheshire Cat. Chester, a balding man nobody remembers well, apparently masterminded sales of nonexistent Canadian Underwriters policies to large corporations and despite the magnitude of the crime, was never again seen and is thought to have created a false identity and name for the precise purpose of committing the crime. Or take the case of headless Gretchen of the Green Feet, whose death is tied to a silk factory where that precise shade of green was being used on a line of blouses. Why the dye was on her feet has never been explained, but her naked unmarked torso was found . . .

Old material. All of it. I felt a flare of anger—a what-does-Jake-think-he's-pulling? rush. But the real question was what I thought I'd been doing.

I was reading last month's copy. Bad enough, but it had taken me forever to comprehend the words I was reading and still longer to realize I'd read them before, including the surfeit of *more*s.

At his desk, Jake studied the paper in front of him. I suspected that its words made as much, or little, sense to him as the old column's copy had made to me.

Griffin had returned to cropping photos. Their conversation was over, because Griffin was wired to a radio on the table. He must have been listening to a news or call-in program because there was none of the usual humming, foot-tapping, or finger-jiggling of the plugged-in young.

Jake felt my glance and looked up. I smiled and nodded. He started to stand, but Griffin pulled off his earpieces and grabbed Jake's arm, whispering rapidly while handing Jake one.

Jake inserted it without pausing to wipe it off. That might be one definition of a really good friendship.

He listened, closed his eyes, and sucked in his bottom lip. After a moment, he pulled it out, handed it back to Griffin, and shook his head slowly, as if in disbelief. Then he came over to my desk.

"Sit down," I said. "Here, next to me." I waited for whatever had so dismayed him. Of course, it could have been nothing more than a losing sports score, but Jake's reaction had seemed personal and tinged with shame.

"My mother," he said. "She's talking to radio and TV stations. Crying to them. I just heard her." He looked down at the desktop and pressed his thumbnail into it, cutting a tiny channel. "They told her they were questioning Mother Vivien, and my mother called her a harlot and the Whore of Babylon and said she'd killed Harvey, as a woman scorned."

He looked haunted. When I didn't respond quickly enough, he said, "She's my *mother* and she's coming off like . . ."

Like an hysterical, self-centered jerk who never thought of how her public ranting would affect her teenaged son. Or what earthly good it would do except momentarily relieve the pressure inside her and make strangers who didn't care feel sorry for her.

Jake's bony nose and cheekbones flushed. "Why'd she have to call the TV and radio people?"

"They probably called her," I said, as if that made everything all right. I shook my head, glad that we'd passed the point where I had to give Jake any opinion of his mother or her actions.

"She—Mother Vivien—called us early this morning. I mean, Harvey hadn't been dead but a few hours. She wants our house. The Moral Ecologists own it. She said we couldn't live there anymore. And my mother just told the entire world that, too." He closed his eyes. "Like I want everybody to know I'll be homeless soon."

I cleared my throat. "Jake," I said. "I promised to talk with you about—"

But Griffin walked over and waited next to the desk. "Yes?" I asked. "What's up?"

"Mind if I cut out early, Miz P.? I could crop those shots next time and print the ones from this morning. There's a whole lot of other stuff I have to do."

Jake, who'd seemed lost in private thoughts, swiveled. "Hey, man, you said we'd talk more first, that you wouldn't go ahead—"

Griffin waved him off. "No problem," he said, still with that vague smile. "It's under control, so chill." He looked at me and grinned. Griffin was not a grinner. "Jake likes to worry, doesn't he?" He sounded mildly amused. Griffin wasn't one to utter an unnecessary word to a teacher, either.

He was conning me. Playing the role of a hail-fellow-well-met regular guy. But why? What were the two of them hiding? "It's okay," I said. "Do what works for you." Journalism, an elective, is a loose after-school activity. No need to be rigid.

Jake sent one final, fiercely emphatic glare and shook his head, *No!* Then, after catching my eye, he focused down on the desk, at the canyon his thumbnail was digging.

"What's . . ." I began. "You guys need to talk to one another?"

Jake kept his head bowed.

Griffin looked at him, then at me. "Not necessary." Another smile. Why start with the happy face now, close to the end of his stay here, facing virtual exile? "It's like this," he said to me. "I have to do stuff for my parents. I promised to help them, and they're waiting. Jake's disappointed—he wanted to do something together."

Definitely a con. Griffin's parents were out of town looking at boarding schools. Tea Roederer had told me so.

"Griffin, I haven't had a chance to say how much we'll—I'll miss you. I'm really sorry you're transferring."

"Not as sorry as I am," he said, but his expression remained slightly benign. "I'm not the boarding-school type."

"You'll be a big asset to whatever newspaper they produce," I said. "And a major loss to ours."

"Thanks. Whatever." He shrugged.

Jake continued to watch him, his features tight with concern.

"So . . ." Griffin said. *"Adiós."* He left the room.

"Maybe you should head home, too, Jake," I said softly. "It must be hard to concentrate and your mother probably needs you." And a muzzle. "I've given your situation thought." That sounded adult and considered, almost judicial. It suggested contemplative retreats in paneled studies, with considerations of precedent, and it bore no relationship to the moth-thoughts that had fluttered in meaningless confusion through my brain all day.

As a child I believed that wisdom was a secondary sex characteristic, guaranteed to develop to some degree, like breasts, after puberty. My failure to achieve anything akin to it was one of the bad surprises of real life.

"If what you've told me is true, Jake, if you're sure that's what you heard, positive it was said precisely that way—"

"I know what I heard. Jeez. Don't you believe me?"

"Of course I do."

"Then why're you—"

I stopped this detour. "Sorry." I'd sounded as legalistic and quibbling as a shyster lawyer. I had to be braver about this. More straightforward. "I think—even though we don't know whether your—the reverend—ever spoke to Mr. Roederer, and despite the possible harm to innocent people—" I could not stand hearing myself! Maurice Havermeyer was speaking through my mouth, using me like a ventriloquist's dummy. "Tell the police," I said. "Let them decide if it's relevant or not."

He looked at me bleakly, his features immobile. After what felt like a long time, he nodded. I could almost feel his marrow dissolve in exhaustion. There'd been the long fatigue of divorce and separation, followed by pretending that out-of-sight, out-of-mind didn't apply to his long-distance dad. The battle with Harvey, the consistent unreliability of his mother, and now the escalating consequences of her second husband's death.

I hated to add to that bone- and soul-weariness, but he needed to be warned. "One other thing." I took a deep breath. "You should be aware that Miss Finney overheard you express, um, serious hostility to your stepfather on Monday. While you were in my room, before homeroom. Remember?"

He shook his head, then shrugged. I was sure he remembered why he'd come into my room, but not the words his discomfort had produced. He waited, visibly confused about where I was headed with this. I hated what I had to say and kept looking for loops and detours.

To Jake's blank expression was now added exasperation and impatience. *"And?"* he prompted.

"I know it was nothing more than talk, Jake. Blowing off steam. I'll speak on your behalf about it, I promise you, but—"

"Speak on my behalf? About what? Harvey?" Silence for a moment, and then, "You can't be serious. She thinks I killed him?"

I sucked in my lips, as if forbidding them to compound this with more words. "Not necessarily. But maybe."

"Why would she?"

"Because you said people got killed all the time and why not him. Things like that."

"Wait." He stood up. When he was sitting, and close to my eye level, I always forgot how tall he was. "Why are you telling me this?" He loomed over me, his hands in tight fists.

Say no, I silently pleaded. Say you wouldn't, couldn't have because it'd be wrong. Say no.

Instead, he said, "She heard me shoot off my mouth and she took it seriously. Is there more?"

I nodded and stood up, but at six-two, he had a solid six inches on me. While my new position felt more equitable than facing his fists had, we were nonetheless not seeing eye-to-eye anymore. Not metaphorically or literally.

"What?" he asked, although I was sure he knew.

"She, like you, feels that what she heard may be relevant to the case and that she therefore has a duty to tell the police. About you."

He stared at me, his mouth half-open, the metalwork of his braces glinting incongruously.

He was a boy. Tall, broad-shouldered, man-shaped, but nonetheless, a boy. "I told you," I said. "I'm in your corner. You can rely on me. I'll be more than glad to speak on your behalf, to go make a statement now."

He looked at me bleakly. I could almost hear his unarticulated thoughts. Or maybe they weren't his at all. Maybe they were the sound of the air currents around us, of how it was. Or of my own pulse, the inside of my mind.

"Anytime," I repeated. "I promise."

But I ached for him. My feeble promises were not nearly enough to make up for the repeated insults that he had been and was still being dealt. All term I'd wanted to rescue him, but nothing I could do was enough to compensate for the tiny kernel of doubt that even I held.

It was not enough. But it was all I knew how to do.

I WAS JUMPY and melancholy all evening, unable to concentrate on any one task for long. The loft felt fine as long as I knew

Mackenzie would ultimately be home to boom around in separate syncopation, fill it up, soften its distant corners, provide motion and color. That was not true tonight.

I went over tomorrow's lessons to be certain they were observer-worthy, but lost interest halfway through and didn't care whether that happened to my visitors as well. I tried watching sitcoms, but they were reruns, even though it was only March. There was a new and unfathomable programming theory, as far as I could tell, making viewing a game show, the object of which was to guess which week a new episode would be shown. I didn't want to play.

I read for an hour, the words sliding off each page as I turned it. I wished Sasha were not so consumed with Dr. Perfection and that I was out with her, enjoying human companionship. "I am seriously bored," I told Macavity.

He stalked off. Another country heard from. "I'm sorry," I protested. But the truth was, his snoozing was also a rerun and not sufficiently entertaining.

I paced. Tidied things that were not messy. Relocated objects and stood back to test the effect. I considered the tall windows facing the street, their plain shades. Window treatments. There was a boring topic that could occupy a lot of time. Mackenzie's shades were stark and institutional, near-clones of those in my classroom. I didn't like lowering them because then the street side of the loft looked blank, as if its eyes had been blinded.

Nonetheless, I needed to enclose this too-large space that made me feel vulnerable and exposed. I went over and looked down at the street, several stories below, to see what was happening in the greater world.

And saw a man happening. That man. The one who'd been across from school too often. The shy lurker. The round one with a pale face that stared up at me. His head, covered by the Russian-style hat, ducked quickly.

Coincidence, I reassured my suddenly quaking self. He happened to be around here and he stopped and unkinked his neck muscles. He hadn't really been looking up here. It wasn't me he'd been watching from the Square, or now. After I'd repeated the idea several times—and lowered the shades all the way—I half believed myself.

By the time Mackenzie called, I once again had turned the TV on, waiting for updates on Harvey Spiers' murder, fearing I might see Jake or Neddy Roederer being hauled off in handcuffs.

I muted the set and wandered around the loft with the cordless phone, listening to C. K. offer the unsurprising news that he would not be home tonight as hoped. Even in Kansas, red tape could hog-tie a man, hairs could be split, and insignificant clerical errors could delay the extradition of a multiple murderer.

He asked about Spiers, whose manner of death had been sufficiently grotesque and innovative to win it national coverage.

I transmitted what little I knew, pacing and talking. Touching pieces of furniture as I passed, as if their constancy and stolid reliability turned them into talismans.

And every time I was near the front wall, I peeked outside, through the side of the shade. The Russian hat was nowhere to be seen. He'd been a symptom of my jumpiness.

"Roederer," Mackenzie said. "You'll see."

"Vivien is the prime suspect, but Jake, oh Lord . . ." I updated him on that fog-filled possibility, which led us to the issue of Jake's telling the police about Harvey's blackmail threats.

Mackenzie's ethical system was shaped around the letters of the law and didn't include many shades of gray. It differed in subtle ways from Caroline Finney's, but like hers, it was clear-edged and definitive. I wanted his take on Jake's obligations.

"Absolutely," Mackenzie said. "He has to tell them. Just 'cause somebody loves books doesn't mean he can't kill. Especially when facing the threat of prison."

"Come on. That was Harvey Spiers' craziness talking. Has anybody since Oscar Wilde gone to prison for sexual preference?"

"How about scandal, then? How about having his wife—the one with the money—find out about extramarital affiliations? How about the possibility of deadly viruses?"

"Neddy Roederer is not the murdering type. He has good

values. Even just the news of it—he looked ravaged this morning."

"You sure it was the news? Or fatigue? Or remorse?" His voice was far away and uninvolved. I resented his ability to be dissociated.

Maybe he also regretted the distance because his voice softened, came closer. "I love his library, too," he said. "And his aesthetics. And his charity. But don't let that interfere with what's staring you in the face."

What was truly staring me in the face at the moment was Mother Vivien on TV. QUESTIONED, it said under her head shot. Her cascading curls were more incongruous than ever, as the hard-worn, painted face grimaced. "Wait a sec—" I turned up the volume.

"—have revealed prior convictions. The self-proclaimed Mother Superior of the Moral Ecologists, a.k.a. Vivien Sessternass Devine Butterick Conkle, was previously convicted for fraud, as well as assault and battery."

My, oh, my. I transmitted the news to Mackenzie.

"No wonder she only uses one name," the man with no name said.

Vivien was shouting, the veins ropy on her neck, her cerise lips grimacing. She looked like a gargoyle with blue eyeshadow.

"You know," C. K. said, "if you'd get online, you could e-mail me every detail when I'm out of town."

This was not the time for a tech vs. no-tech debate. I hadn't even included the computer in my talisman-touching routine. It seemed happy with its own company, its bubbly screen saver looking like a party it was giving itself.

Mother Vivien's tears didn't match her words. "God will smite anyone—will send them to eternal damnation—who doesn't forgive past sins well-atoned for and respect spiritual love! What we had was God's own gift to us, and we were partners in this holy crusade. The reverend was my other half, my—"

Even I'd had enough of her lies. Harvey hadn't seemed God's loving gift, her other half yesterday in the greenroom. Back down went the volume. And in what felt like too few minutes, I was once again alone. Except for Macavity, who was either still sulking at my insult or, more probably, since it happened every time the man left, simply pining for Mackenzie.

And except, when I took a last peek out the side of the window shade, for the round man in the Russian hat, who was back on the corner. Looking directly up at me.

Ten

THE man wasn't there in the morning. That turned out to be the day's only good news.

Otherwise, Friday, a.k.a. Open House, was anything but T.G.I.F. It seemed to last two or three months and felt like a combination of conjuring and tap dancing: all an act.

It was quiet on the streets—the student protests were over and the Moral Ecologists hadn't yet regrouped if, indeed, they intended to return. It was quiet inside as well. At least, inside our brains.

The only rational lesson plan would have been to have the students talk through, then write about the week's events. With both sides taking to the streets, decisions made and rescinded and finally, the murder—there'd been enough to fill entire notebooks and years of therapy. We could have sorted through the tangle of events; pulled out ideas about freedom of speech, censorship, ethics, the meaning of democracy, individual responsibility—tons of big issues; dealt with the emotions generated; and had an outstanding lesson in organizing thoughts. In fact, it would have gone to the very heart of what we were supposedly learning in a Language Arts classroom.

But no. The staff was under strict orders not to mention the "recent troubles" and to have only "active" lessons, meaning in Havermeyerese, "visibly active"—which writing, with its long sighs and hunched-over bodies and one hand moving a pen or pencil over paper, definitely was not. Watching someone else think was boring, and the bored watcher might take his child and tuition payments to a more entertaining school.

Free-ranging, uncensored talk was also dangerous. Ask any dictator. What if, during the discussion (of free speech, in this instance) the students spoke freely and stumbled across concepts that made Philly Prep and its leadership look bad? Couldn't risk it. Had to censor it. I therefore tried to stick with the assigned material. Which, by ten minutes into first-period class, and as I'd known it would be, was impossible. It wasn't that the kids disliked *Jane Eyre* or wanted to make me look bad. In fact, some of them actually allowed themselves to enjoy it. But they'd obviously—and despite my warnings—felt they'd been on a mini-vacation, with picketing followed by their trip to the Mutter Museum. All prior assignments had been vaporized by the sight of Grover Cleveland's jaw tumor.

In theory, they'd been doing independent research relating to the novel, reading biographies of the Brontës, and reporting on Victorian and contemporary critical responses to *Jane Eyre*, along with broad-based views of the literature of the time, as well as the status of education, family life, social class, and so forth. They were scheduled to give oral reports. Very controllable, very unthreatening, and very active, meeting Havermeyer's terms.

Except: that assumed they'd done the work. The real lesson of the day, at least *my* real lesson, was to assume nothing. Scheduled reports were not ready, and I was not about to raise a ruckus in front of skeptical visiting matrons. They already looked nervous, clutching their coats around them, despite the heated room, as if afraid of being robbed.

I was a zoo exhibit. See the teacher—what tricks does she know? But I was also the zookeeper, and there was no telling what the animals would do. They could be koala-cuddly, monkey-clever, or, with a change in their metaphorical stripes, deadly man- and lesson-killers.

So with a gaping hole in the fabric of the hour, we segued into character analysis, which was sufficiently vague as to obscure how unprepared a Philly Prep student is apt to be. Brooding, dark-browed, irrational, unfathomable Mr. Rochester, a man I found annoying, worked for hormone-raddled teenagers. It was amusing to watch him generate girl-heat, and less amusing to speculate about what was wrong with my gender that it lusted for the unavailable, the withheld. It was also mildly heartrending to see gawky ninth-grade males trying to comprehend surly Rochester's chemistry.

I thought we might look good dealing with the easy issue of Mr. Rochester's secret. "Why do you suppose the tree cracked in half in the storm?" I asked.

"Because it was rotten," a pragmatic boy said. His voice cracked, like the tree, mid-sentence. We wouldn't hear from him again today. I wished I could console him for his lack of imagination and grace, tell him it would eventually be okay. Once he finished with the pimples and crackling voice he, too, could be unreachable and remote.

"Good," I said. He blushed, making his acne all the more appalling. You have to love a boy like that. He's struggling against so much, he's going to grow up to be either a sensitive, new-age gem or a freeway sniper.

"Let's look at it from another angle. Why do you think Charlotte Brontë chose to have a tree crack in half just then? On the eve, more or less, of Jane's marriage to Mr. Rochester?"

"Miss Pepper! Miss Pepper!" A hand and wrist crisscrossed with silver and black leather straps waved wildly. I hoped those disdainful women were properly impressed. Look at the intellectual excitement of a Philly Prep classroom.

God bless Caralee Mintz. She pushed back a lock of striped hair—peacock blue and platinum this week. Caralee was always a visual treat. She intended to be a feminist designer, she'd told me, and she wore her works in progress to class. Her latest "line" was formal attire, hence today's tulle combined with recycled plastic, tin, and grommets. She clunked and bristled as she waved her hand.

It was her newly discovered and rather rabid feminism, not her design concepts, that could be a pain, but at least she showed actual academic eagerness. "Yes?" I asked, waiting for her take on the split tree.

"Why's she call him *Mister* all the time if they're getting married? She's Jane, he's Mister. Why is that? What's his first name? Why doesn't she use it?"

Damn. Inquiring minds want to know on the wrong day. "Good question," I said, "but weren't we . . . about the tree? The split tree?" I had no idea what Rochester's first name was. I wasn't sure I ever had. More appallingly, I had never cared.

"I think this is important," Caralee grumbled. "This is about *equality*. See? They're getting married, but he's still, like, the master. *Mister!* She's like his kid or his servant. *Jane!*"

"It's an interesting point, a valid point. Even if that was the practice of the time, it still reflects a basic inequality, and you're correct. But back to that tree . . ." A silence long enough to make me wonder whether they might actually dislike me. And then from the edge of the room came a male voice heavy with scorn. "We aren't talking *symbolism* here, are we?"

I ignored the edge of contempt. "Perhaps," I said. "Or foreshadowing. Remember what that was?" Come on, team! Show those ladies we learn stuff here—and what the hell was Rochester's first name?

A few nods, a frightening spot of dead air, and then a volunteer to talk grudgingly about setting a mood, hinting at what's ahead. As for me, I wished that life as clearly foreshadowed coming events.

Maybe it did. The burning effigy the night of the fund-raiser now felt as clear a signal as a blinking light. But too much clutter and junk made the picture over-full and confusing without a friendly author highlighting which piece of the puzzle was the important one. The trouble with life was that you never knew if something was significant or irrelevant until it was all over.

While these thoughts drifted by, I pedagogically pulled teeth, all the while demonstrating mine in a big smile for the visiting critics, whose numbers waned and waxed, giving me repeated anxiety attacks throughout the hour. "What feeling does the splitting of the tree give you?" I wanted to go home, to lie down and not think. "What mood does it create?"

Somebody finally said "sad." Not eloquent, not even exactly on the mark, but we ran with it until we reached the glimmer of the idea that something bad was ahead, something as yet unseen.

"Those cries Jane hears," one bright young thing suggested.

"So the tree, which is originally one thing, the way, perhaps, a married couple is supposed to be . . ." Come *on*, I'm doing all the work! But zilch was happening on their faces, in their brains. ". . . supposed to be the way Jane and Mr. Rochester will be once they are joined in the near future—or should be, splits in—"

"I got it! It splits! Like marriages do. Hey! Cool."

"And Charlotte Brontë was foreshadowing what?"

They waited, expectantly.

"The secret?" I prompted. Oh, please, they were supposed to have read past Rochester's secret by last week, but I'd never had a chance to check. I know I shouldn't speak ill of the dead—though I don't know why not—but could I spare an ill thought for the educational effects of the dead's tactics? This less than stellar performance was Harvey Spiers' fault. "Mr. Rochester's secret," I said, hoping that my sense that whole seasons had just passed was not accurate.

There was a general aura of recognition, including nods. And eventually, a discussion about what it might do to a person to carry an important secret about themselves around for a long time. "If you pretend to be other than you are," I asked, "are you then truly that something else? Are all lies wrong? Is it the same with secrets? Does secrecy poison the air around you?"

It was sufficiently interesting to even make Caralee forget the issue of Mr. Rochester's missing first name. Or perhaps her creative mind was absorbed elsewhere, designing fiberglass frocks.

The morning staggered on, one yoctosecond at a time. For those not overly familiar with *yoctos*, Alex Fry had informed me that they are the smallest designated unit of time. Think of a decimal point, then twenty-three zeros, and *then* a one. Think how infinitesimal that sliver of existence is, then think of one yocto placed with deliberation next to another, on and on with numbing repetition, and you'll have a hint of my morning.

Afternoon, too. The misery didn't stop at noon. Parents came and went and I performed, pushing the boulder of student inertia up the hill. We never spoke of murder or mayhem or civil disobedience or freedom of speech. Mark Twain's quote—still on the board—was the only hint that anything controversial might have happened. The events and passions of the week were our secret, our madwoman in the attic. I found the weight of it exhausting. By the end of the day, I barely had the energy to move my limbs down the stairs and out to my car. I don't know how actors and actresses keep up their strength to perform over and over, but at least they get more money than I do, and sometimes, a bouquet at the end.

I APPROACHED MY overlarge, overempty building unwillingly, dawdling outside, pondering where else I could go, what I possibly needed to buy, whom I knew who'd be at loose ends on a Friday eve. My status was vague and less than a good fit—not exactly single, but still alone.

It was First Friday, the monthly official ramble through

gallery options in Old City. My turf. A few smartly dressed folk already wandered my streets, peering into windows, deciding on dinner first or after. Their numbers would increase as the nine-to-fivers concluded their work week and the suburbanites commuted in.

Maybe it was time to stop behaving as if one of my limbs had been amputated just because Mackenzie was away. Instead, I'd treat myself to a night on the town and see what was happening in the art world.

I went upstairs to drop off my briefcase and wash my face, calling greetings to Macavity, who clearly considered me the second-best possible returnee home. I wondered how he felt about being alone in this vastness all day. But since he slept through the alone time, maybe he hadn't noticed what, to me, was a space with the disquieting ability to grow and dwarf a solo occupant. Semi-empty, it became a warehouse once again, with no inventory besides me, and I took on the properties of a piece of stored merchandise, which is to say, a lump.

That era had to end, now.

But before I could get on with my new self and my evening sojourn, I had to respond to the enticing summons of the blinking answering machine. Somebody wanted me. More than one somebody.

Unfortunately, the first somebody was my mother. It was amazing how the sound of her voice reversed the problem of feeling adrift in a too-large space. Instead, I felt smothered in a feather comforter wrapped over me with the best of intentions, but nonetheless suffocating.

I had to warn long-distance providers to stop sending her special offers that allowed her to reach out and molest me.

At least she'd dropped the insane idea of my hiring an investigator. Now she wondered if I'd heard about a new bestseller that provided women with rules—a few of which she mentioned pointedly—on how to capture a man. I'd already broken all the ones she mentioned.

The second call didn't want me or anyone here. It was a wrong number, somebody in search of a Caleb. I went to erase the message, then froze, listening to a familiar voice apologize for invading Caleb's privacy.

Neddy Roederer assumed I'd have told the truth about something as basic as my escort's first name. Silly, trusting man.

Why did Neddy want to talk to him? The message didn't clarify anything. ". . . and if you have the time at all in the near future, I would profoundly appreciate it. Sorry to bother you, but you're the first member of the police force I've ever met socially, so I'm afraid I am taking liberties. But I would like to consider any man who admires books as much as you do my immediate friend. If you could call me at my club, I'd appreciate it. If I'm not there, leave a message. The number is . . ."

What was that about? I was about to phone Mackenzie, leave a message at his hotel, if he was still there, to call Neddy, then immediately call me. Then I remembered that Neddy was away, scouting schools and impossible to reach.

So the long and short of it was that nobody—except Mom—wanted me. I could go out with a clear conscience.

Monday, my students would be allowed to write again, and we could explore the subject of secrets. I wondered if anyone else would find the topic as interesting as I did. I thought the internal pressure of secret-keeping would bend your bones and cripple you. Maybe Rochester was once a jolly party animal, now curdled and remote because his insane wife weighed on him like ten times Quasimodo's hump.

And then, of course, there were the victims the secret-keeper created, intentionally or not. Like Jane.

But that was for Monday, two days away. Meantime, I accepted this gift of guilt-free, papers-to-mark-free, man-free time as a boon. I'd do precisely and only as I alone chose to.

I was almost out the door when the phone rang—my faraway beloved. Frankly, his conversation did not meet the level of entertainment I expected from the evening. He had a lot on his mind, all of it revolving around "damned bureaucracies," "damned lawyers," and "damned incompetence." I assumed this was code for

"I'm not there now and I am definitely not happy about it because I love you and miss you."

Finally out of steam, he halfheartedly asked about my day. But as I tried to bring its convoluted tediousness to life, I heard the miles between us, felt each syllable I uttered squeeze through the phone wires and expire unattractively at the other end. He had the Away Syndrome.

I learned about this affliction during a now-and-then (and finally never) thing with a consultant who was forever leaving town.

Basically, those suffering from the Away Syndrome confuse motion with advancement. Mackenzie, for example, suffered under the illusion that because he had relocated his butt to Kansas, he had moved on, evolved, while I was still mired in the same old same old. Stuck in the same place.

Luckily, Mackenzie and I didn't have to contend with the Syndrome often, so I didn't try to deal with his patronizing attitude or shortsightedness. To return home is to be cured.

I abandoned my spiel. Mackenzie didn't notice.

"Incidentally," I said, "I reread Jake's article yesterday and something dawned on me. That Cheshire Cat guy—the embezzler?—his name, or alias for the job, was Chester Katt. He disappeared."

"Yes?" he said with insufficient interest.

"Chester with a *C* and Katt with a *K*. Disappeared from Canada right around the time you with the same initials pop up in this city. You care to explain?"

"You got me, clever girl. And probably you've already found the bags of money under the mattress."

"While I'm on the line with a member of the Association of Missing First Names," I said, "do you happen to know a fellow member's? That'd be Mr. Rochester, Jane Eyre's honey. He doesn't even have initials."

He didn't know Rochester's name. And he politely, but palpably, wanted out of the conversation. I had pity on him and we ended the brief call and said good-night.

While we'd been talking, I thought I'd heard taps on the roof. Did I need an umbrella? Or had it been squirrels?

I went to the window to check the sidewalk.

No rain.

But in lieu of precipitation—the breath stopped in my throat: him. There. Again. A round man in a Russian hat. Not the product of nerves, but there across the street. Lurking. Stalking. Waiting. For me.

Eleven

TAKING deep breaths, I gingerly stepped back from the window. Okay, I said to myself, okay now, okay.

But it wasn't okay. How had I forgotten to watch for him? Nothing was okay. There'd been terrorism, blackmail, murder, tentacles reaching ever outward. This.

Okay, I nonetheless said again. Okay, okay. He hadn't done anything frightening. Hadn't tried to contact me, let alone hurt me. Not today, not earlier. He was just . . . there.

What did he want with me?

I stood in place, not moving a muscle, as if he could see through walls, then I took a deep breath and lifted the shade again.

Still there.

And that was that. I did not enjoy victimhood or fear and trembling. Not from over-lofty lofts and not from a stranger in a Russian hat. I grabbed my coat and keys and change purse, the latter for no reason I could think of, except the habit of taking mad money before leaving home—one of my mother's basic laws—persisted. And God knew I was mad.

Once downstairs, I opened the door to the street slowly, giving the lurker time. And when I was out on the pavement, he was, to my odd satisfaction, back in a doorway, hiding in the shadows.

I walked until I was directly across from the spot where he was trying for invisibility. I checked my surroundings in the dusk and saw enough gallery- and restaurant-goers to suggest safety in numbers. These were Philadelphians, after all. They would respond to a neighbor in trouble. I stepped off the curb, pointed, and shouted at the top of my lungs.

"You! What are you doing, lurking outside my place day after day? You *stalking* me?"

He tried to merge with the paint on the doorway.

"Answer me!" I screamed. A few people slowed their pace and eyed me warily, wondering whether they were witnessing a mundane urban drama, a future episode of *Unsolved Mysteries*—or just another street person off her meds.

They gave me further courage—or fed my insanity. "You!" I shouted.

"Lady?" a passerby asked tentatively. His date shushed him, told him to leave me alone, and they walked along more quickly.

I was too far gone to quit. "Come out of the shadows and answer me!" I screamed.

To my great surprise, the man in the Russian hat complied. Slowly, his head bowed—hangdog, actually—he walked across the pavement, looked both ways and then crossed the street onto my sidewalk, where he faced me in a semi-cringe.

He didn't look capable of passing Intimidation 101. But you never know. I've seen pictures of serial killers who looked just as repressed and terrified as this man. In fact, that very lack of social graces is why they resort to stalking and stealth. "I'm sick of this!" I said.

"Yes," he said. "Shh."

What kind of response was that?

His glance flitted from left to right, and his single eyebrow crinkled even more tensely in the center. "Please," he whispered, "I didn't mean to upset you."

"Not upset me? With you at school and here, too, watching me? *Not upset me?* I've called the police!"

"Oh, please, no. Oh, God, no. Can you call them off?"

"I'm sick of the Moral Ecologists—of people thinking they know it all!" I felt myself reach the far border of self-control. This was it: the one thing too many.

"Huh?" he said. "Listen, please call off the police. They'd ruin everything. It was supposed to be a simple job, and if I botched it and your mother finds out—"

"My mother?"

He looked clinically depressed as he nodded. I could barely breathe and definitely couldn't think. He stood there, head bowed.

But . . . a simple job, he'd said. Job. Now it was clear, if still unbelievable. He wasn't a Moral Ecologist. "You're—a detective, aren't you?"

"Private investigator," he said in his doleful voice. "Listen, could we go somewhere? The police . . . this is embarrassing. Professionally embarrassing."

I couldn't see the harm in a public place. Besides, I was suddenly aware of being hungry, so I nodded and pointed him toward the coffeehouse down the street. Restaurants would be crowded and require a whole meal. Easier and faster at this hour to follow the aromatic trail to warm safety.

The coffee-rich air fed my anger toward my mother. She still used freeze-dried granules to make coffee, so obviously she was capable of anything, including spying on her own daughter.

I had to confirm that. "My mother hired you, didn't she?" I demanded, as we slipped into a booth.

He sighed and nodded. He also pulled off the Russian chapeau, revealing crinkled reddish hair.

"Why on earth put *me* under surveillance?"

"I wasn't," he said lamely.

"What do you call following me, watching me, waiting that way?"

He looked at his fingernails and sighed with heartfelt sorrow. "I was trying to watch your . . . the . . . Mackenzie."

Relief of sorts. My mother hadn't put me under surveillance.

"Supposed to note where he went, what he did when he left there," the round-faced man said.

"He's out of town," I said. "Didn't you notice that? And why my school? Why were you there?"

"I'm not sure, except . . . I can't put police headquarters under surveillance, can I?"

I called over the waitress and ordered a double cappuccino and a ham sandwich. My tablemate, sounding frightened, said he'd have the same. When she left, I leaned forward and spoke softly. "I mean this kindly," I said. "But somebody has to tell you. You're not at all good at this sleuthing thing."

"I know." His hands were now in a prayerful position. "But it's better than what I did before. It's better than telemarketing. You can't believe how mean people are on the phone."

Since I was super-mean when interrupted at dinner, or any other time, I could, in fact, believe it. And approve of it. "What's your name?" I asked.

"Roland. But everybody calls me Skip—just plain Skip."

Skippy, I'd wager, even though he was trying not to say it. Detective Skippy, bargain-basement investigator. "If you wanted to find out about Mackenzie's past, shouldn't you be in Louisiana?" I asked, not unkindly. "Checking records, that sort of thing? He's been here maybe half a dozen years, that's all."

He nodded. "I know that. I wanted to find out about now, too. Like if he, say, was seeing anybody else, or secretly gambling, or . . . you know."

Disgusting. No privacy allowed and suspicion everywhere. As

if Mackenzie were Mr. Rochester, carrying around a profound secret. As if anybody I knew was. My mother had no shame.

Nor did I. "One thing," I said. "In the course of your investigation, you undoubtedly found out his full name, what the C and the K stand for. I'd be willing to keep quiet about your less-than-subtle work—you're not a very *private* investigator—in exchange for that information." I couldn't believe I'd stoop this low, but I didn't retract my offer, either.

"I didn't get that far yet," he said.

Crime really doesn't pay. "Then I suggest you do go far. As far away as possible. Stop this foolishness."

"There's plenty stuff to find out here, too," he insisted.

"And have you?"

"Have I what?"

"Found anything whatsoever of interest?" I said it lightly—I wanted to feel it lightly, too. But part of me was concerned. Mackenzie said everybody had secrets, a dark side. Why had he been so adamant about that, about Peter Schlemiel?

Skippy shrugged. "Not exactly."

"Anything? Scary sexual escapades? Cannibalistic tendencies? A history of mental problems?"

"There was a woman . . ."

"Yes?"

"No. Nothing. He was in college."

I knew about her. About a couple of hers. After college, too. Dozens. But even if I didn't . . .

I had a queasy feeling that I'd fallen into a cautionary fable, and I'd soon ask the one question too many, activate an evil curse made at my christening.

Maybe personal secrets that don't affect anyone else should be the sole property of their owners. I wondered if I could convince my mother of that, make her see the wrongness of this thing she'd started in motion.

"He sounds like a nice guy," Old Skip said. "And a good cop. Except when he got shot once, in broad daylight, by a kid—"

"I know about that."

He shrugged again. It was almost a nervous tic. There was a

film of sweat on his upper lip, on the knitted eyebrow, on his tightly clasped hands. The shrug was the anti-fear, trying to even the emotional score, convey a like-I-care patina.

"Skippy—"

His head jerked up, his eyes wide.

"Sorry. I had a friend named . . . anyway, *Skip*, your impression is correct. Mackenzie's a good guy and you aren't going to find out anything worth your time or my mother's money. All you'll do is be a royal pain. Why not call it quits and go home?"

"I need this job. I need, like, a track record." His hat, Persian lamb I thought, sat on the table like a small, mute mammal.

"Was the job prepaid? Do you charge by the hour?"

"Made her a special deal. Flat rate for the . . ." he paused and seemed to savor the next word, ". . . case."

"Can't you consider the case closed? Listen, Skip—" I had to gulp, to swallow the missing final syllable. "I *hate* being spied on. Having you pry. Let me find things out the way I'm supposed to, through day-to-day life. Let me be surprised now and then. I know the man and there's no evil in him, but this is offensive. This is based on the idea that you can't trust anybody, even the person you love and live with."

If you couldn't trust your partner, you'd be on an emotional fault line for the rest of your days unless you kept hiring detective after detective, updating your files.

Detective Skippy stared at me with the crazed blankness I'd hitherto thought only cats could master. If it meant the same thing it did when Macavity had the look, then there was no point trying to convince him of anything. And yet I did. I do with my cat, too. "You have to stop," I said. "Most of all, because you'll be ineffective from now on." As if he hadn't been all along.

"Why? What do you mean? I have lots of things left to do, sources to check."

"No matter, because I'm going to tell—"

"Oh, please no, don't! You said you wouldn't, didn't you?" He half stood in the booth, only settling down when the waitress put our cappuccinos and sandwiches on the table.

"I never said that." I'd offered it only as a swap for C. K.'s full name. "And how can I not? You scared me. You're lucky I don't have a gun, and I don't react the way he might." As if Mackenzie were a trigger-happy cowboy in the Wild West. But Skippy bought the concept. His eyes bugged out. "He deserves to know," I said.

"He? You're going to tell *him*." He smiled his relief.

"Who else? Oh . . ." And what was my answer there? Was I going to tell Ma? Have it out with her for pathological meddling? Explain that a person's secrets were his own property. If he had them, he also had his own reasons. Let time or Mackenzie reveal them—not a detective.

I was sure my mother considered this her gift to me. A luxury I wouldn't splurge on for myself.

Unfortunately, it wasn't anything I wanted or could exchange. "Why is she worried?" I muttered. "If she'd stop watching day-time TV, she wouldn't have such a warped view of the world."

Normally, I find the humor—at least eventually—in her attempts to micromanage my life. But not this time. Not yet. It's one thing to meddle from afar, and another to have a ridiculous man intrude and frighten.

Detective Skippy waited, jaw dangling, for the one thing that mattered to him—whether or not I was going to tell on him. In all honesty, I was still too shocked and angry to know what I'd do when I simmered down.

"This is not a normal case," Skippy said. "It's hard investigating a cop. It's not like I can question his coworkers, find out if he has another wife, or life, or a criminal background."

"He wouldn't be a cop if he had one, would he?"

"Well, you know, he comes from another state . . ." His voice trailed off with the weight of that statement.

Only my mother, the benign tyrant of Florida, could live hundreds of miles away, yet hover so closely I tripped over her. The good news was that she wasn't hard to figure out. She was, in fact, so obvious, she was almost transparent: every thought, urge, belief up on the surface pushing so hard to keep her children safe that she knocked us down and flattened us in the process.

She was the antithesis of Jake's parents, so you'd have thought

I'd approve. But what about the happy mean between apathy and overprotection?

My body temperature boiled up to the steamy equal of my coffee, and I sipped without tasting. "Skip," I said, "close the case. Write a fake report and hand it over. That way she's happy, I'm happy, Mackenzie's happy, and so are you."

"It's not professionally ethical," he said softly.

"Of course it isn't. But it's kind and sane, so it must be ethical in some other way that really counts."

He nodded several times, as if concluding an interior argument. Then he shook his head, as if he were now hearing counter-arguments.

"Think about it." I had another question, and wanted to push my advantage while I had him at bay. I'd just proclaimed my passionate belief in the right to secrets, but I nonetheless resented his having any. "Meanwhile, tell me one thing."

He swiveled his head so that he eyed me sideways, suspiciously. Detective Skippy was not going to be known for his poker face.

"Please don't take this the wrong way, but even you admit you aren't . . . yet . . . exactly expert at this."

He sighed.

I could understand why she got excited about the idea of hiring a detective. My mother's life lacks event. She collects gossip from relatives and friends but it doesn't fulfill her daily drama requirements. Kind of like Macavity, who, lacking any predators, prey, or competitors, gets bored out of his mind and freaks at dust motes—back arched, tail enormous, ears back. Terrorizing himself entertains him, helps fill his time.

My mother's that sort of house cat, too. Her entire life has been spent in pleasant, nonthreatening normality. Not a standard deviation left or right, and she wants everybody else to squeeze into that safe zone, too.

But she isn't a dummy. And while she loves a bargain, she knows you get what you pay for. "My question is how, out of the whole world of private investigators, did my mother come to hire you?"

"I asked her to," he said matter-of-factly. He looked so relieved by my choice of question, he was able to take a bite of his ham sandwich.

"You picked her out of a crowd? Used your telemarketing skills and made a blind call? Handed her your card? She found you in the Yellow Pages? What?"

"Don't be silly." He laughed, then covered his mouth and chewed.

"Okay. You asked her to hire you—but why did she agree?"

He was obviously at ease now. He picked up a fallen piece of ham and popped it into his mouth before saying, "As a favor."

"Why? What had you done for her?"

"Me? Nothing."

"Okay, Skip. I see you do have job-related skills, after all. You can keep information to yourself. But this is not the best time to choose to do that. Why'd my mother hire you?"

"As a family favor."

"Family? Whose? We aren't related, are we?" Was Skip the Peppers' equivalent of Rochester's madwoman in the attic? A secret until now?

"We're not exactly related. Not so you'd—"

"Cut this out. Tell me why my mother hired you. In plain English. What family? What do you mean?"

"My mother and your mother go way back. Rolaine Belford, okay?" He nodded a few times. "That's how come I got the name Roland. After her."

No bells were rung. I combed through my Bea Pepper files— card-playing friends, food-buying co-op board, manatee protection committee, nearby tenants, distant relatives, former neighbors. My turn to shake my head.

"Rolf Thayer's sister," he said, as if that meant something. "The Thayers were all *R*'s. Rolf, Rolaine, Rebecca, Rothwell, and Regina. And next generation, there's Rachel, Ralph, Robert, and me, Roland, even though only a couple are still Thayers."

He smiled and stopped talking, as if he'd provided a full explanation. "Who is Rolf Thayer?" I asked.

He put down his sandwich. "You're joking."

This had become boring, and I was missing the gallery hours. Who cared who Rolf was, anyway? He'd turn out to be the fellow who washed her car once a month. My mother was forever collecting people like that.

"*Rolf Thayer.*" Skippy said it loudly, as if I were deaf.

I shook my head.

"Your mother's first husband."

My brain's control board flashed and sparked until it shut down from overload. My what? Her what?

Skippy calmly continued explaining. "My mother helped your mother when he got violent. Got Aunt Bea to a safe place. Hid her there. That kind of stuff. Jeez, I've known your mother my whole life from her visits."

Aunt Bea?

"So when Mom mentioned my new career to her—"

My hand went up, like a traffic cop's. "Wait. Halt." I barely had the air to make the request. Something heavy pressed on my flattened lungs, my breath shallow and rapid. "Wait," I said again, even though he was, in fact, waiting. "My mother's—" It was difficult speaking between gasps. "My mother's been married to my father forever. Her only marriage."

"Except for Rolf." He squinted at me. "Are you saying you don't know about the elopement, your grandparents trying to have him arrested, the estrangement all those years? None of her family spoke to her. I can't believe you don't know."

I swallowed hard.

"Weird," Skippy said, "because I've heard our mothers talk about it, about him, since I was a kid. I mean, God, he was bad, but when I was little, even with those stories, he seemed like a desperado to me. I mean, the robberies, the fights, the gambling. And then, especially about when he was killed."

By now, my air supply was dangerously limited, I was lightheaded and my vision blurred.

"Stabbed in a brawl. Awful. My mother's never gotten over it. No matter what he turned out to be, and he turned out to be really rotten, he was still her little brother, you know."

My mother, she who hired people to ferret out secrets, had an entire other existence. Wasn't the person I'd known all my life. Things had happened to her. Indeed. She hadn't been in that cocoon forever. A drunken lout of a husband who'd been murdered in a brawl, and a friend for decades who'd saved her and from whom she had no secrets. She'd even had *Skippy* as a part of her life.

She'd wanted to know—for my sake, she said—if Mackenzie had secrets and all the while, she was the one who did.

Her secret life. I thought the words, but when I saw my mother's open face, her daily telephone updates to everyone she knew, her unofficial role of spreading all and any information up and down the Eastern Seaboard, my image of her spun and turned inside out.

Those calls weren't meddling. They were *making sure*. Reassuring herself and the universe that everything was known and under control, trying to protect everyone from the chaos she'd known firsthand.

"So in an unofficial way—that's what your mother said to me— we're family. I wasn't born then, but if I had been, I'd have been her nephew. Your cousin. If she'd stayed with Rolf."

My mind, overtired, slowly shut down.

"You didn't know," Skip whispered. "You really didn't. I'm— I'm sorry, then. I guess maybe I wasn't supposed to . . ." His eyes widened in the familiar expression of terror. "You going to tell?"

"Tell? Tell what? Tell who—whom?"

"Tell her. That you know. I would never have—I didn't think for a minute she wouldn't have . . ."

I saw Peter Schlemiel's shadow again. It's what made him three-dimensional. Real. The darkness everyone had, according to Mackenzie. But even he would have exempted my mother.

"Are you?" Skippy asked.

She'd kept herself, her life, a secret. For whatever reasons— because she still carried the long-dead stigma of divorce, or because of a misplaced shame at defying her parents for the love of an unworthy man, for having her marriage self-destruct, for the humiliation of needing to hide from him. Whatever.

She'd kept it a secret that she'd made every mistake, done

nearly everything she so vigilantly guarded against in her own children, particularly me. Because obviously, I was the most like her in my willfulness, my resentment of parental advice, my love of adventure. Or like she had once been.

It was her secret motive, I suspected, for excessive protective gestures. It was who she was, and it made me understand her better.

And it made me feel angry, left out, and also eager to talk about it with her, to work on the over-involvement in my life it had caused.

"I can't answer that yet," I said. "I really don't know what I think or what I'll do."

Peter Schlemiel put his shadow hands on my shoulders and pulled me close.

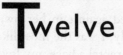welve

ALK about a blow upside the head. I sat in the coffee-house a long while after Skippy made his reluctant retreat. I considered again the weight of secrets and wondered how else my mother's had shaped her. And me.

My entire life needed to be revisited, reviewed, and reinterpreted. I wondered if my father knew. And if he didn't, what that meant about the quality of their bonds.

I wondered until I was wondering in tiny, dizzying circles, and I made my way down the street, noticing the thinning crowds, the increasing cold, and my friend, Sasha Berg, who should have been out with Dr. Perfect instead of balanced on one exceedingly high heel in front of my entryway. Her other heel was up behind her, pressed against the brick wall. She looked like an ad for a B movie.

She also looked like the antidote to Skippy.

Sasha is easy to spot. It's partly her six-foot height—before the heels—partly her voluptuous proportions, and partly her idiosyncratic wardrobe. Tonight, except for her spiky hair, she looked ready for The Hop in a Fifties powder-pink taffeta with a tight charcoal-gray velvet midriff and a pouf of a tulle crumb-catcher above the pointy bustline. And encasing it all, a ratty fur stole. Sasha had never heard of political correctness, or at least had not hearkened to its clarion calls.

But the closer I came, the less she looked like an antidote to anything. Her morose expression clashed with her purple shoes.

"Great outfit," I said. She halfheartedly waved one high-gloved arm. I had a clue as to what troubled her, given the absence of Dr. Wonderful Perfection. And I worried where I'd find energy for Sasha's problems this particular night. She was a high-maintenance friend, perpetually in romantic jams, and I was fresh out of spirit myself.

"Come on in," I said. Silently, she complied. Very bad sign.

Once inside, I poured her a glass of wine before she asked for it, and one for myself as well. I deserved it. I needed it.

She sipped and sighed. "It's been an interesting night," she said. I waited, then prodded. "Where is Dr. Wonderful?"

"Perfect Pete does not exist and never did."

"Okay, so Imperfect Pete. Where is he?"

She shook her head. "I mean he really, truly, did not exist. Neither does the Landauer Trust he supposedly worked for. Neither did his medical degree. So I've been standing in front of your house—and where *were* you, by the way? While the cop's away the teacher plays? But I've been here, freezing and trying to figure out who he was, because he wasn't any of the above. So far, I've come up with a smile to die for, great buns, and an incredibly smooth con."

"Can't be," I said. "Why would he con you?"

"There's the humiliating part. He's a *stupid* con man. An inept, second-rate one who doesn't do his homework if he goes after a woman who doesn't have two dimes to rub together. I think he liked my place and generalized from it."

For some obscure legal or tax purpose, Sasha's father had given her a condo during one of his frequent divorces. The walls around Sasha were those of a wealthy woman. Her wardrobe almost confirmed that. Like Tea Roederer's, it was the eccentric garb of one who didn't care about anyone else's opinion. Only difference was, Tea found her togs at the couturiers and Sasha found hers in the Goodwill bin. Her life as a freelance photographer was hardscrabble.

She finished her wine. "I think his plan was that my rich friends and I would put together a tidy sum for the foundation. He thought it was cute that I was a photographer. Obviously considered it a lark, a rich girl's hobby. I realize all this, you understand, only after the fact."

"Are you perhaps leaping to conclusions?" Sasha was prone to professional gamblers, demolition derby drivers, flakes, and phonies. Dr. Wonderful had been her first appealing-sounding man in recent history. Maybe she was overreacting or picking at nits. "What makes you think he wasn't for real?"

"Mackenzie."

"Excuse me?"

"Mackenzie found stuff out for me. After I got suspicious and asked him to. See, one night, we passed an accident, and Pete got agitated when I asked if he wasn't going to stop and help. I thought that was what they did, had to do, in fact. But he couldn't even look in the direction of the crash. Seemed ready to puke at the idea of blood, and it made me wonder about the medical degree and the work. India has to be worse than I-95. So I asked Mackenzie to find stuff out."

Mackenzie had researched somebody for her—had been a romantic detective, the sort my mother wanted to hire, and he hadn't told me. Not a hint. I felt stranded outside the loop—all the loops—to the point of wanting to bawl. "He never said."

"I asked him not to."

Was that sufficient reason? Was it okay that he agreed?

"He called me tonight. Right before I went out with Dr. Fake. I went anyway, thought maybe Peter and I could talk it through, find the explanation. You know, computer error. Somebody else with his name. Somebody who'd stolen his credit card and was committing felonies under his identity. You read things like that all the time. So we went to this place in South Philly. Had spaghetti with calamari and all was well. A Chianti Classico and much talk about India and the foundation and the grant deadline. Which is when I broached—gently, I swear—the things Mackenzie told me. Peter was perfectly charming, laughed at the idea of his being a fake, excused himself to go to the men's room, and hasn't been seen since. Except by a busboy who spotted him bolting out the back door into the alley."

She was in pain now, but she'd recuperate, and quickly. That was her talent and downfall as far as romance was concerned.

"I wasn't convinced for a long while," she said. "I sat there like a stupid cow and finished my pasta. But upon due consideration, after I'd paid the bill, I decided his failure to reappear might mean that the three warrants out for his arrest were, in fact, true. Because of the other women he bilked." Sasha's voice was low and soft, but that didn't mean it was calm. "Other fiancées. Did I tell you that he'd asked me to marry him? Probably not, because I was keeping it secret, going to surprise you with it." She sighed deeply. "Surprise," she said.

"What a night. I can hardly believe it." I poured us both more wine.

"What?" she asked. "Something else?"

I wanted to tell her about Detective Skippy, to match her story of a double life with mine. She knew my mother all the way back to when we were in high school, and my mother profoundly disapproved of high-risk, bad-girl Sasha.

But I didn't want to play I Can Top That with Sasha's pain. Besides, my mother's half truths hadn't put me in jeopardy the way Dr. Wonderful's had done to Sasha.

"Nothing," I said. "Just . . . I'm sorry about him. He sounded so fine."

"The one I told you about was. Unfortunately, he was also imaginary." She lifted her glass. "Let's drink to the men we make up, even if there isn't a chance in hell they really exist."

We drank to the creatures of our imagination, but also, at my suggestion, to another Peter, last name Schlemiel.

"Who?"

I told her Mackenzie's story: how it turned out that Schlemiel needed his shadow to be accepted as a human, and how people who have no dark side are two-dimensional and false.

She stood up. "You know," she said, "that's probably right. Wise, even. But it doesn't make me feel one iota better. Let's watch the late movie instead. And do you have chocolate in any form? Ice cream? Don't bother with a plate. Just a spoon."

"Two spoons," I said. And that's how we spent the evening until we both realized that we had in fact fallen asleep on opposite ends of the sofa. I offered to put sheets on the sofa and make Sasha's snooze official, but she yearned for the pleasures and miseries of home and left.

HAVING NAPPED DURING the movie, I couldn't fall asleep for a long time, exhausted as I was. With every passing minute, I grew more tense, even though the next day was Saturday, which meant I could sleep in as late as I liked.

That thought must have finally relaxed me, because I was deeply into a mental filmstrip featuring my mother, Skippy, Dr. Wonderful, Mackenzie, and Mr. Rochester—all running hither and yon, wearing masks and saying "Shh!"—when the phone jolted me awake.

"Miss Pepper?" The voice was male and unfinished.

Jesus. A student. Was I late for class? Wait—it was dark—and it was Saturday. Or still Friday. "Who is this?"

"Jake." He cleared his throat. I had the oddest sensation he was fighting tears. "Jake Ulrich." He whispered, as if hiding from someone.

"Are you all right?"

"Not really."

Of course he was not. Who would call his teacher when it was so dark if he were all right? I checked the clock. Four A.M.

"I wouldn't bother you at such a—"

"What's wrong?"

"Miss Pepper? You're the one call they'll allow me. I need help. I'm in jail."

I held out the receiver and stared at it, because from fatigue or stupidity, I didn't get or believe it. I thought it was an adolescent prank: get teach.

And I felt awful. My head banged and throbbed from a lack of sleep and an overdose of whatever hormones doubt, anxiety, confusion, and too much chocolate produce.

Then as I became more fully conscious, I realized what must have happened. Caroline Finney had gone to the police. She wouldn't dawdle or debate or simply intend to do something the way I would. And with that dear old lady reporting her fears, the force of the law slammed down on the boy. I sat upright, ready for action. "Poor Jake," I said. "Don't worry, I'll . . ."

What? Did they really allow only one phone call? And if so— why me? He'd need bail. Big bail—for a murder case.

Wait—did they grant bail for murder?

What was the phone-called person supposed to do? They never showed that part in movies. They cut to her or him charging into the station, knowing what to do.

And while we were on the subject—why me?

"I need an adult to, um, claim me," Jake said.

"They'll let you go? Where do people get bail? Do you need a lawyer?"

"They said I needed a responsible adult. Nothing else."

"I never heard of that before. You're amazingly calm, you realize that? Good for you, I'm impressed." I was babbling noise, in lieu of real ideas, but I couldn't slow myself down. "Okay, the police have you and will release you if—but should I be the one? What about—"

133

"I can't ask my mother. I mean literally. I tried. Twice. She's not answering the phone, and she turned off the machine, so they didn't count that as a call and I got to phone you. Shouldn't I have?"

"Oh, no, sure, no problem." An optimistic alien presence was speaking through my mouth, because I had more sense than to reassure a student that he could call me at four A.M. from jail. "Sure," the alien said again. "It's okay. Just tell me once again—you're where?"

"In *jail*. Gee, I'm sorry—were you sleeping?"

Duh. "*What* jail?"

"Radnor."

Spiers had been murdered in Radnor. You probably had to be locked up where the crime happened, so the police had dragged Jake out there.

Then why had he needed to call his mother? Why hadn't she gone with him to the station?

"That's where the party was," Jake said.

"Excuse me?" What were we talking about?

"Griffin's party. We thought you knew, heard us at school Thursday. I was trying to stop him, thought he was in enough trouble already. He should have listened."

"I'm sorry, I must have missed . . . what does a party have to do with jail?"

"The police arrested everybody. Like three hundred kids. But Griffin and me, we weren't even there."

"Of course not. I'm surprised anyone would think you'd leave your mother to go to a party so soon after your—her husband was—"

"But I did, kind of. Not for the party, for the leaving."

"You went to a party so you could leave it?"

"Leave everything. Griffin and me."

A suicide pact? My breath caught—until I realized it didn't fit what had come before, so I moved from fear back to confusion. There was no comfort in the transition. "Jake, you should have called me. There's no reason to think of such a drastic—"

"Well, we didn't, but that was the plan," Jake said. "Leave in the dead of night. Nobody was supposed to see us or know for a long while, and by then, we'd be long gone and far away."

Running away. I exhaled.

"It was pitch dark, no moon," Jake said. "We took back roads and didn't even turn on the headlights. The car was black, too, like we could just disappear into the night. It should have worked, but it didn't. Not exactly."

Shaking my head wasn't clearing it of confusion, just giving me whiplash, so I stopped.

"We didn't think it through. Plus, the Roederers came home last night instead of today, and when they saw all the cars, they called the police."

I will sort this out, I told myself. Calmly. In order. Point one: Jake's in jail. Point two: this doesn't have to do with Harvey Spiers' murder. Point three: Griffin gave a big party. Point four: Griffin and Jake were not at the party. Point five: the Roederers surprised the party-in-progress. Point six: the police arrested all the partygoers, of which Jake was not one. Point seven: Jake's in jail.

Maybe if I tried it again?

Go to jail, go directly to jail. A roundelay that wound up behind bars no matter where we began singing it. And since we were back to the start, anyway, how about my initial question. *Why me?*

I had to *claim* him, he'd said. Like a coat I'd checked. Or was it more like staking a claim—to Jake? Would that imply future responsibility for him? I'd told him he could count on me. I had fantasized being the semi-mythical teacher of Hollywood fame, the one who'd make All The Difference. I hadn't meant it to involve the wee hours or long drives into suburbia. I wanted to be a sage advisor full of pithy observations about life—not Jimmy Cagney's mother coming to bail the gangster out.

"Miss Pepper? They say I can't tie up the phone anymore."

I stood up, carrying the receiver as I tried to one-handedly pull on jeans and a sweatshirt. Whether or not I understood what had gone on, time was wasting and Radnor Township was not nearby.

And the longer Jake stayed there, the higher the risk that some Radnor policeperson would correlate him with a Latin teacher's incriminating phone call.

"Listen, Jake. In case . . . if the police ask you about anything besides the party, whatever you do, don't say anything. I'll be there as soon as I can."

In this black-and-white movie, I'd been cast not as a war-torn lover at a train station, but as one of those poor but saintly mothers whose only fashion accessory was an apron. Middle of the night, I was going to see my boy in the slammer, brave smile hiding my broken heart.

Top of the world, Ma.

Thirteen

ALL the way to Radnor I argued with myself. I shouldn't be going. It wasn't my role. I was his teacher, not his keeper. And what was I supposed to do at a police station? I was out of my league, and so nervous and irritable, I felt like an ad for analgesics. The *before* part, and nobody held out a remedy.

My mood wasn't helped by a low fog, a miasma rising from the vestigial snow and still frozen earth. Cold steam like the breath of the underworld obscured vision and made the drive look like a hokey, low-budget horror movie.

And why not? Life of late had gone peculiar—histrionic and

overdone. Bad actors, overblown rhetoric, changes and turn-arounds, paranoid fears, betrayals, shocking surprises, and ulti-mately, death.

Curtain.

Where did this call of Jake's fit in? Was it the start of a new act? The finale? And was this a tragedy or a comedy?

The instant I entered the police station, I felt cowed. I had crossed the bridge from good citizenship to the netherworld of baddies. I wasn't alone, though. Scores of parental faces reflected my own shame. The difference was, I told myself, their discom-fort was deserved. Their spawn had gone wrong. I, on the other hand, was picking up an unrelated rental. I fought the desire to announce this significant difference to three testy patrolmen attempting to control the clearing-out process.

"Excuse me," I said, squeezing through a sea of tightly screwed faces. "I need to talk to somebody."

"Who doesn't?" A man wearing a parka over pajamas asked wearily. "Broke my neck getting out of the house, then it's wait, wait, and more wait."

". . . juveniles," a sergeant was telling us, ". . . records sealed and if they don't get in any further trouble, this will . . ."

"Excuse me." I addressed a woman I recognized as the mother of a Philly Prep junior. "Have you already done whatever it is to get your child out?" She stared at me blankly, her eyes blind with that where-did-I-go-wrong mix of shame and fury.

"Is this a line?" I asked someone else. "Am I in line?" The parka man shook his head; the woman next to him barked, "Yes"; and a third parent shrugged.

So I pushed on, unsure whether I was being rude or pragmatic.

". . . not pressing charges at this time, pending a complete household inventory of the damage and theft. They retain the rights to . . ."

In the bedlam of parents, each trying to manage the trick of being simultaneously aggressive, submissive, polite, quick, and subtle, it took forever to be heard, and then to deal with the paperwork and official chastisement that would release Jake from the clutches of the constables.

"Your son—" the cop began.

"I'm his English teacher, not his parent."

He didn't care. These wealthy suburbs suffered, someone clever said, from *affluenza*, and the cops had seen enough smashed and shattered families with kids catching hold of whatever adult steadied them for however long. They didn't understand why I wasted breath establishing nongenetic ties.

The more I thought about it, the less I did, too.

JAKE SLUMPED LOW on the seat and deeply into his parka, imitating a six-foot turtle holding a backpack.

"Where was Griffin?" I asked, as we drove back through surreal ground fog.

"Like I said, we weren't at the party long. Then we were on our way. He stayed on his way."

"And you?"

Jake looked away from me. "I hadn't thought things through enough. I got . . . nervous. I asked him to drop me at the police station. I figured I wasn't in trouble and I could get a ride from somebody. After all, I wasn't at the party when the police came. I didn't do anything wrong. But Mrs. R.—she was there looking for Griffin—she didn't believe me." With that, he sank even lower on the seat. He was in danger of strangling on the shoulder harness. "She knows me," he said. "Why did she think I'd lie? She was really pissed. She got me in trouble like the rest of the kids."

"Let me get this straight—you went to the police station solo."

He nodded. "I realized I needed a passport or papers or something to get over the border."

"You were headed for Canada?"

He shrugged, as if that went without saying. "They could have just made everybody go home. Had everybody call a designated driver. That's what other people do."

"The Roederers? But the police said there was damage."

Jake slid still farther down the seat. Soon his long bones would fold one atop the other and he'd collapse under the glove compartment.

"Was there?" I asked. "Damage?"

Jake sighed. "So the police could have taken everybody's address, like they did, anyway. They didn't have to do that stuff with holding cells."

"How did three hundred kids come to that house? Griffin seems a loner."

"He hired an organizer, a pro. This kid gets the kegs, spreads the word, you know."

I'd thought the swollen, destructive parties that erupted whenever parents were out of town were at least spontaneous. I considered this profession of guerrilla party-planner and wondered if he followed through all the way, let himself be rounded up with the guests.

Jake wore gloves with the fingers cut off; he tapped his knees and seemed deep in thought. "It wasn't Philly Prep kids who did the real damage," he said. "It was the other ones. Like they were angry, right from the start. Before we left, we tried to get them out of there. They were already messing up, putting cigarettes out on rugs and floors."

I winced. I know it's only stuff, but it's gorgeous stuff.

"The chandelier was the worst."

"The one in the hallway? That enormous crystal—not that one!"

"One of those idiots tried a Schwarzenegger kind of stunt. The chandelier came right out of the ceiling and smashed. All over."

I could almost hear crystals shattering on the marble floor, a million prismatic shards blanked out. Murdered.

"It's not Griffin's fault," Jake said. "He didn't ask to live with fancy stuff you have to tiptoe around, and he didn't break anything."

"I'm going to assume you're too tired to think clearly. Whether or not Griffin favors antiques is nowhere near the point. That doesn't answer the issue of what three hundred teenagers can do to a house. Maybe Griffin didn't break a thing, but he made sure somebody would. And you colluded." The cold rage behind their actions frightened me.

Jake didn't try to refute me. "He was really upset. Boarding school's like prison. We sat up half the night last night—no, wait, two nights ago, then night before last, talking about it. He hated the idea, and they knew he did, too, so why do it? Because of what my—what Harvey was doing? What sense did that make? That's why he decided to do that party and leave."

"They probably went to boarding school themselves, so it seems natural."

Jake shook his head. "They don't want him anymore. He was something they borrowed. Now they're returning him. Like he's broken or they don't need him anymore. It's so harsh."

"I'm sure the Roederers mean well." I heard how inane the words sounded the second they were out of my mouth. Childless, I nonetheless sounded like a mother on automatic pilot.

He shook his head again. "They're stubborn, is what it is. Griffin says that when they make their minds up, that's *it*. Whatever they say becomes the Eleventh Commandment. They got really pissed once when he asked them if they thought that maybe God had a Roederer complex."

Something Jake had mentioned had snagged in passing on a corner of my mind, and I needed to backtrack, to find and consider it. What was it? The purchased child? The boarding school? The chandelier?

"Like they bought him to make them look like a family. But a family doesn't send off—"

Two nights ago and the night before last. That's what he'd said. Including the night Harvey Spiers was murdered. And Jake was not at home, as I'd assumed, miles away, but there, pretty much at the scene of the crime. "Jake," I interrupted, "did you say you were at Griffin's Wednesday night?"

"Why?"

How to say this without creating more grief for him? "I wondered if . . . well, since that was the night your—the night of the murder across the road, I wondered if you saw or heard anything."

And also, by the way, did you—or maybe you and Griffin— kill anybody whose actions were, perhaps, destroying a lot of people?

He squinted, as if trying to magnify and read me. "The house is back from the road," he said. "You never hear much in there."

"Did you sleep over? Were you still there when it happened?"

"I don't have a car."

"That's no answer."

He studied his hands, the brown, raveling gloves that covered only his palms. I hoped he'd speak soon for many reasons, one of which was that I needed constant stimulation in order to stay awake. I'd have preferred caffeine, but emotional agitation would do, and Jake seemed able to provide a lot.

"The answer is yes. And no," he said. "I did sleep over. But I wasn't there when it happened. We left for a few hours, Griffin and me."

"Where to?"

"Just out."

I inhaled deeply and slowly. Not exactly an airtight alibi.

"When we got back, it was over. I mean, even the—even the cleanup—I mean, he was gone. We used the back stairway like usual. Nobody noticed."

"Didn't the police want to talk to you?"

"Why would they?"

"As possible witnesses. Even though the house is far back, a fire on the road—if you were upstairs, say, you might have seen or heard something. Noted the time."

He shook his head again. "No police. If they came later or before, nobody told me."

"Nobody asked your whereabouts?"

He shook his head.

"How about Griffin's parents? How were they about your being AWOL?"

"They never asked, didn't know. Like I said, we used the back stairs."

And they never checked. Never caught on about the kids' repeated adventures elsewhere. Never asked if they'd heard anything the night of a murder across the way. Very trusting or very lazy people. Another attack of that old affluenza. "Where'd the two of you go?"

He sucked in his upper lip, unconsciously trying to hold onto whatever answer was in the pipeline. Very bad.

"Reality check, Jake. A man you openly despised was murdered. And as far as anyone knows, you were at the scene of the crime. Don't you think that sooner or later you and Griffin will have to answer for where you were?"

His color drained away and his mouth, held so tightly a minute ago, opened halfway.

"Where were you?"

"Jesus." He leaned forward against the seat belt. "I'm tired. What a week."

Fatigue and suspicion can be a toxic mix. I felt the combination poison me. Everything of late added up to trusting no one, believing nothing, suspecting everything. Add to that the torpor in my cells, and the combination was making me ill. What did Jake's evasiveness hide? Sex, drugs—murder?

"I promised not to tell," he finally said.

"I respect your integrity, but all the same—"

He looked at me with wide, imploring eyes. "We went to Suzy Houston's."

Sex, then. With Suzy Houston, a sweet, if dim, ninth grader. Too young for that, wasn't she? I sighed and shook my head.

"Her mother was out on a date. She'd kill Suzy if she finds out she had people over. But Griffin had a pirated *Jane Eyre*—"

"What does *Jane Eyre* have to do with this? Or pirates, for God's sake?" I felt frayed, and Jake's incomprehensibility—deliberate?—made everything worse. I drove the Expressway, grateful for small favors—no delays at this hour of a predawn Saturday. "Please get to the point."

"That *was* the point. Suzy—is she going to get in trouble over this? She hadn't read the book like she was supposed to for you. We wound up watching it with her."

"That's it? All of it?"

He nodded.

So the evil deed was watching *Jane Eyre*. An illegal videotape copy of the recent movie version. It wasn't officially on tape yet, or I might have shown it to my classes myself. So we weren't talking murder, we were talking grand theft, intellectual piracy. Interesting what seems like good news sometimes.

"I won't say anything unless I really need to, but if Griffin's great technical expertise is being put to use pirating films, I'd suggest he has too much equipment and not enough sense."

Jake shook his head. "Only for Suzy. They're like a big brother–little sister thing."

The closer we came to the paved-over city, the more the ground fog dissipated. I imagined it squashed and roiling beneath the cement. Nonetheless, relief seeped through my bones as driving became less onerous.

"What am I to do with you now?" I asked Jake, when we were on broad and silent Ben Franklin Parkway. Monumental sealed buildings shaped the horizon. "It's not even six o'clock."

I heard a short, nervous exhale, then a longer, more troubled one. He stared out the window into a landscape fuzzed by approaching daylight. "I could say I wanted to get home early, be with her. I guess." His tone would have been the same if he'd suggested that I bury him alive.

"How are you going to explain the jail?"

"Do I have to? If they're sealing our records like they said, why would I have to? She'll get so . . ." His breathing speeded up, and he nervously rubbed the side of his hand across his upper lip. "And if my father hears about this, he probably won't want me to move back with him."

"Is that the plan? Have you heard from him?" My surprise that the elusive journalist had actually surfaced and was offering to behave like a parent must have been audible.

"You think I lie about him, don't you?" Before I could do more than sputter a negative sound, he reached into his pocket and pulled out a piece of paper. "See this? I took it to show Griffin. You'll probably say I made it up myself, typed it onto my computer or something. But how would I get stuff out of his newspaper morgue? It isn't online." He waved the paper near my face.

I smacked it away. "I have to see the road!" Then I took a deep breath and spoke more quietly. "Tell me what it is."

"Sorry," he muttered. "I just wanted you to . . . he did this on his own. I didn't ask. I sent him my column about the unsolved mystery Web site, and he found more stuff about one of the cases I'd mentioned. The Cheshire Cat one. That was Canadian."

I'd found the green-soled corpse and the dishwater drowning more intriguing, but I glanced over because he seemed to require that. I saw nothing except a copy of a news story with a dark head shot in it.

"He sent it to me," Jake said.

This seemed to encompass the dimensions of their relationship— long-distance repartee and an easy bit of research and copying. Nothing that touched the heart. Nothing parental. And meantime, his son was in ever-escalating jeopardy.

I thought about the old child next to me, who had a mother with the emotional maturity of a prepubescent. Who had a father who enjoyed his son at a comfortably remote distance, as long as the relationship didn't get difficult and personal. Who'd had a certifiably crazy stepfather. Who'd thought the Roederers were his sanctuary until one of them tried to jail him. Whose best friend had run away this very night.

Who knew, in short, no safety. "Could you use a little time to get yourself together before you go home?"

He looked at me and nodded, his expression nakedly grateful.

I still had a problem of logistics: The only places I could think of that were open and available for getting oneself together at this hour were park benches and the loft. The latter was warmer.

"Do you believe in him now?" Jake demanded.

"Who?"

"My father!"

Who was Loren Ulrich? Tinkerbell? Was it up to me to make him real? Accumulated fatigue and frustration smacked at my head with cyclone force. Thank God, we were finally home.

I EMPTIED THE cold dregs of coffee into a cup and headed directly for the microwave. "You want half of this?"

Jake shook his head. He seemed untouched by fatigue. If anything, he was wired, hovering around the table, demanding that I believe in his father. I couldn't sympathize much longer. I offered Jake coffee, fresh, and offered some to me, too. I ground beans while sipping my reheated brew.

I tried to remember the steps by which I'd wound up virtually sleepless on a Saturday dawn with an eleventh grader in my kitchen.

"If you tell my mother about tonight," Jake said, "and she tells him, I don't know what'll happen."

He had the agitated look of something caged breaking free. I resented the youth that allowed him to be active and emotional on zero sleep, although he did seem to be wobbling out of control now and then in a way that might take the lid off his raw emotions.

"Why do you have to tell any of it? Even about Suzy Houston's?"

"Because a crime—a *murder* happened."

He shook his head too vigorously, leaned over the table near where I stood, his long frame bent at the waist, his face near mine. "You have to *listen*, understand!"

"Shh." I wanted him back observing boundaries. "You're exhausted, and things are out of proportion."

"No! *You're* the one out of proportion!" He grabbed my upper arms, as if to force me to pay attention, as if I hadn't already been trying my best. I felt weepy with fearful frustration. "Nobody in the whole world listens to me!" he shouted, his grip tightening with agitation. *"You have to!"*

And *blam!* Noise—pounding feet. My scream. A shout, "Let her go or I'll shoot!" Hands grabbing. Then, "What the hell *is* this? Who the hell are you?"

That voice. I exhaled. Jake, on the other hand, didn't seem capable of breath. He looked as if he would crumple right to the floor—if only he weren't being held in a human straitjacket by Mackenzie.

"Please," Jake said. "Miss Pepper? Could you tell him to—"

"He's okay," I said to Mackenzie. "There's no . . . what *are* you doing here? You were in Kansas."

He let Jake go and took a deep breath. "So I was, indeed." He sounded his normal self again. "But it took so long to get the paperwork done that, lo and behold, they meantime invented airplanes, and I took one home. I was in Kansas and now I'm not."

Jake, released, looked like an oversized puppy who'd messed the room.

"I called when I landed," Mackenzie said. "Where've you been?"

"Are you arresting me?" Jake's question was whispered. He kept his head bowed, his eyes on the floor.

"Should I?" Mackenzie asked.

"This is Jake Ulrich," I said. "My student, and not yet a hardened criminal. He meant no harm. Jake, this is C. K. Mackenzie." I don't like sharing my domestic life with my students, so I said no more, but then, I didn't have to. Maybe Jake and I could cut a deal and keep each other's secrets. "Mackenzie also means no harm," I said. "Generally speaking."

"I tiptoe in so as not to wake you and suddenly I see this guy grabbing you. Student or no student, what the hell's going on?"

"Good question," I said. "I wish I knew the answer."

Fourteen

A sullen, recently incarcerated teenager was not the welcome-home surprise I would have chosen, but there we had it. More precisely, there we had him.

Jake and I presented a condensed and sanitized version of recent events, and Mackenzie scrubbed his Kansas adventures of all details good and bad. There had to be more to it than his summary, which consisted of: "Got him and brought him back." Plus a few yawns and the comment that he'd been an "ugly cuss."

I smiled at my hero. So what if he hadn't saved my life, hadn't needed to. He'd thought he was, would have if I'd required saving. That was just as good. But my limbs felt sandbag-heavy with exhaustion born more of the mind than the body. I was tired of worrying about a situation that seemed beyond my capacity, and as a reward for his heroics, I passed him the emotional baton.

"Time for home," Mackenzie told Jake.

"It's just after six," Jake said.

"People do function at this hour. Even on Saturday. Even young people. People get up and jog or farm or practice the tuba or row on the river or write sonnets. People even go home at six of a morning."

"How will I explain?"

"Say Griffin's mom woke you up running the vacuum."

Jake stared. "Mrs. R.? Vacuuming?"

"A joke, son," Mackenzie said. "Say anything, including the truth."

"My mother sleeps in, especially Sat—"

"What is wrong with you? Don't you have a key to your own house?"

"Well, I . . . it's a matter of . . . she's . . ." He gave up and put his hands up in a position of surrender.

And out we went into the morning. The ground fog had gone urban, transformed into gray, watery air.

Mackenzie chauffeured. I was delighted—until he turned left, toward South Philly. "Jake lives in the Fairmount area," I said. "Uptown and to the right. North."

Mackenzie nodded. "Thought maybe breakfast first. I'm starvin'."

He was also allowing Jake a grace period and a less surprising time of arrival. I studied Jake's visible and extreme relief the way an archaeologist might read surface clues to buried secrets, and I saw signs of how deeply and completely unhappy he was. Unlike the archaeologist, I stopped there, unwilling or afraid to dig deeper.

Mackenzie's job demanded knowing off-hour haunts, in this case an all-night diner. I yawned and rested my head against the seat. Total passivity was increasingly attractive.

When we entered the diner, Jake went off to wash up.

Mackenzie and I settled into a high-backed leather booth, from which I studied the decor.

Three walls were resplendent with paintings on velvet, although rather than toreadors or Elvis, the artist was enraptured with overloaded, steaming platters of food. And what retro, incredible edibles! Fat-edged steaks, eggs and sausage, ice-cream sundaes, pie à la mode, twelve-layered cakes.

I waved at the artwork. "Very chic and now. This is the new restaurant trend. The forbidden fatty old standards have become rewards for working out and eating sprouts and zero fat at home."

Mackenzie raised one eyebrow. "Hate to say this, but the art's been up since the Fifties. Nothing's back *in* here—it never left. Never budged." He smiled and took my hand. "I get any interestin' mail or messages while I was gone?"

"Bills and ads." Then I remembered. "You had a message yesterday from Neddy Roederer. I forgot. Sorry. He must have called from the road, because they were scouting schools, and didn't get home till late last night, so you couldn't have gotten back to him, anyway."

"Any hint as to what it'd be about?"

I shook my head. "Not specifically. A delicate issue he thought you'd understand. There was something secretive about the way he asked me for your number, and he didn't want you to call him at home, but at his club. You're the only copper he's ever met socially, and a book-loving one to boot, so you're his pick."

Mackenzie put down his menu. "He wants to confess."

"Confess what? How do you know?"

"Don't *know*. But there wasn't much to do in Kansas besides think about everything you told me the last two days. Spiers was tormenting the man, blackmailing or about to blackmail him about a supposed homosexual relationship that happened behind Tea's back. Then Spiers gets himself killed outside the Roederers' door, saving commute time. What more do you want? If Neddy weren't at the top of the social food chain, he'd have been arrested by now. The obvious is usually the answer."

"I can't buy it. He's too . . . nonferocious. Besides, the police are questioning Mother Vivien. She has a record, too." And there was still, awful or not, an unresolved question about Jake. Or Jake and Griffin together, the strong and angry young men.

Mackenzie shrugged. "You'll see."

I wondered if—when—I would feel ready to talk about my mother's secret. Mine now, too. And that was another problem with tossing secrets, like stones, into the equation. The ripples expanded, touching and involving more and more. As long as I didn't tell Mackenzie, we had a secret between us, too.

That avenue of thought dead-ended as Jake rejoined us.

"By the way," Mackenzie said, "the answer is Edward."

Jake slid into the booth. "What is Mr. Roederer's first name? I love *Jeopardy*."

"Edward Fairfax," C. K. said.

"Franklin," Jake said. "The famous Ben's descendant, remember?"

"Edward Fairfax Rochester! Mr. Rochester's given name," I said. "That's who you're talking about."

"Isn't that who you asked about?"

I gave a thumbs-up. "Kansas was *really* boring, wasn't it?"

"Good library, though. Great research librarian."

"Edward Fairfax Rochester, Edward Franklin Roederer," Jake said. "Their names are really close. Coincidence? I think not!"

"Hmm," I said. "Rich men in enormous homes with similar names. Then the question therefore is: does a madwoman lurk in Mr. Roederer's attic? A dark, broody secret?"

"There's a deaf and toothless dog," Jake said. "Gertrude. She hangs out in the kitchen, not that I've checked the attic much. We hang out in the basement, and nobody's there but the computer." Jake then ordered an all-sugar repast of pancakes, syrup, a cream doughnut, and a soda. Mackenzie, on the other hand, rebalanced the U.S. cholesterol deficit with eggs, bacon, buttered toast, and coffee with cream.

I was too tired to be hungry. "Bagel," I said. "Dry. Coffee. Black." I studied the fourth wall, a mosaic of broken crockery that looked both spontaneous and still in progress.

Jake had youth and sugar in his corner. He was full of energy, and in between bites and sips, he asked the detective about Kansas, extradition procedures, Interpol, and what happened in international chases. He was confusing Mackenzie with 007, but that was okay.

And then, the inevitable Jake question. "So, do you use computers much in your work?"

Mackenzie responded in painstaking detail about data banks of fingerprints, criminal records, and evidence breakdowns—plus God knows what else. Then he segued to his real love: his own expeditions on the Net. This generated a rhapsodic, endless response, and they chugged on with ever more steam, as if techno-talk itself were fuel.

They might as well have been speaking Medieval Bulgarian. I tuned out. Until Jake—apropos of what, I didn't know—pulled the raggedy news story out of his pocket. Yet again. It wasn't Oedipal; it wasn't an Electra complex, so what was it? Had Freud labeled the complex that involved idolization of a father by his son?

But of course, Sigmund the Victorian Papa probably called such adulation standard operating procedure. Normal. And pronounced it good.

"After I picked up on it, my father went into the morgue—you know, where the newspaper keeps its records—and found this, and sent it to me," Jake said.

I would have cried, if I'd had the energy. I hoped Mackenzie realized what it was about. At the moment, he looked confused. He read the weathered copy and looked at Jake blankly, waiting for more information.

"Someday, the Net will have all the articles on it, too. The whole newspaper morgue. Wouldn't need to physically hunt this one down," Jake added. He chuckled. "I mean, what if my father wasn't a journalist?" I could hear how much he liked even the taste of the word *father*.

Mackenzie reread it with serious attention, nodded, and said, "I see what you mean." I'd been wrong. As far as C. K. was concerned, Jake had presented the article not to demonstrate his father's fabulous skills, and not to illustrate tight father-son bonds, but simply as an example of the Internet's possibilities.

"This Katt," Mackenzie said. "Nobody's found him?"

Jake shook his head.

"Picture isn't sharp enough to ID him anyway."

"It's so many generations away," Jake said. "A newspaper reproduction of a snapshot taken at some office party. Maybe never crystal-clear. Then scanned into my father's computer, sent to mine, and printed off the monitor."

"He looks ordinary enough. Easy to disappear," Mackenzie said.

He was indeed extraordinarily bland. Tall and pudgy, with thin, pale hair and a pale mustache. A caricaturist's nightmare, with not an exceptional feature that would stay in your head, except, perhaps, the tortoiseshell glasses frames.

It was interesting to speculate how many unsolved crimes there were around the world, but beyond that, what was the point? Surely not to alert the general populace and have these perps apprehended. If this guy had enough intelligence to change his glasses since the snapshot, he'd be unrecognizable.

I nursed my coffee, the morning's caffeine slapping my exhaustion like an electrified irritant.

Either that or my innate selfishness made me impatient. I was more than ready to deposit Jake where he belonged and get on with the student-free weekend I deserved.

WE DROVE NORTH. Jake lived in the Fairmount area, named, like so much else, by William Penn, who'd deemed the bluff where the Art Museum now stands, a "faire mount." Nowadays, our enormous city park, a major thoroughfare, and this neighborhood all bear the name. Which is lucky, because Fairmount area sounds a lot better than Penitentiary area, a more logical label for this part of town. Penn's rocky bluff is not visible here, but the turrets and towers of Eastern State Pen are. Covering eleven acres, it and its thirty-foot-high stone walls cannot be ignored.

"Another Philadelphia first," Mackenzie said without preamble, obviously feeling the looming presence as intensely as I did. The prison lolled hugely, pressing against the neighborhood. I wondered how the sight of it affected Jake the morning after being behind bars. "The world's first penitentiary," C. K. added.

My man possesses a fund of historical knowledge, and he is generous to a fault about sharing it, so I was familiar with these facts. I tried hard to stifle a yawn, but the contortions such attempts required—flaring nostrils, tight lips, dropped jaw, bugging eyes—felt like work, so I gave up and yawned away.

"Until this place was built," Mackenzie said, "bad guys were tossed in dungeons until they got a physical punishment—a whipping, a beheading, whatever. Here, the punishment was complete loss of freedom and solitary confinement. Once inside, you never saw another inmate. This was a place to do penance. That's why it's called a *peniten*tiary."

"I never knew that," Jake said.

"Books are good things, too," Mackenzie said quietly, turning onto Jake's street. "Once, the governor of Pennsylvania sentenced a dog to life imprisonment here for murdering his wife's cat."

"For real?" Jake smiled, ready to be told it was a joke.

"For real," I said. "Pep the dog went to prison in the 1920s." I remembered historical facts of that sort. The irrelevant sort.

Mackenzie expertly parallel-parked. I had the distinct sensation Jake was fading, that his home would make him disappear like the original Cheshire cat, only without a smile in his case. He took a deep breath, nodded, thanked us both, and got out of the car with the animation of a zombie.

For no good reason, but without saying anything and in unison, perhaps because it seemed polite to see the delivery through to its destination, we scrambled out behind him.

He walked up the three front steps as if he were about to face a death squad. We followed. He turned his key in the lock.

The door flew open without his assistance. "Where *were* you!" his mother screamed. "My *God*! You worried me sick!"

We stood there, Jake on the top step, I, two steps below, and Mackenzie on the pavement. Facing all of us was Betsy Spiers in bathrobe and wild flying hair, waving her hands. Our own drum major.

"Mom, why—what—"

"I didn't know what *happened*!" she screamed.

Of course, if she could control her hysteria, she could have noticed her son in front of her, unmarked, hale, and as hearty as one can be who doesn't in any way want to come home.

But I was being unkind. She was a weak woman who'd been widowed three nights ago. And I still was uncomfortable with how Jake had gone to school the next day, and to a party the following night, although it probably meant he was less of a hypocrite than I wanted him to be.

I peered around Jake feeling damned silly.

"They called!"

"Who, Mom?" Jake's voice was low. I could feel him try to calm her through the power of suggestion. "Who called?"

"They did! The Roederers! I thought you were there—you said you'd be there—I'm all alone here and they called because they said you and Griffin—they didn't know where you were."

"Where I was or where Griffin was?"

She shook her head, negating the question's worth. "Both! I can't remember—Griffin, it was his mother—but what does it matter? You weren't where you were supposed to be, where you said you'd be. I was worried sick."

She'd been inaccessible to her son when he'd phoned, needing her, and now she berated him for not staying in touch. I had to hand it to her. She had self-centeredness down to an art.

Why had she picked up for Tea Roederer, and not for Jake? Had she been out when Jake called? Was she always where she was supposed to be?

"And the *police* called!" she screeched.

She'd answered that call, too. Why not Jake's?

Jake took a step back and away from her and nearly sent me crashing to the sidewalk. "Mom," he said, "this is my teacher. Miss Pepper, remember? And Detective Mackenzie. Could we all go inside?"

"Detective!" She clapped her hand to her mouth, flattened herself against the open door. We took it as meaning that we should come in. "What's he done?" she asked Mackenzie. "My heart won't take this. I can't believe—"

"Whoa! He hasn't done anything. I'm Miss Pepper's friend. We ... I ..."

155

We'd forgotten to make up a cover story. Why were we here? I looked at Jake, then at the walls, waiting for a cue.

The living room was spacious, high-ceilinged, and scrubbed clean, but it nevertheless felt musty, as if its windows and doors had been kept sealed against life. Betsy's putty-based wardrobe palette was also her color scheme for upholstery and carpets. A television on a stand was in one corner. No books were visible.

Jake took a while to come up with a story. "They—we . . ." He looked at his shoes, back at us, and then at his mother. "Sit down, won't you?" he said. I was delighted to be able to, and pleasantly surprised by how comfortable the dun sofa was. I had expected it to be unyielding, a place on which to do penance.

"This is how it was," Jake began.

There were things about Jake of which I didn't approve, most of which had comprised the substance and offenses of this long night. But I definitely liked the way he was trying to soothe his mother. He could have, instead, battered against her, countering her hysteria with indignation. Compassion and a grasp of reality were at work here, and I respected him for it. And had hopes for his ultimate survival and triumph because of it.

"Griffin threw a party," he said in a calming voice. "It got out of hand."

Of all possible explanations—the truth!

"What do you mean, 'out of hand'?" Betsy Spiers demanded.

He shrugged. "Beer, rowdiness, vandalism. Things got hurt."

I thought again of the chandelier, that fragile symbol of opulence, and I sighed.

"Then Griffin's parents came back a day earlier than they were supposed to, and they called the police."

Betsy started to weep.

"Parties like that happen a lot," Jake said. "The police usually calm things down and send the kids home."

"She called me," his mother said. "She just called me."

"Just?"

"No. Not just. An hour, two, three ago. I don't know."

"What about?"

"The *police?*" Betsy had finally registered what her son had said. "For God's sake—you were *arrested?*"

He shook his head. "Not really." Through repeated practice, I assumed, he'd become expert at answering scattershot questions, at running a story through a fragmented field.

"He was reprimanded," I said.

Jake's voice took on more heat. "Which I didn't deserve at all, since I wasn't even there." Too late, he realized his mistake.

"Then, where *were* you?" Betsy sounded close to an actual, thinking mother.

"Griffin was upset because they were sending him away."

"But where were you?"

"Around. Driving around."

"They don't know where he is now," she said. "He left his own party. Why would anybody leave his own party?"

"He's . . . leaving," Jake said.

"Running away," Mackenzie suggested.

Neither of us pointed out that Jake, too, had been driving around, and that he lacked his own car in which to do so, so he'd been another runaway.

"But he called here!" Betsy Spiers said. "Griffin wanted to talk, except he wouldn't say why or what."

"Probably wanted to know what happened to me," Jake said. "We were kind of not getting along when he dropped me off."

"What are you talking about?" Betsy said.

Jake shrugged. "Did he say how I could reach him?"

"I'm so frazzled, I wouldn't remember if he did!"

"Mom!"

"I was rattled by phone calls before it was even light out, and the worry about you. I'm not Superwoman, Jake, and you know how I get when things—"

Nothing improved in this family. Nothing was resolved. Nothing changed.

"You're killing me with your crazy ways!" Betsy's voice approached a register only dogs can hear.

"Mom, please, don't be so—" Jake was interrupted by the doorbell.

"Oh, my God, now what?" Betsy said.

Jake, Mackenzie, and I all looked at each other. Betsy was apparently paralyzed, it seemed presumptuous for either C. K. or me to answer the door, and the remaining alternative was not one Jake seemed to relish. I got the sense that each one of us in the room was remembering that Betsy Spiers had said the police had called, and had never gotten around to saying why.

The bell rang again.

After nervously tapping his fingers on his knee, Jake walked to his front door like an automaton.

Betsy whimpered, her face in her hands, but she peeped through her fingers.

Jake opened the door, and from where I sat on the sofa, I saw his jaw drop.

Betsy Spiers uncovered her eyes and shrieked. For real, and not for effect, this time.

A tall blond man stood in the entry with a garment bag slung over one shoulder. "Going to invite me in?" he asked. "Been a while, I know, but . . ."

"Dad," Jake whispered, as if he were afraid the image would disappear if he spoke too loudly. "Dad."

Fifteen

LOREN Ulrich, newspaper chronicler of mortgage rates and new home starts, confirmed my every prejudicial expectation. A good-looking, well-maintained man, he dropped the leather and canvas overnighter that had been over his shoulder, more carefully deposited a computer case next to it, and stood in a casual pose. He was dressed in white hunter–foreign correspondent clichés: cottony beige garments that would be perfect for a café in Zimbabwe.

Toronto real estate must be wild.

On second impression, he lost some of his slick preposterousness. He halted uncertainly before he entered the living room.

Perhaps that was nothing more than travel fatigue—if The Father of Jake permitted himself such a mundane malaise. So on third impression, my prejudices were back in place.

Betsy Spiers held her hands up like shields against her ex-husband. "What do you want with us?" she said, her voice hoarse. "Why are you here?"

"I said I was coming," he said. "Didn't you tell her, Jake?"

His son lowered his eyes and shrugged. A graceful way of assuming blame instead of reminding Loren Ulrich that he'd made similar promises many times. Why should he have trusted or believed this one?

"Jake e-mailed me about Harvey," Ulrich continued. "I was and am concerned."

"You're lying," Betsy said. "You hated Harvey."

"I'm concerned about what you'll do now. I understand the Moral Ecologists want this house back. So I'm worried about both of you, but particularly Jake." I heard the source of Jake's soft-spoken calming technique. His father used precisely the same modulation and tempo, and it came so naturally, he must have used it back in the Toronto days. For how long had Betsy tottered precariously near the edge?

"You want to take him away from me, don't you?" she screamed. "It's been your plan all along, and now when that harlot is throwing us out into the street, you think you can—but you can't! I won't let you corrupt him, ruin him! I'm staying and he's staying!"

"Betsy—"

"Mom!"

I could not recall a situation in which I had felt less comfortable, but making a reasonably polite exit through the battling trio at the doorway seemed daunting. I cleared my throat. "Excuse—" I was drowned out.

"I can't take this, Loren. Not today, not after all that's already happened, not since—"

"What? What happened? Did something else happen since Harvey? What?"

"Dad, you know how Mom—"

160

"The police, Jake missing, his friend a runaway—that's *some* of what's been happening, just *today*, let alone every other day—and you weren't here, so what right do you have to say anything about any of it? You were *never* here and now you barge in and want to—"

"Excuse us—"

"He didn't say that, Mom. He really hasn't had a chance to say much of—why don't we let Dad—"

"Dad! *Dad!* As if he was ever a proper father to you. And then, when Harvey tried to fill in, to make up for the missing pieces, you *hated* him, treated him like—"

"Mom!"

"Betsy!"

"Excuse me!"

I wasn't the only one to gasp. Everyone wheeled in the direction of The Voice.

Mackenzie didn't often employ that I-am-the-law-and-must-be-obeyed tone, which had the power to realign reality. It belonged in a comic book as a magic attribute of the normally soft-spoken Southern fellow, and had to be used with care. But it worked—even with the Ulrich-Spier clan.

"Your issues are personal, private." His voice was back to its soft-edged melodic self. All three of their mouths hung slightly agape, listening intently. "This's a family thing you three should deal with on your own, without spectators. Therefore, we are takin' our leave. You have that?"

"Who *are* you?" Loren Ulrich demanded.

His question dispelled the Mackenzie magic, restarted Betsy's static and squeaks, delayed our leave-taking and implied that we, not he, were interlopers, that he knew everyone involved in Jake's life, except for us.

"This is Miss Pepper," Jake said. "She's head of journalism class, the newspaper. You know, the columns I send you? And this is her . . . ah . . . ."

My *ah* extended his hand. "C. K. Mackenzie," he said.

"He's a policeman!" Betsy's voice had reshaped itself into a pointed wire that pierced soft tissue. "A *detective!*"

161

Loren Ulrich looked from Mackenzie to his son and back again, waiting for an explanation. Mackenzie provided none.

"We have to leave," I said.

"Wait!" Jake said. "Can't we—couldn't we all sit down again and talk? I would like you to meet my father. Couldn't we have a normal kind of time?" He flashed a look at his mother that combined pleading and fear.

She pursed her lips. *Normal* was obviously a distasteful concept to her.

"What did he do, Detective?" Loren Ulrich asked. "My son—you brought him here because . . . ? Did he do something wrong? He's not involved in this . . ." He shook his head. He wasn't going to finish the thought.

"I didn't do anything," Jake said. That wasn't quite the truth. "Dad, we have to—"

Loren Ulrich shushed his son by putting both of his hands, palms forward, at chest height, then fanning them from side to side like out-of-synch windshield wipers. He was taking charge and he wanted no input except what he requested, as he requested it. I wondered whether Jake found his actions as offensive as I did.

Which led me to wonder whether Betsy Ulrich Spiers had always been an hysteric, or whether it had taken the combination of her overconfident first husband and fanatical second to produce the mess she now was.

I'd always worried why clever Jane Eyre never questioned what had made Bertha Rochester insane. Rochester wouldn't have married a raving lunatic, so the question was the same as it was with Betsy Spiers—did the husbands do it? For the first time, I considered Betsy and Loren with interest.

"What kind of detective are you?" Loren Ulrich's eyes had never left Mackenzie.

"Homicide."

"Jesus." Ulrich's glance shot to his son and stayed there, and his bravado dissipated. Then his expression brightened. He had puzzled something through and he was in charge again. "I've got it," he said. "You're just asking questions, eh? About Harvey, his murder. Awful thing that was. Hideous way to go. Where are you with the case?"

"Not anywhere. That happened out in Radnor, not in the city. I'm with the Phila—"

"Terrible thing," Loren said. He didn't listen well. Luckily his beat was concrete, brick, and steel. He spread his arms wide, embracing the room and its contents. "But you don't, you can't, no matter how . . . grating Harvey was, you can't imagine anyone here had anything to do with it, can you?"

Which made it apparent that he thought either his ex-wife or his son had. And wanted Mackenzie to know that. I wondered which he suspected, and if the idea pained him at all.

"You hate me, don't you?" Betsy screeched. "You've hated me since the day I left, and you want me to go to the gas chamber! How could you suggest that *I* killed Harvey—I'm too weak!"

"Of course you are," he said, his eyes wide. He looked at Mackenzie and me, searching for a sympathetic glance. "No matter how you felt, what he did to you or what you may have said, you are simply too . . . insufficiently . . . *linear* to arrange something that heinous."

Betsy, as well she might, looked stymied.

Was he saying that Betsy couldn't think in a straight line and therefore couldn't contrive a murder? A damnably weak defense, and more like a barbed accusation—as he well knew.

"Are you saying I could have done it?" Betsy screamed. "*Nobody* thinks that except you, because you always act as if I'm insane, but it's you who's crazy! The police questioned me and went away. And how could I have done it? He was too heavy. Besides, everybody knows I never went to those bonfires."

The bonfires the Moral Ecologists said they didn't start, right? Someday we'd have to pursue that line.

"I was here, alone, all night," she went on. "When the police came, they knew—I was here alone. They have the harlot—she did it and they know it."

"Mom," Jake said, "nobody accused you of anything. You don't have to explain where you—"

"Besides, it's impossible. I couldn't lift him."

163

I wondered why she said she hadn't had the opportunity or muscle to kill her husband, not that she *wouldn't* have, wouldn't have wanted to. Possibly because her son knew the reality, must have been here for countless hysterical rants against Harvey Spiers. And it was interesting to know that the police had considered—or still did consider—her a suspect.

But it wasn't sufficiently interesting to convince me to waste more of my day in this unhappy household. "So!" I said. "We'll just be on our—"

"Did I ever once say I thought you'd killed Harvey?" Loren asked mildly, ignoring me completely. "I didn't, wouldn't, couldn't entertain the idea."

Each word was uttered with so little sincerity, it seemed custom-designed to evoke another outburst, further proof of Betsy's instability. But for once, she kept a near silence, broken only by snuffles.

Ulrich turned back to Mackenzie. "You didn't answer me. What's happening with the case? What's your relationship with my son?"

Mackenzie's mouth compressed with annoyance. "Mr. Ulrich," he said, speaking even more slowly than is the norm for him, "it's a waste of my breath to answer people who don't listen." He paused. "You ready to hear me now?"

Loren nodded.

"Miss Pepper and I, we brought Jake here this morning. The reason behind this is simple and has nothing to do with any investigations. The reason is that Jake does not have a car and I do. I was accompanyin' Miss Pepper, and she was accompanyin' Jake, who is her student. Therefore, my presence has nothing whatsoever to do with my professional role. Which fact I tried tellin' you. Furthermore, even in my professional role, I am not involved in the murder of Harvey Spiers because it happened out beyond City Line, which, as you might suspect, defines the edge of the city. I am part of the Philadelphia Police Department. I work on homicides that happen inside this city. Have I made myself entirely clear? Is the geography or anything else about that still confusin' you?"

Loren Ulrich put his palms up in a placating gesture. Then he swiveled one wrist so that his hand was raised like a traffic cop's, signaling *halt*. The excessive hand signals went with the outfit, another international, sophisticated accoutrement. "I don't understand what Jake was doing with you in the morning in the first place. Where he found you, how he got there, why."

"Well, tha's surely puzzlin'." Mackenzie had apparently borrowed an additional Southerner's accent to lay atop his, and he was nearly unintelligible. But gallant. "I admit I initially shared your confusion and surprise," he added in a soft blur of near-English that sounded like, "Ahdmitah nishlysha'ed . . ."

I heard him, though. Confusion and surprise, indeed. Quite a euphemism for racing across the loft and tackling Jake.

"However," he continued, "I came to understand that Jake was at our place merely waitin', delayin' his return here from a desire on his part to avoid disturbin' his Momma too early in the day. Which is to say, it was done from the finest of impulses."

That was grand, since it didn't answer a single question. Grander, when I weighed in the effect of that gibberish. And although Toronto's pretty far from good-ol'-boy land, the soft-summer-nights accent and the guy-thing worked. Or something did. Ulrich didn't rebound with another question.

"In any case," Mackenzie went on, smooth as can be, "you have fam'ly issues to deal with. So, if you'll excuse us."

"I'll explain, Dad," Jake said, moving aside for us. "I'll explain later."

"Sure! For your *dad*!" Betsy snapped. "Do *I* get an explanation? Nobody tells me anything!"

"Thanks," Jake told us again, and we nodded and moved toward the door, freedom, and a student-free day with Mackenzie. A weekend.

However. There's a proverb—Yiddish, I believe—that if you want to make God laugh, make plans. My weekend was providing the Supreme Power a veritable laff-fest because at that moment, the front door was pounded upon, and its bell rung. A very Gestapo effect.

Betsy put her hands to her throat in an odd gesture of fear.

"A door-to-door salesman, do you think?" Loren Ulrich said.

I gave him points for attempting to lighten things up. I, too, tried to help. "The Jehovah's Witnesses around here are really aggressive, aren't they?" For once, I hoped they really were at the door.

"Harvey wouldn't put in a security system," Betsy whined. "He was too trusting—look what happened to him. And there isn't even a peephole, a way to know who is out there, and we could all be killed in a second!"

Jake opened the door.

"Jake Spiers?" I couldn't see past Jake to get a sense of the speaker, but he spoke with great authority.

"Ulrich," Jake said. "My name's Jake Ulrich."

"Correct, sorry. Jake, can we come in? We're with the Radnor Township police, and we need to talk with you. We'd as soon keep it off the street, away from the neighbors."

He said it nicely enough, but it didn't meet Betsy's standards of acceptability. As the two men entered the living room, she shrieked "Po*lice*?" The word achieved glass-shattering pitch.

"Mom," Jake said, and then his shoulders sagged. He looked too weary to try anymore.

To their credit, the policemen, both of whom were rugged and well-worn–looking, central casting's good cops for your basic TV series, nodded and smiled as if they were quite used to cater-wauling as a greeting. Maybe, in fact, they were.

"What is this?" Loren demanded. "I'm Jake's father. What do you want with him?"

"Father?" the younger cop said. "His father died Wednesday."

"This man's not Jake's father, except biologically," Betsy snapped. "He's never behaved like a father. He's so involved in his career, he doesn't even live in this country."

Follow that logic. I dare you.

"His stepfather was killed," Mackenzie said. He introduced himself, showed his badge, and explained he was here socially, not professionally—an explanation that surely increased the confusion, given the company Mackenzie was opting to keep.

"Why are you badgering my boy now?" Betsy said. "He was

asleep when it happened. Griffin Roederer can vouch for that. All the Roederers can. Besides, everybody knows that harlot was behind my husband's death. Harvey told her it was over. A woman—a tramp—scorned. So leave Jake alone!"

"Mom, please. You're making Harvey sound . . ."

"Or Neddy Roederer. Look for the sinner, not for my son. Neddy Roederer was a fraud. A morally corrupt fraud, and Harvey knew it."

"Mom!"

I assumed Jake was trying to remind her that her late husband's whoring and blackmail plans wouldn't help anybody's cause. She seemed to belatedly comprehend this, and tightened her lips again.

"I know what this must be about," Jake said in a small voice, his eyes focused on the mud-colored carpet at his feet. "It's about my . . . the stealing. Last night at the station, she was angry about everything, including that."

"Stealing? Oh, my *God*!" Betsy screamed.

"I took two of her china boxes a while back. She has, like, a million. Tiny suitcases and typewriters and pincushions and globes. They all have hinges and open up, but they're too small to put stuff in. I took a dog and a cat. I'm really sorry. I meant to put them back last night, but in the confusion . . . and of all the bad luck—that's when she noticed them missing."

"Why would you steal anything?" Loren asked with his first show of real interest. "And why on earth a china cat and dog?"

Jake swallowed. "It was kind of a joke, because I'm not allowed to have pets. But more because . . . I don't know . . . they're . . . silly. And pretty. They don't *do* anything, aren't useful. The Roederers have a lot of things like that, just because they like them. We don't have any . . ." He shook his head. "I know it was wrong. But they were so little, so easy to take, and I did it, bor-rowed them. I can't believe they noticed, they have so many of them. They're in my backpack. Could I give them back to you now, maybe, and not have to . . . ?"

The cops looked sad, but impassive. It seemed improbable that they'd traveled here in search of a china dog and cat.

"If you still need background, any kind of help, about Harvey Spiers, maybe I could be of assistance," Loren said. "I knew him way back when he was a clerk in an insurance company, before his great religious conversion."

"Loren!" Betsy yelped. "Don't make him sound—"

"Yessir, thank you for the offer," the younger detective said.

Loren searched his pockets. "My card," he said. Then he shook his head. "That's useless right now. Sorry. I don't know where to say you can reach me. I came right here from the plane."

"Don't imagine you can stay here!" Betsy muttered.

The older cop handed him a card. "If you think of anything, call. Meantime, we need to speak to you, Jake. Do you feel comfortable talking to us?"

Jake nodded and shrugged, a conditional *yes*.

"Do you want an attorney to be present?"

"I didn't do anything wrong except take those things," Jake said, sounding near exhaustion. "I don't need a lawyer—unless you're accusing me of something else. Are you?"

The younger cop smiled and shook his head.

"Am I some kind of a suspect?"

The cop shook his head again. "If you'll get a jacket," he said.

"You're making a big mistake if you think Jake helped her," Betsy Spiers said. "That slut didn't need help. Those ropes and pulleys make hoisting a dead weight easy. Have you thought about that instead of persecuting my son?"

I watched with fascinated horror. Didn't she realize that anything Mother Vivien could have done, she could have done as well? Vivien was large with fat, not muscle. And how did Betsy know about the efficiency of the ropes and pulleys if she never went to the bonfires? I looked at her with new interest.

She seemed to realize some of this. In any case, she changed tacks. "Do you realize what you're doing to me, taking Jake all the way out the Main Line when he isn't even a suspect? My car isn't working right. I'm a nervous wreck. My husband was murdered and now you're taking my son. Why are you doing this to me?"

"I'm sure they have good and legal reasons, Betsy," Loren said.

"And it's only for a short while. They need Jake to verify something, isn't that what you mean?"

Jake had on his jacket and a Phillies cap.

"Good," the younger policeman said to Jake. "It's still chilly, and they're saying a chance of rain later, too, so the hat's a good idea."

Did the law require them to be completely honest about their reasons for taking Jake with them? They couldn't think of him as a murderer and be so paternal and concerned, could they?

"I have a right to know what's going on," Betsy Spiers said. "I deserve to know what is happening concerning my husband's"— with this, she shot a lethal, squint-eyed look at her ex-husband— "murder."

"Yes, ma'am, and we'll surely try to tell you whatever—"

"Well, you aren't telling me *now*!"

"I'll come get you, son," Loren said. "Don't worry."

"You don't even *know* the area!" Betsy had the ability to scream without raising her voice, a genuine talent. "How can you promise? It'll be another one you break, just like all the—" She wheeled back to face the cops. "You aren't going to tell me, are you?" Betsy said, pointing her finger at the cops. "He was my *husband*!"

By now, I was hoping for a show of police brutality. Unfortunately, those suburban fellows were unstintingly polite. "Ma'am," the older one said, "we definitely will, when and if we get any news about your late husband."

"If you don't have news now—why take my son?"

Jake shook his head. The night's overload showed in the blue hollows below his eyes.

Mackenzie smiled and nodded at the cops, in a way that reestablished that he was part of the same fraternity. "You can see there's a lot of anxiety around here—are you able to let us know any more of what this is about?"

"We need a statement from the boy," the older officer said. "A full statement." He looked down at his belly, pleating his chin into a series of chinlets.

"You want custodial interrogation," Mackenzie said.

The cops both nodded.

"Yet he's not charged with anythin'."

"Correct."

"More like he's a material witness, then?"

I thought about the night of the burning, about the two boys across the way with a probable view through winter-bare tree-tops to the scene of the crime. Two boys who hadn't been asked about their whereabouts by either the police or the Roederers. Until now.

"Hope I'm not out of line," Mackenzie said softly to his sub-urban counterparts, "but this early of a Saturday morning, two days after his stepfather's demise, this seems somethin' new and serious, and it's surely not about china animals." Neither of the other policemen moved a muscle. "A homicide, it'd be, wouldn't it? Another one."

Both officers nodded.

Another murder? Another murder to which Jake was some-how connected?

"And the victim would be . . . ?" Mackenzie continued.

The two men looked at each other, and then the younger one nodded, cleared his throat, and spoke. "The victim would be Edward Franklin Roederer."

Neddy. Gentle, charitable, book-loving Neddy. Mackenzie's pick as Harvey's killer. Instead, Neddy was a victim himself. I felt a wave of nausea at the only thing that was evident: two angry boy-men with two now dead, despised, surrogate fathers.

Mackenzie, who is generally a master of looking impassive—even dreamily absent—no matter what's going on behind the facade, reflected my own shock on his face.

Neddy, the elegant and refined, who'd tried to call a cop, who'd had something he felt needed telling. I turned hot, then cold with guilt—I hadn't speedily transmitted his message—a call for help? It didn't matter that Mackenzie couldn't have re-sponded in time. Neddy, whom I'd involved in the politics of our school, whose generosity—prompted by me via the school paper—triggered what now felt like an endless series of conflicts and deaths. Neddy was dead. I felt partially responsible.

But for all my growing apprehension, other muscles relaxed that had been in a state of tension since I'd seen the burning effigy and said nothing fatal had happened *yet*. As if I'd always known something was waiting even beyond Harvey's murder, which was never the end of anything because whatever caused it wasn't over.

Now, the second shoe had dropped. The something else had happened. There was a chilling comfort in the news.

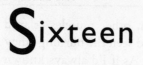Sixteen

" **G** OES to prove they have too much time on their hands in the sticks," C. K. said. "Comin' all this way to retrieve the kid for a statement. Why didn't they take it here, on the spot? For that matter, they could have called it in, an' I could have taken it." Mackenzie, Loren Ulrich, and I were on the pavement in front of the Spiers' home.

"With . . ." I glanced at Loren Ulrich, then mentally shrugged. "Betsy? She'd make it—"

"Impossible." Ulrich finished my sentence. "Betsy makes most things impossible. Flighty, we used to call it. It even seemed cute once, a kind of giddy hyperreacting. Then it stopped being charming or bearable. And now, she's a whole lot worse."

I wanted to say what I thought of a father who could describe his ex that way while leaving his son with her. If Jake was involved in the murders, then Loren and Betsy were coconspirators.

C. K. busied himself with his cellular phone, trying to learn more about what was going on. Neddy Roederer was headline news. If the departments were cooperating, somebody would know.

Betsy had taken to her bed after we collectively promised her that Jake would not be locked up, and that we—I wasn't sure about the graduation to a plural pronoun, but *we* it was—would make sure he was returned from the police station.

"You don't think they're lying, do you?" Loren asked. "I mean, when they said he wasn't accused of the crime. Or the other one."

Mackenzie covered the mouthpiece of the phone with his hand. "It was a hit-and-run," he said.

"Roederer?" Ulrich said. "Then why question Jake? He doesn't even have a car!"

"Between midnight and dawn," Mackenzie continued. "Except there are inconsistencies." He listened again. "Roederer was walking the dog on one of those dark lanes around there."

"Gertrude," I muttered. "The old blind and deaf creature." My stomach felt bloated with sickening possibilities.

"Griffin Roederer's car has damage, blood . . ." Mackenzie said.

"Then they have him? Have Griffin? They've found him?" I asked. Mackenzie shrugged.

"Then question Griffin, not Jake!" Loren insisted. "Stop picking on my son."

I knew that Griffin's car did have to do with Jake. He had been with Griffin on a night when the pressure had been ratcheted to explosive levels. They'd had a falling out, but Jake hadn't said about what. Could it have been the result of a hideous accident? Or worse—of something that wasn't an accident at all? Could Jake have gone to the police about that, not for a ride home at all, then realized he'd walked into a mob of partygoers and their parents and let his real mission go?

Was anything that Jake had told me true? That whole story about the party, and the guilt, and the aborted plan to run away—was that a fabrication to hide the fact that he'd been in a car that killed a man? He'd said they drove without headlights on back roads. Intentionally or not, a perfect stealthy way to kill and disappear.

Both their oppressive parents were dead. I heard echoes of one of Jake's favorite expressions: "Coincidence? I think not." But he meant it as a joke. All I said was, "I was with Jake from four A.M. on. And he was at the station before that."

"For how long?" Loren asked. I shrugged.

Mackenzie's ear was still to the phone, then he said, "Right," and turned off the power. "Time of death's vague. The weather was cold and wet, and the dog could have wanted out any time at all, no matter its regular routine. Or not wanted to go out at all. After all, the R's came home, found the place wrecked, had to deal with police, missing kid, theft, vandalism. Roederer might have wanted to get away and walk it off with the dog as an excuse. Dog's alive, by the way. A broken leg, is all."

"Wouldn't Tea Roederer know what time her husband left the house?" I asked.

Mackenzie shrugged. "Apparently not. She assumes it was after two o'clock, but she's not sure because they have separate bedrooms, and in her words, the whole night was a 'tangle.' "

So time of death was murky and would remain so for a while longer. And meantime, Jake's story became less and less invulnerable.

"Where's a decent hotel?" Loren Ulrich asked. "I figure I have time to check in and dump my stuff before picking up Jake."

"Stayin' long?" Mackenzie asked, although given that the Canadian was carrying only an overnight bag, a daypack, and a computer case, the answer seemed obvious to me, despite my not being the one of us who was trained to detect.

"Overnight," Ulrich said. "I didn't expect to find Jake in trouble. I came because Harvey was killed and Jake seemed worried about where he was going to live. I thought, foolishly, Betsy might finally be open to reason."

His stock rose a few points. He was actively, if belatedly, involving himself in his son's future welfare.

"That was wishful thinking on my part." He shook his head in mock-exasperation with himself. "Betsy does not like reason and she's incapable of making plans."

I remembered. Betsy had impaired linearity. Whatever. "Poor Jake," I said.

"What's that?"

"He's lost two significant people in four days. His stepfather and a man he liked very much."

"What are you saying? You make it sound like he's connected to these deaths."

"Poor Jake is what I said and meant." Well, mostly.

Mackenzie glanced at his wrist. "I have to get back. Where are you parked?" he asked Loren. "If you follow us, we'll lead you to a hotel."

"I'm not," Loren said.

"Not what?"

"Parked. I took a cab."

We should have realized. He'd been carrying his luggage all morning, had no place to leave it.

"I didn't know the area, and I wanted to get here as quickly as I could—Jake's message sounded urgent. Thought I'd rent a car after, and I thought the house would be more central. The kind of place you could always hail something."

It made sense, but so do a lot of things that are based on false premises. Mackenzie could call a cab with his cellular. Or, as seemed more fitting in the City of Brotherly Love, we could give the man a lift.

"How about you drop me off," Mackenzie said to me. "Then get Loren fixed up with a hotel and car rental, and I'll meet you later, back home. I won't be long—have to tie up loose ends about the Kansas guy, take care of a few other things. I'll call."

I had hoped for time with him, for catch-up and a sense of what I wanted to think of as normality with us, but I made do with a quick kiss and a "see you later" as I dropped Mackenzie off. Maybe that was the real normality and I'd better get used to it.

I'd been wrong about the daypack. It wasn't Loren's, but Jake's. When the two of us were driving toward the center-city hotels, Loren apparently realized he'd taken it with him. "Damn," he said. "I should have left this at Betsy's."

"No big deal. Give it to him when you pick him up."

"I'm sure he'll love being handed homework."

"I suspect that's the least of what's in those bags." I knew part of the contents were the china cat and dog.

Jake's motive for thievery made me sad. He'd wanted pets and other impractical, beautiful objects. His home and home life were so unrelentingly bleak that whimsies represented hope, tangible proof that life could be lived differently.

Ulrich cleared his throat. "I feel awkward asking, but would you tell me about my son? He's changed physically, emotionally. It hasn't been all that long, maybe two years."

"Two years is a big proportion of his lifetime." My surge of righteous anger—that such a question should be necessary—wasn't simply about the sins of Loren Ulrich. He'd become my scapegoat for all parents who earned failing grades, and their numbers were legion. Maybe Ulrich didn't deserve the full force of my fury, but he was available.

"It's been difficult," he said softly. "More than I ever anticipated, living in separate countries."

"Come now, the Canadian border is almost a formality. We're not talking Checkpoint Charlie," I snapped.

"In Betsy's mind, it's international espionage."

I shrugged. Betsy's mind could not an argument make.

His tone became confidential. "Plus there's a woman in my life again. A serious relationship, and she . . . there isn't a whole lot of time for me to fly down or anything."

My rage-ometer skyrocketed. What I heard was a man justifying A New Beginning. Running through meadows with one who isn't particularly fond of secondhand adolescents, who may in fact be almost an adolescent herself. And then there'd be a new family, with Jake relegated to ex-child.

"Betsy's made it nearly impossible, making all kinds of Harvey-type claims of moral turpitude. Or saying I planned to kidnap him. Harvey was convinced that Jake was bad, and I'd corrupted him. He had to keep us apart to save Jake's soul. And Betsy . . ." He shook his head in ongoing incredulity. "Betsy let it go on. Betsy agreed with him."

I was a hanging judge with no interest in the defense's arguments. I didn't want to hear about extenuating circumstances. I wanted all parents to be like Scarlett the cat, she who'd gone into the burning building five times to save her kittens. She hadn't talked about difficulties, complications, or extenuating circumstances. All she knew was that her offspring were in danger. All she did was insure that they survived until they could be independent. I wanted Loren Ulrich to have the level of heroism and concern of a stray cat.

And a bit of that anger just might have been in privately acknowledging that my mother, in her own way, wanted only to be that cat and save her kittens. And that in real time and real life, it could be a royal pain. And very complex.

But not where Loren was concerned. So while he may have been waiting for me to commiserate about Betsy and life, I said nothing. Together in silence, we waited at an intersection, while a trailer-truck tried to back around the opposite corner. The light changed from red to green and back again without our moving on in any sense. Finally, I was able to drive again.

"You don't like me, do you?" Loren asked so abruptly and aptly, that I felt my cheeks flame. "Why is that?"

I clenched the steering wheel and stared straight ahead. "I don't even know you. But I do know Jake, and I care about him. He's been put in an untenable position, pushed to the extreme, his options cut off. It's awful for him."

"You sound like somebody explaining what drove a kid to murder. Is that what you think?"

I looked sideways to see if the man was serious, and he was. This was not the first time he'd touched on that idea, which infuriated me because, of course, it brushed against my own fears. "That wasn't what I meant at all," I said. "I meant that Jake's been seriously depressed. With reason."

"But when he e-mails, he sounds like he's having a great time. The newspaper column, his pals—"

"Pal. Griffin Roederer. Your son is shy. A loner."

"Jake? He was never—"

"That was then. He's had his life revised at a difficult stage. He's awkward around his classmates. He and Griffin were—are— best friends, very tight. Otherwise, there aren't hordes of pals, from what I can see. It would be hard for him to get close and to keep his stepfather's identity a secret, for starters."

"No wonder he likes you so much. You're his defender, his friend, aren't you?"

"I'm his teacher. That's a long shot from being enough."

"But the computer. He was always excited about that. It worried me, his interest in crime: writing about it, finding that Web site, sending me things, asking me to do research about people who got away with crimes. Then, with Harvey's murder, I panicked, and now—"

"For Pete's sake! He's not interested in the Cheshire Cat or any of those crimes. He's interested in *you*. Desperate for attention. A Canadian crime was a way to reach you, and he probably searched long and hard for it because you might care about it, about the news story itself, about what your paper had done with it—anything. The caring was important because maybe then, you'd care about Jake."

His voice was a low whisper. "I always care about him."

"It doesn't count unless he notices." We'd reached the Omni Hotel on Walnut Street. Convenient to movies, theatre, and a multitude of historic sites, should he not really want to spend his time here with his son. "I'll wait here until you're registered, then drive you to a rental place," I said.

He shook his head. "I've put you out enough. I'll be fine." He opened the car door, and exhaled audibly. "Thanks," he said. "Not that what you said doesn't hurt like hell, because it hit the mark. Things I didn't want to hear, didn't want to think about because they felt too complicated. So thanks. You're obviously good at your profession, because you taught me a lesson I won't forget."

I watched him walk into the hotel, and I wondered if the lesson would stick when homework was required. I am leery of revelations and dramatic transformations, and Loren Ulrich seemed a man who had charm in place of a backbone.

Home wasn't far, and I drove toward it trying to remember what Saturday plans I'd had. Surely there'd been something in mind that didn't involve adolescent jailbirds.

Sometimes, it felt as if an autopsy of my brain would reveal a bulletin board pocked by overburdened thumbtacks barely securing layers of lists. Lists of lesson plans, meetings, problems with students, plans to make, and deadlines to meet. Lists of the depleted resources of my home. Lists about life—reservations to make, tickets and gifts to buy, people to call, letters to write. By comparison, Moses seemed lucky, having been given precisely one to-do (or not-to-do) list in his whole life, and that with only ten items on it.

I remembered that we needed unglamorous items like onions and tissue. Restocking them seemed a waste of energy, but not having them was worse. I forced myself to stop at the market near Fifth and Spruce. I gave a dollar to a woman who stood by the doors reciting a pathetic set of woes. But once inside, my mind went on free fall, rolling through the past week as I lifted boxes and jars off shelves. I thought about the precipitous tumble from golden Neddy Roederer reverently holding a precious copy of *Pilgrim's Progress* to Edward Roederer, dead under the wheels of his runaway son's car. From madcap Tea in her spangled flapper's dress to the Widow Roederer in her separate bedroom, unaware of her husband's permanent leave-taking. From Harvey Spiers' all-powerful ability to upend the universe to Harvey Spiers, hoisted by his own petard.

And Griffin, the boy Cinderella, a runaway and perhaps a murderer. Even Glamorgan, the stone mansion that had seemed the citadel of safety and permanence, even its treasures were now scarred and depleted.

And Jake.

Seven days and the world unmade.

Only Betsy seemed in stasis—hysterical at the start, hysterical at the end. I stopped in front of the frozen food section, thinking about that perverse craziness, her manipulation, accusing Jake of the very "crimes" she created, like not calling her when—

But he had called her and there'd been no answer, although later last night, she'd spoken on the phone several times. Now that we knew Neddy Roederer had been killed, Neddy, who she thought might have killed her husband—the question grew in urgency. Where had Betsy Spiers been last night when she didn't answer her phone?

And where was Griffin? Why had he phoned Jake? Where had those boys driven?

I stood in the checkout line watching my bill add up, but I was concerned about the things that didn't add up. There'd been too many of them this past week.

And yet, there were rules of cause and effect. Everything ultimately made sense—once you knew enough about it. Right now, pieces rolled around at large while the connection, the center link, was missing.

I wrote a check and the cashier summoned the manager, who nodded gravely and signed off on it. Yet another unsolved mystery. What did that second person see on that check that the cashier didn't? What made him approve it?

I drove home, still absorbed in a futile attempt to connect the dots. Somewhere, somebody knew who had wrapped Harvey Spiers in straw and cloth, and why. And somewhere, somebody knew why—I wouldn't even let myself think a name, I wouldn't accept the obvious—somebody knew why, when he heard and felt his car hit a human body, he fled. Or worse, knew why he deliberately ran down Neddy Roederer and left him to die.

And then, all I could think of was of not thinking. Of home and a nap and forgetting, at least temporarily, all of them and their complicated woes. I was too tired to decide whether I was a part of the *them* that was in trouble.

Seventeen

I slept precisely one hour and sixteen minutes before I awoke from unpleasant reruns of earlier, overpopulated dreams. Everyone was whispering, unintelligible messages—Mackenzie, Mr. Rochester, my mother, Dr. Wonderful, plus a new cast member, Neddy Roederer. This time, my mother was carrying what I'd thought was a dead body, but was merely pants and a jacket. That's what jolted me awake—a maternal reminder, even while I slept.

I was supposed to be at the seamstress' who was altering a suit I'd bought at a secondhand store. How had my mother known that when I'd forgotten?

I sat up, awake and guilt-raddled and convinced there were entirely too many things I didn't understand.

The pantsuit, of course, wasn't ready. The seamstress' cat had been ill and in need of surgery. I should have phoned instead of coming over, she said. I walked back toward my place, hoping Mackenzie would surface with a workable idea as to how to salvage this weekend. I considered possibilities as I crossed the street—until the blare of a horn at my side so terrified me that I levitated, arms flailing, like a figure out of a Chagall painting, if Chagall were having a really bad day.

"Amanda!" a voice called, but I was too busy palpitating to identify the source. Or care. Earthbound again, I scuttled to the curb.

The blare of horn again. "Amanda!" the voice called, and this time I turned and saw a hand waving from the driver's side of a sizzly-blue car that had reduced my life span by at least five years. "Didn't mean to scare you!" Loren Ulrich shouted. "Just wanted to catch your attention."

"And that you did," I gasped, my hand to my chest.

He pulled into a loading zone. "I need to talk with you."

I bent and looked in the car. "Where's Jake? What are you doing here? And how did you know where I'd be?"

"One at a time?" He tried for a grin, but failed. "You showed me where you lived, remember? We drove past after we dropped your—uh, Mackenzie, off."

We had.

"I didn't know where else to go. Betsy's hysterical. I don't even know if there's a problem."

"Meaning?" Talking into a car is distinctly uncomfortable, and definitely undignified. My back whined. "Is Jake all right?"

"I don't know," he said softly. "I don't know where he is. When I got to the police station, he was gone."

"Gone? Didn't they question him?"

He shrugged. "I was a little late, and meanwhile, some aunt of his came for him. A name I'd never heard of. Did Harvey have a sister I don't know about?"

This was not the day to ask me about the extended families of strangers. I stood up straight. "Why don't you find a parking space? I'll wait here."

He had an expression of desperate pleading—as if I had magical answers that would save him and the day. He'd been late, is what I'd registered. Had once again failed to do the right thing by his son. Betsy had been correct in her prediction. That made me still angrier.

I waited a goodly amount, but I didn't put that in Loren Ulrich's column of offenses. It wasn't easy finding a spot on a clear Saturday when winter seemed finally willing to go on hiatus. The promised rain wasn't happening and the air was chilly but fresh. The street swarmed with people exploring the nearly forgotten sensation of not fighting the elements.

Finally, I saw Loren walking toward me at a pace that was either leisurely or hesitant. He dragged a lumpy fabric bag. Jake's pack. Which reminded me of its owner and its owner's father's incompetence, and made me angry all over again.

"I couldn't help—" he began, as he moved within earshot.

"Don't," I said. "Wait till we're upstairs. I want to hear this through. I need to make sense of it."

He was silent until I unlocked the front door and we were in the loft. "Nice," he said. "Really nice."

Which it was. The airy spaciousness was accentuated by our lack of furnishings. But we did have an oak table that served as dining room, emergency desk, and whatever else was necessary. Mackenzie's computer was on it, along with the morning paper, still folded, and the full bag of groceries, plus the mail I'd picked up on my way in the first time. I gestured toward the ladderback chairs and he sat down. I moved aside the litter, both electronic and not. Loren dropped Jake's backpack to the floor and looked as if he, too, would like to lie there inertly.

"What happened?" I put water on to boil. It seemed the thing to do in a situation that felt fraught. With hot water, we could have coffee, tea, or a baby.

"I rented the car," he said.

I unpacked the grocery bag. "Horrible color." Irrelevant, yes, but I was in a mean spirit and it's so easy to wound a man via his car, even when it's a rental.

He shrugged. "It's what they had. I went directly from the rental office to Radnor, but I got lost, so I was late. They must have rushed him in and out."

"Hold it. Lost?"

"I had a map, but those roads are insane. One crossed a creek, I swear. You drove directly into the water. I couldn't believe it! I backed off, tried another route, got all lost, and finally drove through the creek."

I knew that road, had grown up with it and its odd situation. It was a practical road, the shortest line between two points. A wet line, true, but such a trickle of a stream that constructing a bridge to ford it would have been pretentious. Very un-Philadelphia. But an idiosyncratic road wasn't the point. "Lost!" I repeated. "For how long?"

"I don't know. Long, maybe."

I sat down and silently counted to ten. Only then did I dare ask. "Did you ask directions?"

He contorted his mouth and bobbed his head forward in male body language that translated as: *Ask?* Do you take me for the kind of man who can't hack himself out of the wilderness? *You* can ask. You're a girl. But not when I'm around.

"What is it with men?" I stood up. The kettle made asthmatic sounds. So did I. "The woolly mammoth wouldn't get you if you'd admit you're lost! The—"

"I read the book, too," he said. "It's stereotypical, it's stupid." He looked at me sternly. "And it's what I did. Or didn't do. Can we move on? When I finally found the place—and it is amazingly obscure for a police station, like you should just know where it is—Jake was gone. Gotten a ride from the woman he said was his aunt."

"Said?"

"He doesn't have one that I know of. Betsy has a widowed brother in Tennessee and a bachelor brother in Oregon. I'm an only child."

Why was I not surprised by that last fact?

"And I don't think Harvey has—had—family outside Canada. Betsy never hinted that he did. Plus, the aunt was black. Who was she?"

"You have a name?" I filled a glass teapot with hot water and put in the tea infuser. I forgot to ask if that's what he wanted, and when I remembered, I didn't really care. "Aunt who?"

"Margaret Pail or Pael or maybe it was Paet—they just turned this book around for me to look—they were pretty busy, or acting like they were. I couldn't make it out. Only a P and a tall letter at the end and vowels in between. I thought for a minute—hoped that somehow, Margaret was your real name and that you wrote *Pepper* in an idiosyncratic way."

That would be interesting—a dyslexic English teacher.

"He phoned her."

"Then we have two good pieces of information. They can't think he's criminally involved in the hit-and-run or they wouldn't have waved him off that way, and we can assume he wasn't kidnapped. He went voluntarily."

"But why? I told him I was coming to get him. Why didn't the kid listen? Why didn't he wait?"

He looked earnest and confused. I waited for him to reach the obvious conclusion, but his head-shakes and expression indicated ongoing befuddlement. I poured us both cups of tea and pushed the sugar bowl and creamer into his sight line. He didn't react.

I didn't see the point of stating the obvious. That would be cruel.

Then he muttered about irresponsible teens, and I lost the last of my charitable patience. "I'll tell you why he didn't wait." I kept my voice level by dint of admirable self-control. "He didn't wait because as far as I know, you have never shown up when you promised to. At least five different times this school year Jake told me about plans he had with you. You were coming to Philly to visit, meeting him in New York. Once you had tickets to a game in Pittsburgh, and you were sending plane tickets. I can't remember the rest, but—"

"Do you realize how erratic my schedule is?"

185

"Real estate emergencies? Last minute scoops? Give me a break."

"I have deadlines, a column. I cover for people. That's how it works there. I never deliberately set him up. You don't have children, you don't know what it's like to—"

"You're right. I don't know that—but I do know your son, and I know why he didn't wait for you. Because I suspect there were more than the times he told me about. After a while, he stopped going public with those plans because he was mortified when they didn't pan out. Today he didn't know how or where to reach you, and everything he did know indicated that you once again weren't going to show up. That you meant to, but something interfered. And by golly, Loren—it did. Did you call the police station when you were lost? Did you tell somebody you were on your way so they could tell Jake?"

He exhaled so loudly it was like a snort. "I didn't want to waste time, make myself even later looking for a phone. And I didn't know the number of the station, and—"

"And he left. He didn't want to say that his dad is a flake, his mother an hysteric, so instead, he called somebody reliable."

Loren had ruddy patches high on his cheekbones. "What do we do now?" he asked in a low voice. "He didn't go home."

"We find him. What's in his backpack?"

"I didn't look. It's Jake's. It's private, it's—"

I had already retrieved it. My rules of privacy are strict but shallow. If you are so private that you disappear, then the only rule left is: Whatever Works. "Maybe it'll have a clue as to who Margaret is."

If it did, it was buried within an aromatic mass including worn socks, each wrapped around one of the china animals. They were actually fanciful boxes, Limoges china, and as Jake had said, pure fun. The St. Bernard opened at his neck, and inside was a tiny spare keg. The grinning cat opened between her teeth. I also found a paperback on computer graphics whose contents included "Three-D Data Visualization! Digital Image Manipulation! Advanced Morphing! Blobs!"

High time "Blobs!" got excited recognition.

And papers. Lots of them. "More of these damned unsolved mysteries." He pulled out a dog-eared sheaf held together by an oversized green paperclip.

On top, I saw the now familiar pale-faced embezzler. I didn't think he had much to do with Aunt Margaret.

"Look at these," Loren said. "A kidnap in Missouri, the disappearance of middle-aged twin women."

I shrugged.

"An empty Navy blimp that crashed in San Francisco in 1942."

Like father, like son. How could he question Jake's interest in old crimes when he was detouring into them himself? "Loren," I said. "Your son is missing."

"What else can I do about it? I am surely not going to call the police on him! It was your idea to investigate—this is all we have to go on."

"A blimp accident more than fifty years ago can't be—"

"The parachutes were inside, but no people. Never found them, either." He spoke rapidly—the words didn't matter. He simply didn't want to allow space for thoughts about his son's disappearance. "Like the *Mary Celeste*." He sounded like a tape on the wrong speed. "The ship floating in the Atlantic back in the eighteen-hundreds with all its passengers vanished. Remember?"

I did not, but I imagined the story had appeared in countless boys' adventure stories.

"Look, a notebook," I said. Both of us eagerly grabbed for it. I let Loren turn its pages, waiting for a revelation.

I might as well have waited for world peace. Or Godot. We found sketches—one that looked a whole lot like the principal, Maurice Havermeyer, wearing a dunce cap and writing *I will learn to speak English* over and over on the board. We found brief passages—quotes and wisdom as revealed via hip-hop. We found checklists concerning the digitalization of the photo of a donkey. I feared finding out for what that was intended.

But we didn't find *Margaret*, an *M* or even a phone number with no name attached. In short, nothing. "If not her, I'd hoped to find something that might take us to Griffin," I said.

"Why? We're looking for Jake," Loren snapped.

I wasn't going to tell him all my reasons for wanting Griffin around. "Griffin might know who Margaret is. Might be with her. Where else would Jake go? Where is Griffin? I'll bet Jake knows. In fact, what if Griffin wore a disguise, pretended to be Aunt Margaret in high heels and a wig—"

"Doesn't he have facial hair? Wouldn't he look ridiculous? Don't you have to show ID? And Margaret was black."

"It was just a . . ." It had indeed not been meant to be taken seriously, but having said it, I gravitated back to it, feeling as if I needed to touch the idea again, get something from it I'd missed.

"Just a what?"

I shook my head, held up a hand while in my brain, a frantic voice repeated, "Wait a minute, wait a minute, wait a minute!" So I did. And then I had it—via Griffin, friendship, wigs, Limoges boxes. "I don't know who Margaret is, but I think I know where Jake would have asked her to take him."

Loren stood up. "Tell me."

I stood up, too. "Have your map-reading skills improved dramatically in the last ten minutes? Or your ability to ask directions?" I started refilling Jake's pack.

"Do you think he's in danger?"

"Not at all." I didn't want to touch Jake's socks again, let alone put the china cat and dog boxes back into them. Instead, I pocketed the *objects d'art* and finished repacking. "He went to the only friendly place he knows. Knew. But they don't know you, and you are not Canada's answer to Lewis and Clark. You need a guide." I put the pack over my shoulder.

"You?"

"You see somebody more qualified?"

"All right, all right!"

We made our way to Loren's appalling car. "It's the color of electrocution," I said. "It buzzes."

"I told you, it was the only—stop picking on it." He opened one screamingly loud door. "Hurry up," he said, when I wasn't in my seat quickly enough.

"Get this," I said, when I realized I had no idea whether Loren Ulrich was a competent driver. "There's no danger. No emergency. No need to speed or be reckless." This radioactive car would be stopped immediately if it were speeding. I closed my eyes, but the blue shriek of color remained on my retina. "No rush," I repeated. "I wonder what they put in the paint to make that blue so painful."

"How can you know Jake's safe?"

"You don't want me to talk about your car's horrible color?"

"It's moving, right? The color of a car doesn't matter."

Color. The color of a car. That was it. And it could matter.

"You never said how you know where he is," Loren said. "I'm not a chauffeur, I'm his father. Don't you think I'm worried, don't you—"

"It doesn't take a Sherlock. Jake's resources and options are limited. I'm sure he wants to comfort Tea Roederer. Her husband's dead, and the poor woman thinks her adopted son murdered him."

"Didn't he? Accidentally or not—what more evidence do you want? His car had blood on it."

"That's just it. The color of the car is wrong."

"For Christ's sake! You have an obsession with paint jobs!"

"Last night Jake told me Griffin was driving a black car. They wanted to disappear, you see. But Griffin's car is that washed-out, unattended, dull-finished, rusted-up no-color. A junker."

"Interesting," Loren said. "But if he had taken one of his family's other cars, they'd have noticed."

"I didn't say he did. Other times, he did. But not last night when he was leaving for good. That would make the car too easily traced. I think he stole a car. It's the only thing that makes sense, but Jake didn't know what to do with that. Griffin didn't commit manslaughter, because he was not in his car when it killed his adopted father. But he did commit grand theft auto. Jake wasn't about to tell the police, at least not last night. All the same, I'll bet he wanted to tell Tea Roederer, to set her mind at rest a little, tell her that things aren't as completely bad as she thinks. An act of kindness. He likes her, and she was furious with him last night. As well she might be. I think he wants to begin to make amends."

I might get at least a Saturday night with Mackenzie. Jake would be with his father or mother, the paperwork on the con from Kansas finished, and the detective at home. At this point, I'd even share him with the computer.

"You said Tea Roederer. Tea isn't short for Margaret, is it?"

"Theodora."

"Then the question remains, who's Margaret?"

"Maybe she's the woman who works there. The housekeeper. I think Margaret was her name. She was the boys' friend. Jake was probably afraid to call Mrs. Roederer directly."

When I leaned back, I felt the bulge in my pocket, and I took out the china pieces that had caused the rift with Tea. I held the St. Bernard on my right palm, the smiling cat on my left. Expensive bibelots. I'd seen them in catalogues. Several hundred each, and the Roederers had tabletops full.

"The Cheshire Cat," Loren said, glancing at my left hand.

"No—there's an entire cat here," I said. "The Cheshire Cat was only a grin."

"Eventually. But I'll bet that's what it is, with that gigantic smile. Do you think Jake made the connection?"

"He didn't say." I looked at the little figure with the big smile and felt as if I were being sucked in between its square teeth, pulled into the maw of something I didn't understand at all.

I closed my hand around the cat until I couldn't see it. Fatigue, I told myself. That's all my vibrating nerve endings meant. I gave Loren the remaining directions, then closed my eyes and tried to doze.

Eighteen

THE house by daylight was as spectacular and inviting as it had been by moonlight. We paused at the base of the long driveway, across from where first the effigy of Neddy Roederer and then the body of Harvey Spiers had burned. There were still remnants of the yellow Crime Scene tape that had roped off the area. Nothing else was left besides charcoal blocks, formerly known as books. We looked instead at Glamorgan's sun-warmed stones, the old trees protecting it from the elements, the acres of wooded countryside surrounding it. This house made me understand the point of money.

And I definitely understood why Jake, boxed in by walls the

color of depression, in a home from which all joy and sensual delight was removed, would consider this place heaven. It had the comforts of home—as long as you didn't mean his home. I put the Limoges boxes in my pockets. He could return them today, close that chapter.

I thought Tea Roederer would understand what the "borrowings" had been about. She certainly understood the power of beauty. Proof was on her walls and tabletops and in the many gifts of the Roederer Foundation. Also, she had struck me as a woman who listened carefully, tried to hear what really was being said. She even tolerated Griffin and Jake's cyberspace jargon, about which she admitted knowing precious little. The important thing was that she paid attention, which must have provided a delicious reprieve for Jake's vocal cords, so long used to shouting into a void.

I tried to think what it would be like to be Jake. I took my recently shaken faith in what I thought I knew about my mother, something that felt like a betrayal by omission and stung just a bit, and I set it alongside Jake's family.

There was no equating the two, or the pain they could cause. I had lost nothing except a certain smug assurance, because of unburied historical data that was actually irrelevant to my life. Jake's loss was real, ongoing and massive.

"Some place." Loren's tone was a mix of awe and resentment. I could almost read his thoughts. No wonder his son had opted not to wait for him. Poor Loren couldn't compete with a castle.

"It's not too late to get him back," I said.

"Of course not. Once we find out where he is—once he sees us, he'll come back with—"

"I mean into a real relationship. With you, wherever he lives. I mean his affection, his trust."

Loren Ulrich set his jaw and pursed his mouth with resentment. I had known too many others who, like him, suffered from Chronic Fatigue of the Heart and Will. Not a contagious condition, but definitely unhealthy for people close to the infected party, and it is my opinion that carriers are dangerous to children and should be quarantined or, still better, neutered.

"He's your son, and he's a terrific young man." Still no response. I changed the subject, opted for pragmatism. "You can park over there on that turnaround," I said. That was the only suggestion I made to which he responded.

I could see his disappointment when he met the lady of the house. She was not up to the standards of her surroundings. Tea Roederer looked haggard, and while she was too polite to say so, she obviously was not glad to see us and probably not desirous of seeing anybody.

Usually, her plainness was softened by her energy and graciousness, but not today. With fatigue and grief her only makeup, and with her reserved and chilly greeting, she seemed a poorly chiseled stone carving.

"I'm so sorry about your husband," I said. "I liked him very much. It's a great loss to the community as well."

She nodded, acknowledging that I had said something polite. Her face arranged itself in a blank, patrician expression that managed to say I would be tolerable if I kept my mouth closed.

Silently, she ushered us into the entry hall. I glanced up at the spot where the glorious chandelier had hung. Only a hole in the plaster now. Someone had swept up the shattered crystals and carted the remains off.

Tea Roederer's glance followed mine, and she bit her bottom lip. Then she looked at me directly. "What is it you want?" she asked. I wondered if she meant to be rude, or she was simply beyond niceties. And where was Margaret? Why was the exhausted and grieving lady of the house answering bell-ringers at a time like this?

"Mrs. Roederer, this is Loren Ulrich. Jake's father."

She studied him. Looking for resemblances, perhaps. Or waiting for something else.

I studied her as she studied him. Makeup would do wonders to reduce her growing resemblance to Young Abe Lincoln. And somebody should tell her to chuck the wig affectation. Hire an in-house hairdresser if she couldn't be bothered blow-drying. The thing on her head, askew, was ridiculous. A nice enough style, and surely the best hair money could buy—but on a tilt,

193

obviously fake. It took a lot of misdirected money and energy to have a bad wig day.

"I was supposed to pick Jake up at the station, but I was delayed, and when I got there, Jake had gone with someone he referred to as Aunt Margaret."

Tea Roederer's eyebrows rose and her austere and unadorned face softened into something near a smile. "Aunt Margaret, indeed," she murmured. "I assume neither you nor your wife has a sister named Margaret." Her voice, and the attitude propelling it, in contrast to her face, hair, and gestures, was remarkably unruffled. Cool, calm, self-possessed. She'd be a good person in an emergency.

"I don't have a wife," Loren said. My estimate of his IQ dropped. "Oh," he said, too late to redeem himself. "You mean my ex-wife." He shook his head. "No sisters, and not Harvey Spiers' either. He might have family, but they'd be in Canada most likely, and even if they came down for the funeral, which isn't even scheduled yet because of the investigation, how would they know where Jake—"

"Margaret Peek," Tea said. "The housekeeper. The boys are her good friends, despite the fact that Margaret's a black woman in her late fifties who knows even less than I do about computers and whatever else obsesses those boys. And isn't it interesting, don't you think, that he told the police she was his aunt? *Aunt* would be an insensitive term to use, wouldn't it? Toward a middle-aged black woman. In movies, bigots talk in that dismissive way. But I suppose it would be difficult explaining the relationship in any more direct manner."

"Then Jake called her here?" I asked.

Tea Roederer tilted her head side to side in a speculative, "maybe, maybe not" manner. "Margaret answers the telephone, so perhaps. She's actually on vacation today, but she came in to help clean up some of the mess. She's off now, finally. Everybody is. A few vacation weeks while I get away from here." She pressed the heel of a hand against her temple, as if *here* gave her an excruciating headache. "If Jake called Margaret, then I suppose it must have been here, because I doubt that he'd have her family's number."

"Mrs. Roederer," I said, "do you know where Jake went with Margaret?"

She looked startled. "Of course. I assumed you knew, too."

"Where?" Loren asked. "We don't, so where was it?"

"Here, of course. Why else would you come by?"

"When did he leave?" Loren asked. "Where did he go, do you know?" There were moments when the man sounded like an actual father. I wondered if there were ways to fan those small embers.

"Yes," Tea said, "to several of your questions. He didn't leave at all. He's still here."

I couldn't decide if she'd been oblivious to our sense of urgency, if we hadn't made our concern clear, or whether for lack of any other pastime, she'd simply been toying with us.

"He came to tell me why Griffin couldn't have run over Edward. To set my mind at rest on that point."

Just as I'd thought. So Griffin was still in trouble, but not the very biggest kind.

"The discussion of Griffin led to many topics," Tea said. "Including—I hope this doesn't upset you—my accusations against him, to which he admitted his guilt and attempted to explain about the Limoges box. The cat, you know."

I reached into my pocket. I could return her stolen goods right now. But Jake should be the one. I took my hand out, empty.

"I told him to keep it," she said.

Them, shouldn't it be? Keep them?

"As a symbol, a souvenir."

Of what?

"He thought Griffin might have left a clue as to his destination in their hideaway. With all our bedrooms—Griffin has his own recreation room upstairs—the boys treated a hole of a closet in the basement like a clubhouse, the kind kids had in old movies. A place to take things apart, build them, go online, Lord knows what. They spent a lot of time down there."

Less time than she thought, I bet, remembering Jake's reference to sneaking out by the back stairs.

"And he's there now?"

She nodded. "Seems to feel Griffin's running away might be half a test, a serious prank, but that in his heart, he wants to come back. That may be wishful thinking. I know the boys are close and Jake must be experiencing a sense of loss. But Griffin does not have Jake's common sense, more's the pity. The school we found him is excellent. And it would give him stability, particularly now, when we—when I—will be moving, and he'd have to readjust to another school in any case."

"You're moving?"

"I can't stay here. This has become ... bitter. I've told the entire staff to take two weeks off, close up the house while I'm gone. I suspect that will become a permanent condition."

"It's supposedly not a good idea to make decisions right after you've suffered a great loss and are ..." Her raised-eyebrow expression of incredulity stopped me. Who was I to give Tea Roederer advice?

"Where will you go?" Loren asked, as if he hadn't noticed the deep freeze that had greeted my intrusions into her private life.

"Anywhere but here."

I wanted to say how much it grieved me that this city that was so profoundly indebted to the Roederers now felt inhospitable. But her expression froze me out. It wasn't my place to offer such sentiments—I didn't have the credentials to equate my feelings with hers, to *presume* with my betters. Some horrid ancestral worldview that last served a purpose in the Middle Ages had been reactivated by the manor house and its mistress.

"Forgive me," Tea said. "I don't mean to sound harsh. This has been the most dreadful—and talking about it makes it worse. I appreciate your concern."

We nodded. Loren cleared his throat. "Jake," he prompted, bringing us back to our purpose. "His mother is worried sick."

Tea Roederer nodded. Her mood had softened, her attitude toward us warmed. "Yes, of course, but please excuse the mustiness and clutter. It is a basement, after all."

It was humorous, seeing the aggrieved aristocrat lapse into a flustered and apologetic housewife-mode. Her basement could be any damned way it wanted to be. It was a Roederer basement and I was sure that its discards and excess—even its trash—would be exceptionally fine.

"Follow me," she said.

We were led to a cramped landing at the back of the house. The fabled Back Stairs, route of surreptitious expeditions. The landing ended at a heavy door with a troublesome knob. Tea juggled the key in its latch, mistakenly locked the door, and muttered, "Sorry." Finally she unlocked and opened it. "Be careful on the steps," she said, as she worked the lock. "They're sturdy, but the whole place gives me the willies. I have a phobia about spiders, and despite all good efforts, we do get them down there." She shuddered. "I never go down those stairs except in dire emergency, and we've never had a sufficiently dire one."

Has never done laundry, is how I translated that. Has someone else pull the circuit breaker if a fuse blows. Is rich enough to have parts of her house she never visits and household functions she refuses to know about.

"Downstairs, there's a sort of hallway off to the right of the laundry and heating area. Down it a few steps you'll probably find Jake glued to a computer monitor. Forgive me for not leading you to him, but as I said, I simply don't."

"No problem. Thanks," we both said.

"I'm going to close the door behind you," she said, "if that's all right. Those spiders, you know."

As if arachnids, seeing the open door, would make a run for it. Nevertheless, we said everything was fine and walked downstairs. The treads weren't rickety or dangerously unprotected, as in so many old basements. They were solid wood with a decent-enough handrail, and I didn't know what the fluttery-housewife fuss had been about.

The open space into which we descended was unfinished, with pipes crisscrossing the ceiling, and large mechanisms—heaters of home and water, the guts of the house above it—bulking in corners. From what I could see, it was less overstuffed than most basements, but then, the Roederers had spent most of their lives in transit, and would have disposed of the redundant. So while there were a few trunks visible and at least one upholstered dining chair with a sprung seat propped against a wall, mostly it was concrete flooring and naked lightbulbs. Despite the wealth above us and its relative cleanliness, the basement managed to have a dingy subterranean ambience, with the lightbulbs losing the struggle against architectural gloom. I spotted only two windows in the large open area, and those were high up and small.

We walked into the hallway, which was lined with closed storage, and eventually reached a side room that looked like it, too, had once been a closet. Tea had been right. Inside the small room, Jake intently studied a computer screen. I could see the photograph of a man, plus the image of a newspaper that flipped pages as Jake clicked the mouse.

The room was makeshift, and in contrast to the open area we'd just left, knee-deep in clutter. Griffin and Jake had apparently used this place not only as hideout/clubhouse, but also as Dumpster. Sweaters, baseball hats, books, a boom box, CDs, a chair in need of reupholstery, newspapers, fast-food wrappers and containers, a printer.

Loren stepped over the discarded pages of a joke-a-day calendar, avoiding treading directly on them, as if following a magic incantation. "Jake," he said softly, "you gave me quite a scare."

Jake whirled around, eyes as startled as if we'd set off a siren under his chair.

"Are you all right?" I asked.

"Didn't expect to see you here!" He looked shaken and pale, although it could have been the dim light cast by the computer screen.

"I thought you'd be glad to see me," Loren said.

"I *am*, Dad."

"I wish you'd have waited for me, then."

I needed to dilute the father-son tension or we'd all get stuck in it. "Are there all that many spiders down here?" I asked. "I mean, I'm not over-fond of them myself." That was an exaggeration. I am not afraid of spiders. Not much, anyway.

"Spiders?" Jake shook his head. "Why?"

"Mrs. Roederer. Isn't that why she never comes down here?"

"Where'd you get that idea? She comes down. She stores some of her clothes down here, and Griffin and me"—I didn't think it a good time to stop and correct his grammar—"spent an hour with her here last week trying to explain what the Web was. Maybe she meant afraid of the Web, not spiders."

I let it go, but not far. It hovered like a spider on a thread in front of my eyes. Why would she lie about something so inconsequential?

Loren seemed too far out of it to even notice the inconsistency. He leaned over his son's shoulder, studying the multicolored screen.

"Can you show me that conference?" he asked Jake. "The one you got your column from?"

"I didn't get the column from it, Dad. I wrote the column about it. There's a difference." Despite his grumbles, he clicked his way around the screen toward his father's requested destination. "Incredible, isn't it?" he said.

"Boggles the mind, eh?"

Eh. That Canadian trademark. The first time I was in this house, it was a topic of conversation. Harvey Spiers used it and Neddy Roederer commented on it. And now they were both dead. But surely not for the sin of regional speech patterns. Nobody had clearly related the two deaths, but both were dead, and they'd known each other, or at least, Harvey said they had. I was sure there was a link.

Eh. Because of which sound, Harvey later said he knew Neddy, knew the man Neddy lived with. But how could he have? They wouldn't travel in the same circles, ever. Loren said that Harvey had been an insurance clerk before he found God, while Neddy . . .

Jake found the Web site. A low male voice, audibly serious, talked about the crime- and solve-rate in various developed countries.

I was more interested in the voice inside my head. Canada. Insurance, it repeated. Something, Harvey said, that would put

Neddy Roederer in jail. I'd thought it was Harvey's religious hysteria, thought it was about homosexuality. But that wasn't it. It was the Canada connection. It had to be.

I felt short of breath, so near to something I was dizzy. "Aren't you supposed to be looking for a clue?" I asked, while my mind spun.

"See?" Jake was oblivious to me. His dad was paying attention. He had expertise that interested his dad. "You choose a kind of crime, or a region or country, or a time period—you can go a whole lot of different ways. They aren't all violent, either. Like the one you sent me the clipping for. That was embezzlement."

Embezzlement. Canada. Insurance.

Embezzlement must have struck a familiar chord with Loren, too. "Speaking of which, Mrs. Roederer says that you and she, ah, cleared up the matter of the bric-a-brac, is that right?"

"She said I could keep it," Jake said.

"It or them?" I asked.

Jake swiveled around. "What's that?"

"It or them? You took two pieces. The St. Bernard and the cat."

Jake shrugged. "She meant both of them. I'll double-check."

But "it" was not "them." That's what she'd said upstairs, too. *It* was the cat. Only the cat. And how had she noticed one missing trinket in a vast household that had been trashed? *Why* had she? She hadn't noticed the dog.

The screen blinked and so did my brain. Canada. Enormous embezzlement. Insurance company embezzlement. Disappeared. No such person ever as Chester Katt. Insurance. Harvey Spiers. Chester. Cheshire Cat. A small and grinning china cat. The only missing piece noticed. Spiders. And, oh, God—Edward Fairfax Rochester's secret about his wife.

"Jake," I said, still more breathlessly. "Should you be doing that? Aren't you here to find out if Griffin left a clue as to his whereabouts?"

"Huh?" He swiveled and looked at me. "Why would he? I know where he's headed, but you can't tell."

I promised not to, hoping I could keep that promise.

"He found his aunt in New York State. On the Internet. When he was a kid, she was too young to take care of him, then she didn't know where he was, but she's cool now as a guardian."

"Does his—does Mrs. Roederer know that?"

Jake shook his head. "Of course not. Griffin'll get in touch when he's ready."

"But she said . . . then why are you down here?" his father asked.

"Mrs. R. said I could have the computer. I was figuring out how to transport it, what software to take. Some of it's already at school and I have copies of other stuff . . . why?"

"You know what a griffin was in mythology?" Loren asked.

"Not now." My pulse steadily gained speed.

"A monster," Jake said. "That's what Griffin said."

"Only because it combines the head of an eagle and the body of a lion. In heraldry, griffins symbolize vigilance. In mythology, griffins guarded gold mines and hidden treasures."

I looked over Jake's shoulder at the multicolored screen. I saw headlines, a colorized photo of the headless, green-footed corpse, private body parts blocked off.

"Well," Jake said, "this computer is the treasure he guarded."

I was not at all sure he was right about that.

Also on the screen was the man called the Cheshire Cat, with his pudgy, nondescript features, his pale mustache, horn-rimmed glasses, and sparse hair.

Not possibly strong-featured Neddy Roederer by any stretch. Besides, if it had been, Harvey and he would have instantly recognized each other.

I looked at his thin hair. "My God," I whispered.

"What?" Loren asked.

"Let me ask you this—why would a woman wear wigs all the time?"

"Don't pick on Mrs. Roederer," Jake said.

"She wears wigs?" Loren asked.

"No," I snapped, "her hair just slides off her head the way it did today. I'm asking a real question, and trust me, it's important."

"It's a fashion statement," Jake said. "Isn't that what it's called?

A kind of look? And freedom—I've seen her with short hair Monday and long hair Tuesday."

"Are wigs relevant to anything on God's green earth?" Loren asked. "You're on my case when I said what Griffin's name meant, but now you—besides, let's talk about it in the car. Jake, can you turn off that thing so we can get it packed up?"

"No!" I said. "Don't turn it off yet—look at it, and my question, my question—think about it."

"About *wigs*?" Loren sounded testy.

"Yes! Look!" I pointed at the screen. Surely somebody else would make the connection.

"At what?" Loren said. "The bald guy? Is that what you're getting at? Can women get bald that way? Young?"

"Yes," I whispered.

The silence in our little room was many decibels loud.

"Impossible," Jake said. "Ridiculous. He's a . . ."

"He's Chester Katt, that silly, made-up name. Don't you think he meant the name as a joke, an apt one, too, because that cat knew all along he was going to disappear."

"I'm sorry," Loren said. "I'm not following."

"What if he didn't exist at all?"

"No, really, he was there. He had a job. People knew him. He was real."

"But he wasn't really Chester Katt."

"We already know that. Listen, I'm pressed for time. I've got to get back to Toronto."

"What if *he* were a *she* in disguise? Wouldn't that be brilliant? Nobody anywhere would be looking for a woman, especially a patrician, long-married woman with a son. They wouldn't occupy the same universe."

Jake stared at me.

"You're the one who always said they bought a son like something they needed," I reminded him. "And named him Griffin. Guardian of the treasure, your father says. Interesting, isn't it?"

I could feel Jake's effort to walk this through, figure out each step. "And then, it was because Harvey knew?" he asked.

"Knew something and was therefore dangerous. I suspect he knew less than he thought, and way less than she feared."

"He thought Neddy was gay and connected with the real Chester Katt. He thought Chester was real," Jake said. "And he knew Chester had embezzled millions."

I nodded.

Jake digested this and nodded again. "But then, her own husband. She wouldn't—"

"I think it all became too much for him. He seems to have always been the passive one. I think when she escalated into murder—maybe even got him to help—it made him snap. He was going to tell." The message for Mackenzie. The need for private consultation, for her not to know. "The secret was getting too hideous to hold. He knew who'd killed Harvey and why. He, like his almost namesake, had a mad wife in his attic. So she killed him that night. And tried to frame Griffin by using his car."

Loren was blinking hard, computing at a slow speed. "Jake," I said, "you once told me Griffin could scan and change pictures. "Can you? Can you see what Chester Katt would look like thinner, without the glasses, the pasted-on mustache, and with a wig?"

"What a complete waste of—just leave the computer and let's get out of here," Loren said.

Jake tapped at the keyboard. The back of his neck was still too thin for the large man he'd someday be. It—he—looked vulnerable.

And I suddenly saw something I should have realized more quickly. *Jake* was the connection. He'd never, out of shame, mentioned his stepfather in this house, so when the secret was revealed at the party, Tea would have seen him as Harvey Spiers' secret emissary, or spy. Jake, surely seen as knowing too much, torturing the Roederers with that Web site, his fixation on the Cheshire Cat story. Asking for a tape of the TV show—a visual check—to send to his newsman father in Toronto. Even the china trinket—the one she noticed—that he took.

"Keep at it," I said. "I have to check . . ." She was leaving. Her remarkable coolness had let her say so. I'd thought it was aristocratic, when it was just the calm of the con. I walked back down the hallway double-time.

No servants, she'd said. Leaving. Permanently, I was sure. Just as she had done in Toronto and who knew where else? Tea Roederer, that renegade strand in the social fabric that nobody had been able to trace would disappear the same way Chester Katt had.

I had to give them credit for the style and bravado with which they'd invented the Roederers. Ben Franklin's descendant, indeed! Brilliant. Who could suspect people with such exquisite taste, such correct social values, such elegance, of being thieves?

How stupid I was! How slow! How blinded by surfaces, fictional credentials, and aesthetic values of which I approved.

The basement door had been difficult to open not because she'd accidentally locked it then. It had been locked when only Jake was down here. He'd become part of her plan, maybe saved her time by simply appearing and not needing to be hunted down. He knew things, the significance of which he didn't yet understand, like Griffin's alibi for Neddy's death. But she knew.

By now I was at the top of the stairs, my hand on the knob, my lips forming a yoctosecond's worth of prayer—let me be wrong, incredibly wrong—my hand, turning.

Nothing. I wasn't wrong. Another attempt, another definite nothing. A serious, total nothing.

We were locked in the basement. Margaret was on vacation, as was everybody else who worked here. And Tea Roederer, whatever her real name was, was about to disappear.

I walked down the stairs. No need for major consternation yet. There were windows.

And previously unnoticed grillwork over them.

And no sign of another door, of any other exit. No sign of anything that could break a locked and solid door down. Where were the usual basement tools? In a lean-to outside? Damn the rich with their overabundance of space.

Don't alarm Jake or Loren yet, I decided. They were male. They'd rush into action, any action, however stupid and futile. Think. What's the worst that could happen? The basement was spacious. We wouldn't run out of air. We wouldn't die of starvation. Margaret would probably be back before the two weeks, anyway, to cover furniture and do those things rich people mean when they speak of "closing the house."

A washer and dryer sat side by side in the corner along with a rack for air drying and an enormous open hamper with a dish towel hanging out of it.

We could get drinking water from the washing machine supply line. I was proud of my basement-wilderness survival techniques.

There was no reason to panic.

Maybe there was food storage down here. Perhaps even mansions stocked the canned and preserved haul of summer, the way a farmhouse would. And if not, that was okay. It would be hardest on Jake's rangy, ever-growing frame, but for me, it'd be the affordable equivalent of a spa. I'd finally lose those five pounds.

Or Mackenzie would figure it out, and as soon as we heard a sound above, we'd pound on that door and shout. Nothing to worry about except inconvenience and boredom. A bad plan on her part. Not worthy of the Cheshire Cat, not wily or complete enough. She was losing it.

I headed toward the computer room, ready to reassure them, but was stopped by the sound of shattering glass. I turned back. Maybe we were locked in by accident. Maybe she was sending help through the window. At least a warning through the bars of the window.

But help didn't look like the enormous something now blocking all the light from one of the windows. Nor did I understand how it could look like a board being hammered over the other window. The one she hadn't broken. And help didn't look or smell like the smoky fumes—like car exhaust, like a poorly maintained car's exhaust—pouring through the broken window.

All right, I told myself. *Now.* Now was as good a time as ever. Now was the *perfect* time.

I panicked.

Nineteen

I was a natural at panic, a potential virtuoso, but given our specific situation, I tried to stifle it as I made my way down the hallway toward Jake and his father. I had heard that if you opt for the gasping-for-air or screaming thing, you gobble available oxygen at warp speed. So I worked hard to stay calm. Either because I was concentrating on that, or because I was nonetheless panicky, my progress felt exactly like the nightmare where I need to run for my life, but my legs are underinflated balloons and each laborious step takes an hour.

"Guys," I said, when I entered their lair, breathing rapidly, "we have a—"

"—perfect fit!" Jake said. "It's primitive, but look."

There she was on the screen in her dark wig, the glasses gone, the shape of the face slimmed down, the pale mustache removed, and color on the lips and eyes.

Loren Ulrich patted his son's shoulder. "Quite a detective we've got here. Quite a computer genius."

Jake squirmed and swiveled around on his chair. "This makes sense of what Harvey said before he . . . oh, man . . . if . . ."

I waited before sounding the alarm, trying meantime to think of a plan, of at least a suggestion of how we'd get through this alive.

"If she was Chester Katt, that explains why Harvey thought Mr. Roederer was gay. Mr. Roederer told me that they'd been all around the world. They went to Bali after Canada, I remember, but to Canada after Nairobi. Hot to cold to hot places, he said. So if they were together when Harvey met her—disguised as a him—it would have looked like they were two men."

His head moved from side to side in tiny arcs, like a tremor that denied what his mind was telling him. "I thought Harvey was going to try blackmail."

"Maybe he did," Loren said softly.

"In which case, they'd think his ranting about Neddy's sins meant the stealing, like he knew the truth about the disguise and that Mrs. Roederer embezzled seventeen million dollars. Even though I don't think Harvey had a clue," Jake said.

"Seventeen mill." Loren let out a low, appreciative whistle. "Buys a whole lot of living." He looked up at a thick pipe with seams of duct tape, but I knew he was using X-ray vision into the palatial living quarters.

"Look, guys," I interrupted. "I hate breaking up the conversation, but maybe we've been too clever by half. We have a problem. A biggie."

"What kind?" Loren asked.

"For starters, we're locked in. She locked you in first, Jake, knowing you wouldn't notice for hours. So when it was our turn, she jiggled the key and pretended to have turned it the wrong way first. In any case, she did it. And it's a solid door."

"They knew how to build 'em in the old days," Loren said. "Unfortunately."

They were reacting with remarkable and unexpected calm, so I moved my tale beyond the introduction. I informed them of the added attraction—the exhaust pipe aimed at us. "And remember, Margaret's on vacation," I added lamely. "Along with whatever other help might otherwise be here. There's no way to phone 9-1-1 from the basement, is there?"

Jake shook his head. "No phone."

I hadn't expected anything else.

"How could she have known we'd figure this out? Or even that I'd come here?" Jake asked.

Such questions didn't help our escape, but since my last opportunity to teach looked like this moment and in this basement, I shared whatever data I had with my student. "She didn't know you'd show up. Your appearance was the frosting on the cake. She'd not only get away, she'd get rid of the one person left who was likely to connect the dots and understand what had gone on. Or maybe your arrival just saved her time. Maybe she was going after you next." I gave him a minute to silently digest that idea.

"I can't believe she'd leave all this," said his father.

I gave up on Loren. "We have to figure out what to do."

"If what you said is true, then there's nothing we can do," Loren said.

I vowed that if I lived, I would no longer make sweeping generalizations about men springing into action too readily.

"We don't know that yet, Dad," Jake said quietly. "Maybe there's another door somewhere."

"Wouldn't she have locked that, too?" Loren said.

"Let's check the entire basement," I said.

"Luckily for us, it isn't small," Jake said. "It'll take a while to kill us."

"Slow death," Loren said. "Lucky us, indeed."

Those closed storage areas made the square footage available to the carbon monoxide smaller and made its work more efficient. "Maybe we should try and stop the damn stuff from coming in," I said. I headed for the large space and took inventory. Then I pushed the overstuffed, under-upholstered side chair beneath the high window. The weight of my foot sent the sprung seat almost down to the floor.

I sat down on it, discouraged.

"The washing machine!" Jake said. "That won't mush up." He was already starting to move our future water supply.

"The dryer, instead," I said. "It's lighter, anyway."

As soon as it was pulled out, we saw the small hole into which the dryer exhaust had once fit. The tube was missing. I looked up at the barred window and suspected I'd find it up there, connected to the exhaust pipe of a car. Unfortunately, the hole was too small to let more than our fingers get through it, but it still would have let some of the fumes escape, if it, too, had not been covered by a piece of plywood. She was a lot handier than I'd assumed. Must be from her prearistocratic phase.

Jake kicked aside the woven hamper blocking his way and he and Loren lifted the dryer and relocated it under the window, then Jake, the tallest of us, hoisted himself up top. The metal bucked and protested, but he put one foot on each side and found stability.

"Push the dryer tube out the window," I said.

"I'm trying, but it's—damn!" he said. "I wedged it into the car. I can't move it at all now."

"Can you pull it the other way?" I asked. "Toward us?" At least then, the exhaust wouldn't funnel as directly into the room.

"It's too big. The metalwork is too close."

The Roederers' basement window grilles were in poor taste—too ornate, befitting a hacienda, not Welsh Glamorgan, if you asked me. And what did their curlicues deter besides squirrels and raccoons? Do forest animals or even thieves really require intricate patterns and spiky swirls? Damn and more damn.

Jake pushed and pulled and neither gesture made a difference. The exhaust poured in, close to his face.

"Get down," I said, and he did.

"Sorry," he said between coughs.

"Not your fault, son. You gave it a good try."

"That's Griffin's car out there," Jake said. "I saw the accordion."

PLAY THE ACCORDION, GO TO JAIL, Griffin's bumper sticker said. It had become his trademark.

We heard thunks above us. The busy feet of Mrs. R.

"She's still here," Loren said.

That seemed odd only until we acknowledged that for her, there was no rush. She could gather her favorite possessions, pack at leisure—dead visitors don't interfere much—and leave when she chose to. It wasn't as if she were ever going to be seen again. We were hearing, if not watching, the disappearing Cheshire Cat, The Sequel. No more black wigs. On with something that would divert the eye, off with something else, and she'd be invisible again. A woman or a man, and either way rich, with the money probably safe in a Swiss bank. I hated her then, hated that she could calmly get on with her life while knowing that ours were ending one floor below. As if she were the Sun King—or Queen, depending on mood and wardrobe. As if she had all the rights and privileges of the world and we had none.

Which is pretty much how it was.

"Off with your head," I muttered. "You're nobody." A pretender, an equal-opportunity con who saw a way to steal big and enjoy the take to the hilt. A woman with thinning hair, a talent for creative accounting, and a fondness for the arts, that was all.

And we'd been blinded by it. An entire city. By counterfeit credentials, supposed connections, real money, and amazing largesse. Ah, that was clever of them, that sharing of their bounty. Just enough, and for the right causes, so that we'd need to believe. There was something extravagantly bold and splendid about stealing a vast fortune and being so open about spending it left and right. Still, I hated us for being gullible, for not questioning the wigs and vague background, and the way she said "liberary," for being deafened by the cry of "Money!" The Roederers bought us with almost no effort.

I sent killer rays of loathing through the floor and wished I knew a curse to put upon the soles of her feet, burning them as they calmly walked above my head.

"Let me make sure I have this straight," Loren said. "We're doomed, right?"

"Dad!"

"Grow up, instead of giving up, would you?" I shouted. "God, but you're a pain! *Do* something—anything!" This was hypocritical, given that I'd earlier condemned all men for doing just that, but so what? When facing death, I permit a dash of hypocrisy. The thing I regretted was making a loud noise. I didn't want Tea Roederer to have the satisfaction of overhearing our misery.

"We haven't checked out the rest of the place." I moved back to the makeshift corridor. "Look for anything," I said, as we moved down the hallway. "Something that could batter a door, or get through those window bars. Or for another room or cubby or closet that might have a window she forgot, or a trap door—"

"Why on earth would there be a trap door?" Loren asked. He was not going to be my new best friend, that was for sure.

"Why *not*?" The man was useless, nothing more than deadweight. However, a clash of wills wasn't going to get us out. "People in England used to build weird and useless parts of their homes called follies, didn't they? And turn hedges into mazes. Rich people do peculiar things, Loren. And what about the places where they hid escaping slaves on the Underground Railroad?"

"This doesn't seem the kind of house on the escape route," Jake said.

We didn't have time to check whether the grossly rich had done their bit. Instead, we had the dimming of the light. Worse. Its extinction.

A bulb was out, maybe two, and the irregular shapes of the walls with their jutting storage closets became hazards. We found a small bathroom at one point, not much bigger than an airline facility, but with a stall shower, a mildewed shower curtain, a commode, and a tiny sink. No window. Good enough, I could imagine some grande dame declaring, for the likes of them.

Jake groped his way, touching padlocks we passed, peering up and over whatever he could.

We reached a peculiar wide structure, a sort of snout coming out of a bricked-up square on the wall. "Coal chute," Loren said. "In olden days, a truck backed up to where the window was and dumped a ton or so down it. We're standing in the former coal bin. Then it'd get shoveled into the furnace behind you. Early central heating. Very posh."

There was no heat operating of the central or local variety, and the subterranean basement was chilly, more and more so as we moved away from the large room under the kitchen. I was glad of my windbreaker and the sweater beneath it.

Jake reached into a door he'd unlatched. "Christ!" He nearly knocked me down as he leaped backward. "What *is* it?"

I took a deep breath and looked. "What *was* it," I said. "An entire village of minks, and I think a beaver and, oh shame on her, that looks like sealskin. If it gets too cold—here's our heating system, folks."

"Fur storage. What next?" Loren said.

Next was a lowering ceiling. And, as one by one we tumbled on them, three steps down. A smaller space and a still lower temperature.

Loren's eyes adjusted first. "Wine," he said. "A wine cellar. Hundreds of bottles. Thousands, maybe."

"We could go out drunk." Jake sounded interested. Nothing like a party, no matter the circumstances. I considered the idea of seeking oblivion here before it hit me in the bigger room. I had always heard the Roederers had, among their countless assets, a good cellar. I looked at the bottles, all on their sides on racks. Good wine, maybe, but this wasn't a good cellar. This was a good dungeon.

"No windows," Jake said. "Let's move on."

"She's going to blame our deaths on Griffin, too," I said as we walked. "His car again."

"But he wasn't—it wasn't—"

"And we are the only ones who know that," I said. "Except for her and I don't think she'll tell."

"If only she hadn't bricked up the coal chute," Loren said. "That'd be perfect."

Would have been, should have been. Of course it would have been perfect. That's why it had been boarded up long before the idea of the dungeon was formulated. What can go out can come in, and that chute would have been large enough for a deer to slide home on. What was the point of "if only"?

On the other hand, it was the first sign that Loren was activating his brain. He was trying.

"Too bad about the chute," I agreed, to encourage him. *"Chute!"*

"We don't have guns!" Loren snapped.

"The hamper—above the hamper. A thing—what was it?" I'd been so focused on getting to that window, trying to stop the fumes, that I'd brushed off the boxlike structure that the hamper half hid. It had blended into all the exposed household arteries down here, the pipes and conduits pumping the house into life. But this one was square, made of wood that looked aged and used. It ran ceiling-ward at a slant, just the way the coal chute had.

"Thank you, Loren," I said.

His smile was puzzled, but he followed me.

It's amazing how much smaller the basement felt now that we had a mental map of it. In an instant, we were back at the laundry, now redolent of exhaust fumes. Not the place you'd choose to be.

"A laundry chute?" Loren asked.

"Yes! Your idea!"

He looked baffled, he looked . . . Lorenish. "It goes up into the house," I said.

"It might be boarded up," Loren said. "It's probably left over from a hundred years ago. It—"

"There's a dishcloth in the hamper below it," I said. "That suggests the thing is still in use. It's surely worth a try."

Jake looked at me, then at the chute.

"Granted," I said, "it's not a great idea, but it's our only idea. What are our options?"

"We could have a little dignity about this," Loren said.

"Being gassed by Griffin Roederer's car in his basement is *not* what's meant by death with dignity," I said.

"Well," he said, "I don't have any choice, do I? I certainly can't fit in there, so what's the point?"

How had an hysteric and a dodo produced Jake? "Only one of us has to go up there," I said. "Then he can let the others out."

Of course, I meant Jake, with his long legs and arms, his strong muscles. And he knew it, too, because while Loren and I were sparring, he'd pulled the washing machine over so that it was below the chute, and had gotten himself on top of it and was easing his head inside.

I heard huffs, puffs, and a soft *thunk*. And then Jake scrunched down and emerged again, red-faced. "I'm real sorry," he said softly. "My shoulders won't fit. I don't know how to get around that."

I thought of friends' stories of giving birth to the ever-feared big-shouldered baby. The laundry chute wasn't all that different, except that it had zero flexibility and nobody could do an episiotomy on it to ease the way.

"So it's me." It's I. Who cares? The point was, I was the only candidate left. I could barely believe myself. I was going up a wooden chute? My sports were reading, dancing, a bike ride now and then. This was akin to rappelling without a rope. I was too old, too weak, too frightened.

Besides, what if I didn't fit? I climbed up onto the washing machine, then positioned myself in a crouch and slowly stood up. My head went in. So did my shoulders.

I thought about my boobs, about all those years of worrying over their size, or lack of it. I was still worrying about the same issue, but with more urgency now. Would I fit? Would they? If not, would I be trapped through eternity, found someday by a mourning Mackenzie, stuck by the boobs in a laundry chute?

I fit. They fit.

Time to obsess about hips. It helped stave off a newfound case of claustrophobia. The chute was dark, with the smell of age and maybe of all the unwashed laundry dropped through it. The sides were smooth wood running at a sharp angle. I supposed I should be grateful it wasn't completely vertical. I could feel the edges of planks. Hell on stockings and fine lingerie. Snags galore. Probably the laundress did them by hand.

Well, too bad for the laundress and her delicate garments. I was the one in trouble now. My upper torso was in the tube and I could maneuver my arms enough to push against the sides—but coming up was potential mortification. I could stand up, in fact, but my hips—what if they were too big? Squashed in a tube by the hips or butt was far more humiliating than being trapped by boobs.

Please, Lord, I begged. I've been meaning to take off a few pounds, be more rigid about wine and chocolate, although they are so much fun. But please? I imagined myself swelling, the Michelin Man in a laundry chute, a laughingstock even in death.

But I fit.

That was supposed to be the good news. I got a sneaker firmly planted on each side and tried not to think about how impossible this was and how relieved I was that my body parts were in proportion. If I lived, I'd try out for Miss America.

But I wouldn't live because now, totally encased in the wood, hearing only the murmurs of the men waiting for me, I was paralyzed, every sinew terrified into rigidity. I knew what I looked like in a cross section. Those mountain climbers you saw in pictures, in a vertical tunnel, a whatever-it's-called running down the mountain. And they had ropes. Besides, even looking at those photos turned my stomach.

I couldn't do this. I wasn't meant to. I was weak and cowardly.

I was also out of options. I could stay in the basement and die, or give the chute a chance.

I grabbed for purchase higher up, then quickly moved each foot farther up inside the chute. If I could do this, I could probably qualify for the Olympics.

The men—*my* men, even terrified Loren—gave a small whoop.

Then one for the Gipper. One for me. I would do this. Sometimes all you can hope for is to die trying.

215

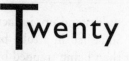

Twenty

I climbed as arduously and gracelessly as an inchworm. With each crawl, each grab, each press against the sides, each silent attempt to make my lumpy-bumpy human shape become a hard-sided wedge that couldn't be dislodged, I oozed upward, heart beating triple-time.

I was grateful this was an old chute, made of natural material. I had to assume that nowadays, it'd be plastic or metal, and I'd never be able to scale manufactured smoothness. On the other hand, if the house had been newer, perhaps its ceilings would have been lower. I had never realized how high one story could be. Half a story, actually, because where on the first floor would the opening be? Waist-high, I'd hope. Just right for chucking table-cloths and dish towels.

I climbed—one hand, the other, one foot, the other—over and over, trying not to be daunted, and nearly failing when there was no sign of an end or opening. I almost released my hold and let myself drop. Why exercise if you were going to die before you showed the results?

I heard something from below, an almost-word or two—a pooter? A net? It sounded as if they'd trapped something. Or were singing some arcane nursery rhyme. The low hollow sound repeated, annoying the hell out of me. I had to concentrate or I'd fall. Loren's voice didn't do well in a wooden tube, especially when he tried to speak softly so Mrs. R. couldn't hear. His words dissolved in the wood grain. I ignored his rumbles. It was all I could do to climb and listen to my own gasping breath.

"Mandy year?" was easier, unraveling into "Mandy, you hear?" on Loren's third try. I didn't know how to answer. Yes, I heard, but no, I didn't comprehend and would not shout and alert Tea Roederer. "Cuter!" it sounded like this time. That I was *cuter*? Was that Loren's stupid way of cheering me on? Hand, hand, foot, foot. That was all I had room to think about, what with big blocks of brain reserved for fear and panic. I was not up to the task. If I'd had time, I would have prepared, worked out with weights. I would be buff, strong, the new woman.

But I hadn't and I wasn't. I was a large package of insufficient muscles with which to defy the laws of gravity.

How had I gotten myself in this unnatural position, hanging in a tube like a giant insect whose wings had been pulled? And with three lives depending on it.

Hand, hand, foot, foot.

The other two gave up on sending messages, probably by reason of being asphyxiated because I couldn't move fast enough. I forgave Loren his sexist *cuter* remark, his failings.

Hand, hand, foot, foot.

And then—one hand was on something new. Slightly recessed. With a metal band running horizontally.

A door—what else could it be? *The* door. I braced myself more firmly and pushed with my right hand.

And pushed.

Nothing happened except that my wrist sent strong signals that if I insisted on pitting it against a solid surface, it would be the contender that broke.

The door was locked. Maybe always, maybe not even having a single thing to do with me, maybe having nothing whatsoever to do with this particular instance. Locked to prevent accidents from the other side.

In a rage, I pounded, then panicked anew. What if she were still there, and heard? What if she flung open the door? I'd plummet a story down in a wooden tube and if that didn't kill me—she would.

Don't have heard me, I begged of her—as if her main drive in life was granting my wishes.

What would she do next?

For that matter—what would I?

I looked upward. The chute continued skyward, dark and high above. I wanted to cry, felt my eyes sting and water, but with not a free finger to dry them, I couldn't afford tears.

I was too tired to go on, and what if I did? Why wouldn't all the other exits be locked, too, as further safety measures?

Damn Tea's sudden caution! She had courage to defy the entire world, violate most of the commandments—then she obsessed about laundry chute accidents? What was *wrong* with her?

Loren shouted up the tube again. Then he was still alive, and hearty-enough sounding that I was sure Jake was still with us as well. The bad news, of course, was that between the deafening tom-tom of my own heartbeat, and the wooden absorbency factor, I still couldn't understand him.

It wasn't the cute business anymore. Now it was baths. Or grass. Fins and baths. Sounds like . . .

"I don't care!" I screamed, then re-remembered the resident murderess and froze even more stiffly against the walls of the chute.

And became aware that, with the worst possible timing in the world, I urgently felt a call of nature.

The horrific possibilities were endless.

That was *not* how I was going out. Now, with every single muscle tensed, I moved forward, or rather, up. Hand, hand, foot, foot. I pictured the soaring ceilings, the bas-reliefs at the top of the walls, the spot from which the chandelier had hung. I pictured myself as a creature with adhesive palms and magic sneakers that stuck to all surfaces.

I focused my attention on the top of my head, the most *up* spot I had the power to imagine, and thought only of upness, the state of uphood. Be as uppity as all get out! And get out!

And no more than one second before I knew I would give up, let go, accept fate, plummet downward and die, one single yoctosecond before my brain and body would have to give up, I felt the wall change again. There it was, another slatted segment.

No lock, no lock, *no lock*, I whispered. Only then did I dare to try, once again wedging myself at three points as much as I could as, holding my breath, I pressed with my right hand.

It gave.

I was so flooded with relief, I nearly let go and plunged downward, but nearly doesn't count. Instead, I inched my feet up the wall, keeping my head at door-level until I was in almost a fetal position, so I could propel myself through the opening, into the room.

Now I had a new mantra—don't be here, don't be here, don't be here now. As I made my way, I had a few sub-mantras, depending on where precisely I was. *Don't step on my hands as they appear. Don't hurt my head as it appears. Don't kill me as I appear.*

I wondered if this constituted a rebirthing experience. I wondered if I'd been as worried the first time I encountered the world.

And then I was through, out of the claustrophobic dark into the blindingly light openness. I landed, headfirst, on bare, waxed floorboards, which groaned and squeaked greetings.

I don't know why babies cry, unless it's for joy. It's a hell of a lot nicer out in the open, even with a slightly sore forehead. I wanted to laugh, to pound the floor and kiss it. I was alive, and I was out.

At which point I realized that getting the gentlemen in the basement *out* had been the reason for the climb, and time and oxygen were both running out.

But first . . .

This never happened in the movies. Superheroes never had to excuse themselves and hit the lavatory. I was inferior stock, and profoundly worried that someday people would be able to say that two men died while I visited the Roederers' facilities.

The chute had deposited me in a hallway, centrally located between bedrooms, the better to dispose of their linens. There were an awful lot of doors, open and not, lining the hall on both sides. A small but exquisite art collection graced the landing, on the papered walls and on dark wood pedestals. The Roederer money was ill-gotten, but well spent. Closest to me was a rose-quartz statue of Shiva, the many-armed Hindu god of destruction and reproduction, an interesting combo. He didn't look troubled by his dual nature. He looked lit from within, cool and hot at the same time, the four arms exquisitely graceful.

I wondered what would become of the treasures when Mrs. R. skipped. I wondered which, if any, of them she'd take along.

This is not to suggest I was dawdling, because I did my speculating while trying doors. To my momentary amazement, all the doors were unlocked—but when opened, most revealed nothing. Empty shells of rooms in desperate need of a human touch to bring them to life.

The wealthy couple hadn't put even the minimum in these rooms. Not a bed, a lamp, a table. Because the Roederers didn't have houseguests. They probably didn't have friends. Their entertaining had been public and for public causes. Main floor only. Why waste two dimes on rooms no one would see or use? It was interesting that in this one area of their life, they saw no need for subterfuge. I wondered if Jake had noticed the unfurnished rooms, and whether he'd just accepted it as the sort of frugal economy his family would approve of. If, of course, people in his situation ever suffered a surfeit of bedrooms.

Luckily, bathrooms, even if unused, didn't need furnishings, and I found and used one, locking the door behind me, just in case she was around, waiting.

She wasn't.

Detour completed, I was on my way to Jake and Loren who, please God, had not expired in the last two minutes.

In the relatively small area I had to traverse between the bathroom and the stairs, I passed a very Cézanne-looking painting, a suit of armor for a tiny medieval warrior, an ornate Southwestern storytelling figure, a mask made of silver, gold, and turquoise, and a blue and white Chinese vase. I walked over two small rugs, one patterned with flowers, the other with interlocking geometrics, both the zillion-knots-to-the-inch sort with the sheen of woven silk.

The best in the world. Nothing less. The collectors turned out to be fakes, but their knowledge and appreciation of art was real. Even the old flooring, creaky and tired as it sounded, was a work of art with inlaid parquetry. I tiptoed, afraid of setting off protests from the boards under my feet, then I gave that up in favor of expediency. What difference could it make?

Seconds later, I had my answer. Probably neither the tiptoeing nor the strides had made a difference. The clunk of my headfirst arrival would have sufficed. And following that trumpeted announcement, my side trip had given Tea Roederer time to arm herself before confronting me.

I froze at the top of the stairs, although inwardly, everything was in motion—pounding, clenching, spasming—because there she was, two steps up the grand staircase. No longer madcap, just mad. Her wig was more askew, and she'd misbuttoned her black velvet dress and accessorized it with a gun aimed directly at my stomach. She looked like doom, like inevitability. She was only a decade older than me; how had she become a force of nature, mythic and unstoppable?

I was inside my skin watching me—watching us—as if we were a show, played in slow motion. I didn't and couldn't move, but she could, a step at a time, one hand on the banister, the other carefully maintaining her grip and aim. She scowled, visibly peeved either by my presence, her forgetfulness in leaving the chute door unlocked, or both.

From my strange observer's distance, I heard my voice say, "Don't do this. There's no point."

She shook her head briskly, annoyed, not wasting words on the likes of me.

Her vast arrogance revitalized me. Systems *on*—racing, scurrying, doing their best, all at once and instantly, but to no avail. I couldn't remember a place to run to or hide where I wouldn't be trapped. Even if I gained a moment by locking myself into a room—a lock she could shoot through—that would only add to the danger downstairs, where minute by minute, the cellar filled with poison.

This was her house. She knew its closets, windows, and exits. That's how she'd been able to calmly attempt the murder of three people. This was her call, her game. I had to find a way through what she knew. Or be what she didn't know.

"I don't like loose threads." Tea Roederer paused and raised her gun.

I swayed, I stepped side to side, I did deep knee bends, then stood straight.

I looked like a dancing duck. I added hand motions, anything to confuse, up, sideways, above the head, down, like a bargain-basement imitation of the Shiva.

Tea Roederer, the local god of destruction, waved her gun. Behind me stood Shiva, who owned the title. I whirled and grabbed the statue and held it in front of me like a hostage. "Don't do it!" I shouted at Tea Roederer, and I hoped so much she wouldn't.

She would. She came up another step, squinted, and raised the gun.

With all my might, with whatever power was left in my exhausted arm, and with a silent apology—to him and to his carver—I hurled the statue.

He flew. And destroyed.

Tea gave a great *whoof!* of escaping air and toppled backward, down the stairs with the many-armed god. Except for the staircase runner, the entry was all hard surfaces—wood, plaster, and marble, so that each painful bounce against a riser was clear and loud.

A deafening explosion drowned out our human sounds. I stopped, crouched, screamed, a reflex of pure terror. Was I shot? Pieces of plaster fell silently, dustily, from the ceiling. No pieces of me followed suit.

I started down after Tea, apologizing again to Shiva, who'd been amputated twice as he bounced.

Tea tumbled all the way to the bottom. Shiva had gotten one of his remaining arms stuck between two of the balusters. I pulled him out as I passed and set him upright. He looked a lot better than the woman who'd thought herself a god.

But she still looked too good for my liking. The floor of the entry hall was marble. Very hard stuff. Tea lay on her back, blinking and stunned. But incredibly resilient. Any minute now, she'd shake herself back into place and be at me again.

I dove at her, knocking her back onto the marble, hard, and then I stood up and planted one foot on her chest. If she'd try to get up, I'd stand on her.

She bled from an unfortunately nonfatal bang on her nose. But I didn't want her dead. I wanted her in court, explaining what would be otherwise unbelievable. That the patrician so eagerly clutched to Philadelphia's breast was, in fact, faux. A murderer, making Tea/Chester both a wanted man and now, a wanted woman.

But I had more important things than her to consider. Jake and Loren were in the basement with time running out, or already dead. I looked around. The detonating gun had flown out of Tea's hand, bouncing on its own trajectory down to the floor, just out of reach.

I looked at her. Her skin was ashen, her breathing shallow. She wasn't going to pop up this instant, so I took my foot off her chest and grabbed her weapon. She struggled to sit up. I aimed the gun. Wasn't there something I had to do before being able to pull the trigger? Was it in the right position now or had the fall pushed it back?

Only way to find out . . . I aimed straight up. This is a test, I muttered, this is only a test. In case of a real emergency . . .

It worked. I stood in a small hailstorm of plaster dust and fragments.

Tea fell back down, her eyes wide.

"Do not move," I said. "Do not even think about moving." I felt John Wayne–ish now, able to speak calmly and carry a big gun. I pointed the weapon in her general direction and tried to figure out what to do with her while I got the guys out of the basement.

But as I thought about it, I heard footsteps. Whose? Too many feet and steps for two people. And sirens? Loudspeakers and breaking glass? And all from the wrong direction in the house, the front of it. Near me.

And wait—Jake and Loren couldn't get themselves out, that was the whole point, and if I hadn't unlocked that cellar door, who was it pounding toward me—

"She! She—" Tea screamed. "Get her! She attacked me!"

I was grabbed from behind. "Drop it!" an authoritarian voice bellowed directly into my ear.

"I'm not the one—"

He didn't seem in a mood for discussion. "Drop it!" he shouted, real menace in his voice. This was how cops got bad reps. I'd just been through hell—the least he could be was polite.

Nevertheless, I dropped the gun.

"She! She—" Tea said. "Arrest her! Look at her—she—"

"No!" I said. "She's the—" My version was going to be a hard sell. Tea, rumpled and bruised, had a pathetic, victimized aura. Her wig was off and her semibald head made her look much older and a whole lot feebler than she was, but still patrician. Still the lady of the manor. All the same, couldn't they let me explain how I'd climbed a laundry chute, tackled an armed murderer, and saved her prisoners?

Maybe not that last part. I didn't hear any sound from below. "The basement," I said.

"Yeah, yeah," the cop muttered.

"No, listen, the back stairs—locked—there's two men down there and exhaust fumes coming in."

"Lady, we know." But how could he? He did nothing except snap handcuffs on me as if I hadn't said a word.

I tried again. "You don't understand, there are two men who will die if you—"

"Hold it a minute? We're busy." The policemen—not a female among them—swarmed, one helping Tea Roederer sit up and shakily attempt getting to her feet, another studying the bullet-aerated ceiling, another making note of the de-limbed Shiva, another wandering off, presumably to inspect the manse.

"You have this backward," I said. "I'm the goodie!" That apparently lacked convincing power or finesse. "I'm not the villain!" Now I sounded old-fashioned, out of a twirling-mustache melodrama, the wrong century's drama. "There are men in real danger down—"

"Let her go!"

Loren! Loren? Loren with the policeman who'd left the room. And Jake right behind. Loren, looking more physically rumpled and scattered than he ever had, but stronger inside—taking charge for the first time. Facing down men with guns. The man had possibilities. "She isn't the one!" he said. "She is." He pointed at Tea.

"You the fellow got in touch?"

"My son did. This boy here. My son." He put his arm around Jake's shoulder, a touch to reaffirm that Jake was a real person. The light of belated comprehension in his eyes was so bright, you could have read by it. "He saved the day," he said.

What had happened between them because of the crisis was good. Even great. But what he was saying didn't make sense. *I'd* saved the day, hadn't I?

"Hey—you're the kid was at the station this morning." Jake had been singlehandedly justifying the Radnor Township police force's payroll. "About the mister here. The hit-and-run."

Jake nodded.

"Well, you're a smart kid. Fast thinking." The policeman actually cracked a smile. All was forgiven. And all of me forgotten. I was still handcuffed and unacknowledged and they were deep into an incomprehensible conversation. "The call we got was from Idaho." The cop chuckled after he said it.

"Jeez," Jake said. "I thought there'd be somebody closer. He did it by phone?"

"She, and the answer is yes. Her 911 dispatcher did it."

Loren saw my befuddlement. "I told you. You know, in the chute."

"Shoot?" one of the cops said. "You talking about those holes in the ceiling? Good thing nobody got hurt, but you want to explain, Miss?"

"We're talking laundry chute," I said.

"I forgot to lock the upstairs door." Tea sounded on the verge of tears. "I never thought anyone could climb up there, but she did. She got out."

"Stop whining!" I snapped. Lord knows Tea had made me feel bad for presuming to be her equal, when all along, I was her better. "You're a phony. I don't mean the money you stole or the murders—I thought this was about banned books, while it was about cooked books. Your special talent. The truth is, you don't believe in free speech. Not for Harvey Spiers. Not even for your husband."

"Run that by me again, lady?" the cop said. "Maybe backtrack to the robbing and killing part?"

"About my arms," I said. "Loren, Jake, tell them again. Tell them I'm okay." I turned to my cop. "Couldn't you take these things off me?"

He looked fuddled. Jake and Loren had somehow passed muster, but I'd been aiming a gun at a social icon. Nobody was ready to release me. It was possible I'd be in cuffs forever.

And I might have been, except that at that moment, Mackenzie walked in. He didn't have a big white horse, but still and all, there he was. Like magic. I turned so he could see my handcuffs and rescue me.

"Hold it, mister!" a cop said.

Mackenzie identified himself. I waited, full of hope.

Jake beamed. "You read your e-mail," he said.

Mackenzie nodded while he scanned the room—the guys, the police, Tea—me. I smiled at him, flooded with relief. He scowled back. My jaw dropped. Nothing made sense.

"What's this about mail?" the cop asked.

"The computer has a modem," Jake said. "I should have realized sooner. That means a telephone line, even though there's no phone. That's how I get online, where we already were. Dumb of me not to get it sooner. So I e-mailed everybody I've ever had on my list, even you, because you gave me your address." He nodded toward Mackenzie, then looked at the policemen. "I said this wasn't a prank and to get help fast. I figured somebody, somewhere, would get the message. I told them the address and the name of the police force and said to call them. And they did."

"By the time we left the station, at least a dozen people had called," the cop said. "I'm sure there's been more since then."

Computer. That's what Loren had been trying to say. Not that I was cuter. Internet. Jake.

So my climb, the terror, the exhaustion, the fight on the stairs—all that had been an exercise in futility. I was a downsized hero, replaced by electronics. I never got my fifteen minutes of fame. Not even fifteen seconds.

"And here we are," Loren said.

"But the fumes," I said. "So much time went by—I was sure you were dead. How did you survive?"

"Weren't you listening?" He laughed. Mackenzie still looked grim. I wanted to slug both of them. I was concerned about my increasingly violent fantasies, but that might be a possible side effect of climbing up a laundry chute to no applause. "Loren," I said, "I was busy—and you didn't speak clearly, and I will kill you if they ever uncuff me—"

Mackenzie made a barely perceptible nod, as if he were the Caesar of Radnor, sparing my life. "She's misguided," he said. "Overfond of drama and hyperbole and often weird. But not a

227

criminal. Of course, all this could have been less melodramatic if she'd left a note. *Said* where she was headed."

"Sorry," I muttered. That's what he was miffed about. It wasn't enough to scale the heights if I messed up on basics, like cohabitation etiquette.

"Why keep your whereabouts a secret?" Mackenzie asked.

Secrets again, those slippery shape-changers, even when unintentional. Sometimes good, just as often, bad. This time, dangerous.

"You could have died!" He cared.

"It won't happen again," I said.

"You mean next time you're in a locked basement with poison coming through the window you'll write a note tellin' me that?"

The cop uncuffed me. My wrists hurt even after that short time. "Loren?" I redirected my amorphous hostility his way.

But he only grinned. "I tried and tried to tell you that Griffin's car ran out of gas."

Gas, not grass. Griffin, not fin. Ran out of gas!

Tea Roederer said a nasty Anglo-Saxon word. Something had finally rattled her.

Jake smiled. "He never remembered to fill it. She—" He pointed at Tea, whose skin was maroon with rage. "Mrs. Roederer was always on his case about it. Sometimes she'd have to come get him when he'd run out, and man, would she be furious. That's why when we'd sneak out at night, we'd take one of the other cars. They always had gas."

How pragmatic those imaginary Roederers were, always fully tanked and prepared to cut out on a moment's notice.

Tea fumed, practically erupting into lava flow. She had stolen millions and killed two men—one her own husband. But everything paled beside the fact that her adopted son had once again failed to keep his tank full. Teenagers can indeed be infuriating.

"When you're living with me, you'd better be more conscious of your gas tank than Griffin was," Loren told his son.

Jake beamed.

"It was a kind of dramatic learning experience," Loren said to me. "Clichéd, I suppose. Don't know what you have till you nearly lose it. That kind of thing. I'm not putting him in danger again. I'll work it through with Betsy."

"I'm glad," I said. And I was.

AND I STILL am. It was all—the part I believed for too long—a fairy tale. And in an oddly fitting way, it had a mostly happy ending.

Harvey Spiers is, of course, beyond happiness or sorrow. But since he believed he held the copyright on morality, I must assume he's reaping his just and eternal rewards in whatever segment of eternity he earned. That makes some of us happy, if not Harvey.

His erstwhile stepson's letters sent by e-mail via Mackenzie make it clear that life with his father is easier and saner than life here had been. Jake also writes that Griffin is thoroughly enjoying the life of an ordinary kid in an ordinary house with his extremely ordinary relatives.

My mother's happy because she doesn't know a few things. She's gotten a glowing report on Good Citizen Mackenzie, and she doesn't know there was no investigation. And she's happy, even though she doesn't know it, because I have decided to keep her secret about a time when she was desperately unhappy. What I've come to feel is that her history is her property, to share only when she so decides.

So I suppose I've made Detective Skippy happy, too.

Betsy, of course, is not happy, but since being unhappy apparently gives her pleasure, that's not a sad outcome, either. She's wearing makeup and bright colors nowadays, has found a new residence, and is reportedly dating a corporate executive of the shark variety who will surely provide her with sufficient misery to keep her motors going.

And Mother Vivien is free, no longer under suspicion of murder and now the sole ruler of the Moral Ecologists, so she got what she wanted—the right to be the boss of making everybody else unhappy.

As for me, I'm happily learning more about living with

someone. I think we might get it all straightened out about the same time as the Arabs and Israelis do, but we're having more fun than they are with the learning process.

Sometimes, I sit in the loft and think about Tea and Neddy. Not the shabby people they really were, but the myth it was their genius to create, that fabulously wealthy, fun-loving, globe-hopping, party-giving couple with the right values and a sense of noblesse oblige that royalty would envy. Who needed reality when such extravagant make-believe was available?

Now their house is empty, and its contents sold off. Neddy is dead and Tea's in prison for the rest of her days. I don't miss them at all—but I do, now and then, remember the art and the priceless books and her beaded dress and the merriment and the extravagant gestures that expanded the possible and were fun, even vicariously.

Of course they were pretenders, but they played their roles with such zest and bravado they became what they were miming. Neddy and Tea were the Roederers. Figments, yes. Wearers of extravagant masks and disguises. Fabrications. But also, as real as it gets, even if they never existed.

So now and then, as I curl deeply into my comfortable but unspectacular life, wearing my woolly socks, drinking tea, and marking yet another stack of compositions, I find myself day-dreaming about Glamorgan and a great crystal chandelier and the invented couple who existed there for a while.

And I become full of wist. I miss them. I miss their gift of firing our imaginations. I miss their very real generosity. I miss those people who never were.

We nearly had a wonderful time. Wish they'd been here.